WALKING WITH THE ENEMY

THE VICTORY EDITION

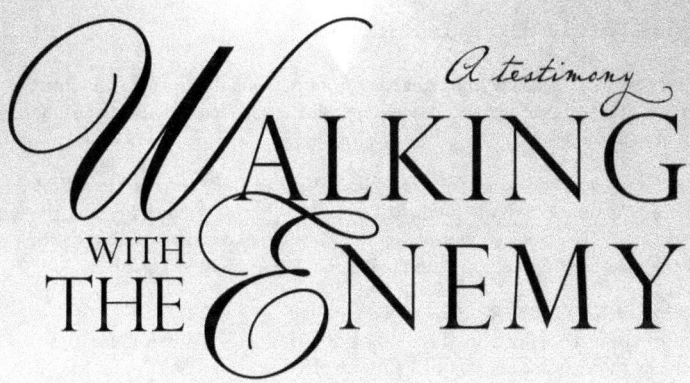
Walking with the Enemy
A testimony

C. READ

TRUE LIGHT
PUBLICATIONS

 | True Light Publications
P.O. Box 98144
Jackson, Mississippi 39298-8144
www.TrueLightPublications.com

True Light Publications and colophon are registered trademarks of the author.

The Victory Edition © 2015 by True Light Publications

All rights reserved, including the right to reproduce this publication in any form, in whole or in part, except in accordance with copyright laws. Please contact the publisher for permissions inquiries.

Scripture references are from the King James Version (KJV) of the Holy Bible, aka the Authorized Version, originally published in 1611.[1] [In this Victory Edition, the words in brackets signify the italicized words that the King James editors added to the text to help clarify the meaning and better relate the original language to English.]

An Important Note to the Reader:
The information contained in this book is of vital public interest for those who are unaware of the extreme danger of being involved with religious cults, and it is highly recommended for youth and young adults to read and understand as well. The Endnotes are a story unto themselves and are very important to read.

Book design by TLC Book Design, TLCBookDesign.com
Cover photo © kevron2002 for Deposit Photos.

Publisher's Cataloging-in-Publication
(Provided by Quality Books, Inc.)

Read, C., 1957-
  Walking with the enemy : a testimony / C. Read. — V edition. — Victory edition.
  pages   cm
  Includes bibliographical references and index.
  LCCN 2010929877
  ISBN 978-0-9672825-7-2 (hardcover)
  ISBN 978-0-9672825-9-6 (paperback)
  ISBN 978-0-9672825-2-7 (e-book)
  1. Cults—United States.   I. Title.
BP604.2.U6R43 2014   299
                             QBI14-2206

Manufactured in the United States of America
10 9 8 7 6 5 4 3 2

In Dedication

To those who have given their lives
for the cross of Christ!

Acknowledgments

I would like to acknowledge my Father in Heaven,
Who is the Lord God Almighty!
The Most High God!
The Great I AM!
All praise, honor, and glory unto Him
and His beloved Son, the Lord Jesus Christ,
Who is my Savior, my Redeemer, and my Friend!
And it is only because of Him
that I am alive and living!
Praise His Holy Name
forever and ever!
Amen!

Special Thanks

I AM SO GRATEFUL to God for all He has done, and continues to do, in my life; and I am especially thankful for the gift of His precious Son, the LORD Jesus Christ!

I thank God for my dear Husband and our seven beautiful children He has graciously given to us. I am also especially thankful for our last two little ones—the LORD knew we needed them to make our family complete! They are a reflection of the fact that the Enemy does not win in the end!

In addition, I am so thankful for all who have helped or encouraged me in this awesome endeavor, and for those who stood by me when it seemed as though no one else would. God knows who you are, and I pray that His love, mercy, and grace will be with all who love our Lord Jesus Christ in sincerity!

Finally, I am eternally grateful to the Holy One of Israel, and for His beloved servants that He has put in my path and for those I am yet to meet.

The Author

"I know that, whatsoever God doeth,
it shall be for ever:
nothing can be put to it, nor any thing taken from it:
and God doeth [it], that [men] should fear before Him.
That which hath been is now;
and that which is to be hath already been;
and God requireth that which is past."

Ecclesiastes 3:14–15

Table of Contents

Preface to The Victory Edition 15
Introduction 21

Chapter One
Churches 25

Chapter Two
Heed the Call 41

Chapter Three
The Devil 89

Chapter Four
Exposed 169

Chapter Five
There Is Still Time 209

Chapter Six
Shining Light on the Darkness 285

Chapter Seven
Then It Will Be Too Late 295

Chapter Eight
Whose Side You Are On 305

Chapter Nine
Christ or Antichrist 317

Final Note 339
Something to Think About 347
Timeline Index 354
Holy Scripture Index 356
Endnotes 359
About the Author 382
The Storms of This Life 383

Preface to
The Victory Edition

This book has been over twenty years in the making, and even though my walk with the enemy was bittersweet and the source of much sorrow and shame, it is nonetheless a valuable gift that I would like to share with others.

This edition is a much sharper and more concise version of my testimony and remains true to the original, which was first published on 2 March 1995. Considering the state of the Church, it is even more relevant today!

If you truly love God, I hope you will read what I have written with a sincere desire to know more about Him. If you are a biblical scholar or learned individual, please listen from your heart and don't let your knowledge get in the way. If you are a skeptic, please hear me out and give me the benefit of the doubt for this moment in time. And if you are a man who will not listen to a woman, I pray you will set your pride aside and seek to hear the truth.

Sin is the doorway into darkness, and so many Christians turn a blind eye to sin or willingly participate in it, which opens the door to error and deception. It is *only* through Christ that we can truly see the reality set before us.

The Wicked One has been very slow and calculated in his evil plan to deceive God's people. He knows that if he moves too fast or becomes too obvious, he may alert his victims to the danger and scare his prey away.

I found myself doing some of the finishing touches to this edition on a seemingly minor but extremely important Biblical holy day, called the festival of Purim. It was during this season, many years ago in the days of Queen Esther, that God's people celebrated the great victory that Almighty God had given them over those who hated them and sought their destruction.

I pray that I will always be true to God and never forget what His dear Son has done in securing *my* salvation, and not for me only, but for all men who will repent of their sin and trust in Him. And because I am so grateful to the Lord Jesus Christ, I will earnestly proclaim the truth of the gospel as long as I have breath for such a time as this!

5 March 2015 / 14 Adar 5775 / Purim[2]

PREFACES TO THE PREVIOUS EDITIONS (1995–2002)

I believe we are embarking on a time in history that will be like no other. The world is changing so fast that at times it is hard to keep up. But praise God, the eternal truth of God's Holy Word is timeless.

The Devil is out to lead astray whosoever he can deceive into believing his lies, and he has been quite effective. His objective is to steal from you, kill you, and destroy you in any way possible. But if God's favor is upon you, He can intervene on your behalf, which is why God's grace is so important.

I am certain that everything in connection with this book is under the faithful care and guidance of Almighty God. And it was only through providence[3] that I received my first perfect-bound book from the publisher exactly two years to the day that the True Light pierced the darkness!

One day, all God's people will know exactly what has taken place in obscurity, and then they will realize how God has been working among so many others, *even* the enemy, to have His perfect will accomplished.

I have endured much opposition, from within and without, but I am determined to share what I have witnessed. Moreover, it is *only* by the grace of God that I will fulfill the call that He has placed upon my life.

Preface to the Victory Edition

This book is a collection of transcripts and letters written before, during, and after God delivered me from my enemy; and as you continue reading, you will see how I came to be in such a dangerous and vulnerable situation. I have slightly edited some of the letters for clarity, but I did not alter the content.

Most of the original letters that I had sent out were signed, sealed, and notarized at the chancery clerk's office, by direction of the Lord. I know this practice is somewhat unorthodox, and I have not done it in the past, but there again, I am not the same as I was before. Praise God!

Since the night of 28 February 1993, my relationship with God has taken on new purpose and meaning. The overwhelming desire of my heart is to please my heavenly Father in everything I say and do and to be obedient to Him regardless of whether I fully understand or know all the reasons why.

My purpose in sharing my story is so that others may gain a better understanding of this war that we are in. You might be completely unaware of the danger, or you may not even acknowledge God, *or Satan*, but it is so important that you find out whose side you are on before it is too late.

Please keep in mind that the enemy does not want you to become aware of any of this, since my testimony exposes him for who he really is. Satan will try any means possible to divert your attention away from this book, but I hope you will persevere if you want to know the truth of what I have learned about his tactics.

The memory of what Christ has done for mankind has become so tainted with evil. Apostasy, hypocrisy, and compromise are bringing churches down, and the name of Jesus continues to be misused and abused for personal, political, and financial gain. And it has even gotten to the point where you must have a very guarded approach toward those who claim to be Christian.

Jesus said that many would come in His name, yet they are ravening wolves dressed in sheep's clothing, seeking to lead God's people astray. This is why we must pay close attention to what people do, not just what they say.

It is imperative to come to terms with the fact that as long as you are living in this world, you too are at great risk of walking with the enemy. And only by walking in the True Light can you understand the adversary.

You also need to realize that the true condition of your heart will greatly affect how you will respond to the words that Almighty God has given. Only the sincerely humble will fully appreciate the message.[4]

May you truly grasp what you are about to read, and may God grant you the grace, knowledge, and wisdom you will need in order to comprehend and apply these wonderful truths to your life.

It is not my desire to bring attention to myself or other innocent people, and for that reason, I have changed or deleted names and places so as not to identify specific individuals and their whereabouts.

The deception that I was in could happen to anyone, anywhere in the world. In fact, it is going on at an alarming rate! The only consolation is that God has warned us about it in the Holy Scriptures.

Since my "translation" from darkness into His glorious light, I see that dates and events are important to God, despite the fact that my enemy tried to get me to believe otherwise. Looking back, I see how significant they really are. (See Colossians 1:12–14.)

The Ninth of Av (5759),[5] aka Tisha B'Av, became very meaningful for me in the course of writing this book. According to tradition, the enemies of Israel destroyed both of the Jewish temples in Jerusalem on the ninth day of Av. Reportedly, the first temple was burned down by the Babylonians in the year 586 BC, and the second temple was completely destroyed by the Roman Army, under the command of Titus, during the Jewish revolt in AD 70.[6]

Preface to the Victory Edition

These temples represented God's presence in the midst of His chosen people, but praise God, we don't need a man-made building for our heavenly Father to reveal Himself to us today. And if you will allow the Lord God to purify your heart, He may choose to make His habitation with you! But it can only happen through Emmanuel, the Messiah of Israel.

We are at a turning point in this battle for the souls of men, and it won't be long before Jesus "will swallow up death in victory!"[7] Praise the precious name of Yeshua HaMashiach,[8] Jesus Christ—the Anointed One!

If you happen to find out that you are on the wrong side, my sincere hope and prayer for you is that this testimony will encourage you to get on the side of the Lord while there is still time.

If you are one who is truly seeking God with all your heart, my most earnest prayer for you is that you will come away from here with more of a love and a deeper appreciation for God the Father, Jesus Christ His Son, and the Holy Spirit of the Most High God!

Introduction

THE FOLLOWING DIALOGUE was broadcast from a Christian radio station. It aired the day after the Branch Davidian compound[9] near Waco, Texas, went up in flames while the world looked on in horror as some eighty people, including women and children, were destroyed by the fire.

As you read my letters, you will see a number of similarities regarding some of the things that have come to pass in my life that will coincide with some of the bizarre events surrounding David Koresh and Mount Carmel.[10] My only explanation: *This is a war between God and the Devil!*

Because of my experiences, I am able to understand how Koresh[11] was capable of manipulating, seducing, and deceiving his followers into believing the lies, even though I have never met the man.

My situation involved totally different people and places, but it is just as what a man once wrote to me after reading my testimony of *Walking With the Enemy*:

> "It would take a while to share with you all that I found to be in common with your story. Though they are different, the similarities are undeniable. It's amazing how the enemy's signature is the same."

I am certain that the hosts of this radio station had no idea that they were being used by the Lord to assist me in exposing the hidden agenda of the Devil himself—which is *the peaceful eradication of mankind!*

The following discussion was my first encounter with some of these men, and even though they were discussing a very serious matter, after reading this you'll have to admit that the Lord has such a wonderful sense of humor.

*W*alking with the Enemy

Guest Speaker: Dr. David Breese[12]
Prophecy and Cult Expert / 20 April 1993

Host Let's go to C. Read...Thanks for being patient, and go ahead with your question or your comment.

C. I was just wanting to mention that I had just been delivered from a cult. And actually it happened on 28 February 1993.

Host What took place? What kind of cult was this? Can you give the name of it, C.?

C. [It was a Bible study group.][13] I was with them a little over three years.

Host Dave, is there a question you would like to ask C., maybe to find out what kind of a cult this was?

Guest Yeah, C., uh, first of all, I rejoice that you have been delivered.

C. Oh, me too. It's wonderful, actually!

Guest And I can tell by the sound of your voice that you thank God you weren't beguiled totally and completely into this thing, but something of the clear Word of God got to you so that you came to Christ. Right?

C. Oh yeah!

Guest That is a great testimony, C. I'd be interested to know, did someone come and preach, or did—

C. Oh no. The Lord actually came down by His Spirit into my living room.

Guest Do what?

C. It was a real fascinating experience.

Guest Oh *my!*

C. He, uh—it's kind of a whole long story.

Guest C., *stop* right there! Did you say someone, *or something*, came down and materialized in your living room?

C. The Holy Spirit manifested in a person and spoke. And that person happened to be me. And I hate to—I don't hate to say *me*, but for some reason, it's almost like I am boasting if I claim that the Lord actually spoke through me. But He did...He spoke in a very mighty way, and it happened that same day.

Introduction

The main thing about it is that our leader, my *ex-leader,* was *supposedly* a very godly man. And it was through deception and seduction, and many things were involved.

Host C., can I encourage you, when we get through with our conversation with Dave Breese, to give him a telephone call at his ministry, and you all can discuss this?

I'm sure, Dave, you have some questions relative to what C. is talking about. And C., if you would jot down that telephone number and call Dave. We have another caller[14] waiting, and since you said it's a long story then maybe he can find time to discuss it with you.

C. Okay.

Guest And we'll be happy to send this book, *The Marks of a Cult,* to all who call and request it. So we will welcome your call.

*And He hath put a
new song in my mouth,
[even] praise unto our God.*

PSALMS 40:3a

chapter one
Churches

> "I Jesus have sent Mine angel
> to testify unto you these things in the churches.
> I am the root and the offspring of David,
> [and] the bright and morning star."
>
> Revelation 22:16

I DID CALL DR. BREESE, and I went into detail about many things that took place during my time with the Bible study group. He was very intrigued and said God may use my experience as a ministry for others. At the time, I did not realize that God would have me develop a book that would explain how I was able to be deceived into thinking that I was walking with followers of the Lord Jesus Christ when, in truth, I was walking with the enemy.

I was directed by the Lord to send the following letter to several different churches and individual Christians. It was the first of many letters that God would be asking me to send out to those He had laid on my heart.

I will never forget the response I got from a woman who worked at the post office when I first started mailing this letter.[15] She confronted me one Sunday morning after a church service and said, "You need to quit sending out those letters!" She told me I was wasting my money and that I should spend it on my children instead.

I said, "I would have to deny the Lord to do what you are saying, and I just couldn't do that."

My answer did not seem to appease her, but I wasn't really trying to. My greatest desire in this life is to be pleasing to God, and I am determined to obey Him regardless of who is with me or who may be against me.

5 June 1993

To Whom It May Concern,

I am sorry this is such an impersonal salutation, but I will be sending this letter to people that are related to, friends with, or have had associations with members of Bill's Bible study group. Or you may possibly be someone who has never heard of this group but *needs* to.

If you are unfamiliar with this ministry and their practices, I will enlighten you. They were originally a prayer/Bible study group with Bill as the leader. Many people have come and gone, but the main group is Bill (pastor), Ira (assistant pastor), Candy (elder), Wendell (prayer warrior), and Thomas and Kim (followers).[16]

They consider themselves to be a church and have a listing in the local newspaper.[17] They currently hold their meetings at Ira's home and are open to the public.[18] They meet on Wednesday, Thursday, and Sunday nights.

They have a music and children's ministry, and Wednesday night is usually devoted to prayer. By all outward appearances, this is a nice group of people getting together to worship the Lord Jesus in song, word, and prayer.

Bill and Ira also claim to be prophets sent by God to proclaim His Word.

I had been a member for the last three years, and we met in my home for the last two years, that is, up until the night of

Churches

28 February 1993. My primary responsibilities, as established by Ira, were the ministry of "helps." I was also considered by her to be the weakest one, which is why I needed her and Bill to help me discern the "word" properly.

I walked with these people for three years, believing that they were my friends and that they cared about me. I grew to love and trust them completely and would do anything in my abilities to be a true friend.

Everything that I ever did for them I did as unto the Lord and never expected anything in return. I see why it is so important to have that frame of mind in light of everything I know now.

I felt that God sent them into my life to help me learn of Him and His ways, and *I did* learn very much from my association with these people. *That* is what I would like to share, as much as I am able to disclose at this time.

The following is a letter I sent to Bill and Ira, which explains my feelings toward them at that time.

11 May 1993

Dear Bill and Ira,

I received a letter from Candy the other day. She questioned why I haven't talked to her, but as I mentioned to you, I just can't deal with any of you right now. The wounds of what you all have done are too deep, and I am going through a healing process.

I know when I saw you and Bill at the store, such sadness came over me and I spent the rest of the day crying over all this. I didn't realize that seeing you two would cause that reaction in me.

You know, it really bothers me that I could have special friends like you for three years and come to find out you really weren't the type of friends I thought you were.

I tried to write you two a letter a few weeks after our breakup, but I just couldn't finish it. Besides, my husband kept pestering me until I came to bed. He has expressed that he doesn't want me to talk with any of you unless he knows about it.

I want you to know that I hate that things turned out this way. I really had no idea that it would. I never thought I would be rejected by all of you. I figured I would walk with you forever. It was a very hard thing to accept for a while.

Even when I spoke to you on the phone, Ira, I still had a lot of sadness in my heart concerning the loss of our friendship. I really felt like you two cared about me in a way that nobody ever has in my whole life.

I want to say that I did, and still do, care about what happens to you. I really don't desire anything bad for you, regardless of what you might think or what it seems like. And I know in your hearts that you do believe that.

I am not writing this letter to gain your sympathy, because I don't want yours or anybody's for that matter. I still take complete responsibility for what I do in this body of mine, and I know that I will reap the effects of what I sow.

I just want you to know that no matter what the enemy says to you, I am following Jesus! He is my Lord and my God! And Him alone do I serve! I know you've said that when people walk away from you that they won't continue walking with Jesus, and for some that is very true, but I think you will be wrong in my case.[19]

I hope one day you will see the complete truth and walk in the True Light. That is my greatest desire for you. I hope you will share this letter with everyone and even the children because it's truly my greatest desire for them too. I don't know if you

Churches

will, but would you please tell the children that I love them, even though they don't see me right now?

I will continue to pray for all of you as the Lord directs me. After all, He does know what's best for us. He is the only one who truly knows our hearts' intent. And by the way, I have not judged you. I really don't know exactly what your true intent is, only to the extent of what you have spoken to me. But I know the Lord commands that we look at our behavior, and that of our brothers and sisters. And that's all I have done.

I know you think I am under attack by the enemy. And I am! He doesn't like the stand that I have made. But that's what this is all about, isn't it? Light against darkness! The battle has already been won; we just don't see it yet. I pray that you, in the end, will be standing on the side of truth. But only you can decide.

This will probably be my last personal letter to you. I've written many. Do you ever re-read them? Or have you thrown them all away? If I had to guess I would say that they probably never meant anything to you, just as it is obvious that I never meant anything to you, either.

My last words to you are this: Purify your hearts! Repent! And turn back to Almighty God! So that He can heal you and make you whole again. He so wants to. But you have to confess your sin to Him, and to each other, so He can cleanse you and so healing can begin.

This has been a very hard letter for me to write, and I still have a lot of pain and grief inside of me that I didn't realize was there. But just remember, when I am in public, the Lord is my armor and His angels are all around me, and His Holy Spirit is inside of me, and I have chosen to yield myself to Him no matter what kind of fool it makes me look like. This letter is from my heart, and there are no evil motives behind it.

If you have ears to hear, you will hear!

(Just as I finished writing this letter, I received a phone call from the former husband of one of the members, asking me to appear in court.)

P.S. I just heard that you got a summons to appear in court. I have not received one as of yet, but if I do, don't be concerned, because I will only speak the truth with all honesty and sincerity, as I always have with you.

Let the Lord's peace be with you, and I know it will if He truly resides in you. Because He says, "I will never leave you, or forsake you. I am with you alway, even to the end of the world."

"And behold, I come quickly, and My reward is with Me, to give every man according as his work shall be. I am Alpha and Omega, the Beginning and the End, the First and the Last!"[20]

{End of letter to Bill and Ira}

I would like to apologize for the last part of my letter. There was very much of a sarcastic tone to some of the statements, and that was just not a good note to conclude that letter on. I know they are not living in peace, just by what the Lord has impressed upon my heart.

In fact, I know they are living in fear and torment. And I am truly sorry they have chosen to live that way. I would hope that would show them who they are following. And it certainly isn't the Prince of Peace, who is Jesus!

My relationship with them ended on 28 February 1993. The only dealings I have with them now are as the Holy Spirit leads me into their path. I will go into what happened on that night of 28 February 1993, so you will have a clearer understanding

Churches

as to why I can no longer befriend them or have anything to do with them unless the Lord directs me.

That was a night that none of us present will *ever* forget. It is because of what has transpired *since* that night as to why this has become an issue. I know many of you would rather not get involved or wish you didn't have to face any of this, and I am sorry for the grief and heartache many of you have gone through, and will continue to go through, because of your relation or association with some of these people.

My prayer for you is that you will so learn to trust the Lord Jesus Christ for every aspect of your life and allow Him to comfort, encourage, and strengthen you through all of this. You just need a humble and sincere heart and be willing to receive and obey the truth of the Word of God.

I would like to address the parents at this time. I know this must be very hard for you, and if you are a Christian, you must really be pulled in two different directions. I just pray that you will get before the Lord God and earnestly seek Him with all your heart on what you should do, and just do it!

At times, He asks us to do the hardest things, but He knows the outcome and we don't. And your obedience can sometimes make the difference between life and death. I am speaking of spiritual life and spiritual death. That is so much more important, because it will be forever.

I pray that the Lord will give us all an extra measure of grace to endure what's up ahead.

The Night of 28 February 1993

This was such an unusual night, and when Ira saw me for the first time that evening, she practically fell back and this shocked look came across her face. I asked her what was the matter, and she said, "Oh, nothing."

And then she commented on what I was wearing, but it was an old sweatshirt she had seen plenty of times before and I never got *that* reaction out of her. I knew she was lying, but I just didn't know why yet.

I had given Ira an article from the Sunday morning paper[21] on David Koresh and asked her to read it. It was just telling about his many wives and his claims that he was Christ.[22]

[I was not yet aware of the raid on the Branch Davidian compound by the federal agents, because Candy had kept me busy at her house in the country, and looking back, I am certain it was by direction of Bill and Ira.]

As Ira was reading the article, Bill seemed very nervous, and it was obvious to me that he was very much aware of that situation.

Afterwards, I let Candy read it, and I asked her out of hearing range of Bill and Ira if she knew what spirit David Koresh operated under. She said, "No." And I said, "The spirit of antichrist, the same spirit that is here." She didn't say anything, but she looked at me kind of funny.

I would like to mention that I said many things this night that I did not fully understand or realize the ramifications of until later, and I am still gaining insight on many things pertaining to all of this.

While we were waiting to get started singing, I spoke to Wendell and said, "I see the adversary hasn't kept you away tonight." And he said, "Not that he hasn't tried." And I said, "Well, I am very glad to see you tonight."

And then I spoke to Thomas and said, "I am very glad to see you, too." And I patted him on the arm. (This was a very unusual way for me to be talking, but I really didn't think much of all this until later.)

This is some of the words to the song we were singing when the Lord God interrupted our meeting, and it has been my prayer for some time now. (See Psalms 9 and 68.)

ARISE O GOD

Arise O God, let your enemies scatter. Arise O God, let your enemies scatter. For You are exalted King of all the earth! Riding high above the Heavens! Your Name shall be praised in the mighty gates of Zion! Your Kingdom shall reign forever! And ever![23]

This was the night that the Lord God Almighty answered my prayer and made His presence known in our midst in such a mighty way! These are the people that were present that night of 28 February 1993: Bill, Ira, Thomas, Candy, Kim, Wendell, me and my husband, our children, their children, and the Holy Spirit of the Lord God Almighty!

I am not sure at what point we were at in the song, but all of a sudden I started praying in the Spirit as the Holy Spirit gave me utterance. Then my hands were suddenly thrust up into the air, and I felt as if the Lord God above was pouring Himself into me while my hands shook uncontrollably. (My husband later told me that I did not appear to be shaking at all.)

There was such an anger and rage and hostility coming from my mouth, and I got so loud that I was drowning out the music. So after a while they decided to quit playing the musical instruments. (Bill plays the guitar, Ira the keyboard, and Candy and Kim the tambourines.)

Just to give you a feel for the atmosphere, my husband had a fire going, but it wasn't cold enough so he had the doors and a window open. So while the Lord was pouring out His wrath and indignation through me, it was not limited to just the confines of my living room. It was also for the *prince of the power of the air* to hear.[24]

This went on for a little while and then I stood up and abruptly walked to the front of the fireplace where Bill usually sat to teach.[25] I turned to face everyone with my hands still held high in the air and still speaking in the Spirit, then I suddenly stopped!

There was a dead silence in the room and every eye was on me. As I brought my hands down directly in front of me, I made a sweeping motion to the sides as if to say, *enough!*

The first intelligible words out of my mouth were, "Oh, Jesus, You are so beautiful!" At that moment, it was as though I just melted to the ground, and then I bowed down and put my face to the floor. At that point, I began praising the Lord and giving Him honor and all glory and thanksgiving.

I told Him that I am nothing without Him, and anything that I have that is worth having is because of Him. I told Him that I love and adore Him and that He alone is my Lord and Master.

After that, I lifted my face up from the ground and saw that everyone was staring at me. I started to get somewhat nervous, and I began to mumble something about how I didn't like to be the center of attention and how this really wasn't like me at all. Bill interrupted and said, "Well, give the interpretation." I was intimidated for maybe a fraction of a second, and I just closed my eyes and said very firmly, "I will."

Usually I was very intimidated by both Bill and Ira, but this night was different. There was such a boldness about me that I was actually intimidating to both of them! In fact, there had

CHURCHES

been a fear growing in them for some time now that I didn't really understand until after this night and the subsequent confrontational meeting we had on 2 March 1993.

It would have been nice to have gotten this prophecy of 28 February 1993 on tape, but it didn't matter. On 7 May 1993, the Lord brought everything that was addressed that night back to my memory almost exactly word for word.[26] As I spoke these words, it was quite different. It was more in love and compassion, but with much boldness and conviction.

PROPHECY OF 28 FEBRUARY 1993 [27]

"Many things you have been taught here have been done in secrecy and in darkness." I said this as I was looking at the congregation. *"You have been taught truth mixed with lies, and the* LORD *says it will go on no longer!"*

I looked at Bill and said, *"And you[28] are the one who has taught the lies, and the* LORD *says it will go on no longer in this home. And the* LORD *is giving you a chance to turn from your sin. And He is so forgiving that He will not hold your sin against you if you repent. And if you do not, you will die!"*

While pointing at my husband, I said, *"He is my husband."* Then I looked at my husband and said, *"I love him with a love that cannot be broken."* Looking back at Bill, I said, *"I love you too, but with a brotherly love. And I beg you to repent!"*

Then I looked back at everyone and said, *"Everything you have learned here has been tainted with evil, and you can't hold on to any of it. The only thing that you can hold on to is the fact that Jesus Christ died for you, and by His mighty power, God raised Him from the dead. And if you believe that in your heart and claim Him as* LORD, *He will put the same*

Spirit that raised Jesus from the dead inside of you to lead you and guide you into the truth!

Light will overshadow darkness, and darkness will not be able to stand in the presence of God!"

{End of prophecy}

I went on to say that anyone that wanted to come and pray and just read the Bible together would be very welcome here. But it would no longer be a two-man show run by Bill and Ira.

I realized that was all the Lord was giving me to say at that time, but He also stated that the remainder of this prophecy would come out later; however, I did not voice that to the group.

I started getting rather nervous again and said, "Well, that's all I have." And I went to my seat. They resumed singing, and Bill got up and preached like nothing had even taken place. At first, I was very agitated, but the Lord calmed me down and said, *"It will be addressed at the appointed time!"*

The rest of the prophecy came out on 2 March 1993. I will not go into all the details of that meeting except to say, *they have much to hide.*

[I'd like to stop and mention that the local newspaper has since removed Bill's ministry from its church listing, under much protest from Ira, I was told. Bill has stated to me, as per a phone conversation, that he is no longer preaching; and Ira said they are presently attending their old church. So it appears that the prophecy of 28 February 1993 has indeed come to pass!]

At this time, I would like to address only my family members, friends, and those that are acquainted with me. If you know me very well, you know that I was "born again" to God,

Churches

during my tour of duty in Yuma, Arizona, in November of 1979, while I was enlisted in the US Marine Corps.[29]

I have been a Christian for thirteen years now (as of the date of 5 June 1993), and I am very sorry to say that I've been a very prideful, arrogant, and thoughtless person. And I would like to express to you that I am very sorry if I have demonstrated that attitude toward you.

I would never intentionally want to be hurtful to anybody, even when I wasn't born again.[30] But I see in many ways where I have been. I have been a very selfish and inconsiderate person, and I ask you to please forgive me.

This is truly from my heart, and I am not saying these things to win back relationships or to manipulate you in any way. That is truly not my intent. In fact, I am not doing too good in the relationships that I have in my life now. But with the Lord's help, I am sure we will restore whatever needs to be.

There is also a lot of sorrow in my heart to the Lord, because all the while when I thought I was truly walking with Him in Spirit and in truth, I was actually walking with the enemy! And because I was such an improper representative of Him, I am extremely sorry.

But the Lord is so wonderful, and merciful, and forgiving! He won't hold any of my sin against me, especially since I did it out of ignorance. Like He says in His Word, "My people are destroyed for lack of knowledge" (Hosea 4:6).

But because I love Him so much, He will turn everything around for my good and the good of those who love Him, too. And for that, I will always be thankful and praise God for delivering me out of the power of darkness!

I would like to emphasize that what took place on the night of 28 February 1993 and 2 March 1993 was by the leadership of the Holy Spirit. This was not my doing. And I would like you to also realize that His anointing does not come as I will it, but as *He* wills it.

So don't think I am anything just because He has used me in this way. C. Read is nothing, but *Jesus Christ* in C. Read is everything! In fact, it's only by the grace of Almighty God that I am even able to talk about this.

My prayer to the Lord is that He will continue to show me my sin quickly so that I can see it and repent of it. I always want to have a pure heart before Him, so that I can see and hear Him very clearly.

The overriding desire of my heart is to have a deep, personal, and intimate relationship with our Creator. And I see how sin can separate me from Him, and ultimately kill me, whether I am deceived or not.

One request I would like to ask of you: If you are a Christian and the Lord brings up my name in your heart, would you please pray for me? And not for me only, but for all God's people, whether they have been born again into the Kingdom of Almighty God yet or not.

Thank you for taking the time to read this, and I will always be grateful for your prayers. May the Lord bless you and keep you from the Evil One. He is out there seeking whom he may destroy, and he takes no greater pleasure than to bring down a Christian. But always remember, "Greater is He who is in me, than he that is in the world!"[31] And the same holds true for you if you are a disciple of the Lord Jesus Christ.

You wouldn't believe what it took to get this letter typed. But I praise the Lord, He has given me the ability to put these words to paper. And I pray that He receives all the glory and honor for anything I do that is worth doing.

Churches

Blessing, and honor, and glory, and power be unto Him that sitteth upon the Throne, and unto the Lamb, forever and ever! Amen! (Revelation 5:13)

I attest this letter to be the truth as much as the Lord has given me the understanding, ability, and authority to speak.

A servant of the Most High God,
and the Lord Jesus Christ,

C. Read

As signed by me in the presence of a witness
on the 11th Day of June in the year of our Lord,
One Thousand Nine Hundred and Ninety-Three.

*Arise O God,
let your enemies
scatter!*

chapter two

Heed the Call

"Take heed therefore how ye hear:
for whosoever hath, to him shall be given;
and whosoever hath not, from him shall be taken
even that which he seemeth to have."

Luke 8:18

THE LORD LED ME to send my 5 June 1993 letter to the members of the church we attended before I joined Bill's Bible study group, and also to various Christian organizations and individuals, to total some one thousand copies.[32]

In response, I received some very encouraging letters. The mayor of the city even thanked me for sending him a copy. He wrote, "You are to be admired and congratulated for the stand that you take." He ended his note by saying, "God has ways to deal with things like that. Sometimes we just don't understand." I really appreciated hearing from all of them.

As of 17 October 1994, the only letters that I had received from members of the Bible study group were from Candy and Ira, and basically, most of what they said was that I was wrong and they were right. They still contended that they were walking with God, and that I was walking with the enemy. In essence, that could have been true if their "god" was the Devil, and their enemy was Almighty God.

I had sent a taped message to Candy on 7 July 1993, and it generated quite a response from both of them. I truly spoke what was on my heart, and even now I sincerely hope that I could somehow be wrong in my perceptions of these people I grew to love, but deep down inside, I do not feel that I am.

One very important lesson that I have learned is that the "spirit" in which something is spoken is so much more important to consider than the words alone. And only God knows for certain whether a person's motives be good or whether they be evil. Which is why it is so important to be able to discern His voice perfectly.

Howbeit, there is coming a day very soon (at the Great White Throne)[33] that there will be no more room for doubt as to who truly loves and belongs to the Lord Jesus Christ, and who does not.

The following letter was sent to my former friend, whom I once trusted, and I praise the Lord God Almighty that I am now walking in the True Light, with eyes that can truly see!

12 July 1993

Dear Ira,

I would like to discuss with you many things pertaining to all that has been going on, but I know that true wisdom is knowing what to talk about, to whom to talk with, and when. I truly want to be very honest and open with you, and with all people for that matter.

I really don't have anything to hide, and there isn't anything that I can't talk about that has gone on in my life. That's not to say that there aren't many things in my life that I am very ashamed of, and that I am very sorry for, but I am willing to discuss them if the Lord gives me the freedom to do that.

I would like you to know that just because someone inquires information of me, doesn't mean I will discuss my whole life story with them. I am trying very hard to be led by God's

ℋEED THE CALL

Spirit, and I am not so naive to think that there aren't people out there, sent by Satan, to try to trip me up and use my words against me. But even in that, I am going to just trust the Lord to show me my mistakes and help me to not make them again.

I pray that in speaking with you I will be very sensitive to the Holy Spirit and only speak what He would want me to say to you. I am convinced that the Word of God spoken in truth is the only Word that is worth hearing or speaking.

I am not going to try to quote Scriptures to you like you and Candy have done with me, but I will just speak to you from my heart. And if I speak the Word of God to you in truth, then it will bear witness in your spirit if the Spirit of Christ so dwells inside of you.

Last night when you called, I was almost happy to hear from you, but there was a lot of apprehensiveness there also. Ira, if you can believe it, I am so sorry that we are not walking together. But like you always used to quote to me, "How can two walk together lest they be in agreement?"[34] And we have a *major* disagreement going!

I so want to believe you when you say that you love me, but I am having a very hard time trusting anyone these days. The only one that I really trust is my Lord and Savior Jesus Christ.

I am not trying to imply that you are lying when you say that you love me and would do anything for me; and if I ever find myself needing to talk to you, that you will always be there no matter what; but I feel that my dependence and the complete trust that I used to have for both you and Bill is what got me in the trouble that I was in while I walked with you.

I do realize that we need other fellow believers that are like-minded to worship the Lord together, and to fellowship with, and even to some degree be accountable to, but I know that the Lord God Almighty is my strength, my support, my sustenance, and the One that will supply my every need.

You stated that you feel I am very lonely, but you are wrong there. I do feel that I am standing alone, but I am far from lonely. I truly enjoy being alone with my Father. I am very thankful for the ones that He has put in my life, and I do experience joy in my heart because of my relationships with them, but my preference is to be alone with Him.

I am starting to understand the personality that the Lord has given me and why I've done certain things all my life. He has been giving me insight on many things, and I would like to share some of those things with you, if and when the Lord allows me to.

I believe that is what I miss most about the relationship I had with you—being able to talk with someone about your life and really feel like they care. (Or so I thought.) You know, you and Bill are the only people in this lifetime I have been so completely trusting of.

I spoke to you about things that took place in my life that I would never desire to speak about, but I did with you. And look what happened! I have found out that you both have lied to me about many things.

And the Lord has revealed so much to me about you and Bill's ministry since I have been released from your control. It's a very hard thing to love someone so much that you would give everything that you are to them, and to have that love crushed beneath their feet. I would think you would understand why I have no desire to trust a human being ever again.

That is why I will only put my trust in the Lord for anything and everything. And I can actually be thankful for our relationship despite all the pain, because it has taught me the need to trust only Him.

Not that I don't talk with others, and listen to them, and maybe even take their advice, but the Lord is my final authority.

I want you to know that just because I don't trust you doesn't mean that the love I had for you is completely gone. In fact, I am starting to understand why the Lord has allowed me to love the way that I do. I hope that one day we can share again, but not until the Lord allows it.

You asked me last night what did I mean by the lies and the truth that I had referenced in the tape to Candy, and I would like to go into that as much as the Lord will allow me. I would like to share the transcript of the tape that I recorded on 2 July 1993 so that it will be fresh in your mind.

The words on that tape were truly from my heart, and I just really felt a need to speak to you all so that you could maybe sense and understand that I am very sincere about my feelings toward you, despite all that I know about you.

Transcript of Taped Recording / 2 July 1993

This is a very unusual way for me to talk with people. Usually I talk with them face to face or write a letter. I've never really ever done this where I speak to somebody through a tape.

And the Lord has impressed upon me to speak to you, Candy, and to whomever else you decide to share this with.

One thing I want you to know and realize is that I care about all of you very much. I know you might judge me and look at the things that you've seen me do; the way that I've responded to some of you in public; my seeming rejection of you by not calling you, or even by not writing you at times when you've written me. You might take that as rejection and that I do not care, and that is not the truth.

If you really knew my heart, you would know that I actually do care about you. And everything that I've ever done with you, with any of you, since I've left that group, has been under the leadership of the Holy Spirit.

I know all of you—I don't know all of you. I know, Candy, you have addressed the issue of the twenty-eighth of February; and Ira, you have addressed the issue of the twenty-eighth of February. And you have both stated that it was not of God. That it was not by the Holy Spirit. That it was of demonic spirits.

And it grieves my heart that you could say that. Not because of anything to do with me, but of everything to do with the Lord. My humanness is in much grief and sorrow over you folks.

(Break)

I am going to try to not get too emotional where I can't speak to you, but I am going to share this song with you that I heard on the radio—the new Christian radio station that came out real soon after we broke up...[35]

When I heard this song, I thought about you all, and I just want to play it for you. [Played the recording.] I am not sure of the name of that song, but the part that stands out the most in my mind is the part that says, "Friends are friends forever if the Lord's the Lord of them."[36] *I hope and pray that the Lord is the Lord of you, and if He isn't, that you will allow Him to be.*

One last thing I'd like to say to each one of you: Candy, I truly love you. Kim, I truly love you. Tom, I truly love you. Wendell, I truly love you. Ira, I truly love you. And Bill, I truly love you too.

Heed the Call

And that love is what God put in my heart for each one of you. And it won't matter whether you hate me or despise me for what the Lord leads me to do. I will do it, because I love Him the most!

But I just pray that each one of you will see the truth and make a decision in your heart that you're going to follow God and not believe the lies. That is my prayer for each one of you.

And there's such a sorrow in my heart right now, especially for you, Candy. I don't really know what's going on in your lives. Just by what I feel inside, I feel like you're really hurting, and I wish I could do something about it, but you've got to submit yourself to God. Resist the Devil, and he'll flee from you.

He doesn't hang around me. I don't have fear, anxiety, or torment. I have a lot of sorrow and a lot of pain because of lost relationships and that sort of thing, but God—He's taking care of that. He has replenished that with His strength and His love and comfort.

And in all actuality, if I had my greatest desire met, I would prefer to be out in the middle of nowhere with nobody, just me and God. That's what I would prefer. I don't have to have human friends anymore.

It's nice to have a little support every now and then from people, because God has been leading me into some things that are very hard to do. He's been speaking through me in ways that would seem like I have hatred and anger inside of me, but that's His anger and His hatred over the way Satan has so perverted and mocked His Word and has tried so hard to destroy His people. He's angry about that. And He's displayed that anger through me. And that's His pleasure. And that's His will. And that's my desire, for His will to be accomplished.

And I guess this is just my last chance of maybe pleading with you folks to realize that you're going the wrong way. And I hope that you'll really get before the Lord, the Lord God, and find out what sin is in your life that is keeping you from seeing the truth. Because sin will blind your eyes. It doesn't matter what it is, it will do it.

I don't want you to go to Hell. I would like to know you in Heaven. But that's not something I can decide for you.

And Ira mentioned in her letter—I have not written her back yet; I will when the Lord allows me and gives me the time to sit down and write her a letter—but she says I will suffer a lot because of the stand that I've made. And that's probably very true, but I know inside my heart that any suffering that I do now, it will be for Jesus's sake that I am doing it, that I am suffering.

The things that I suffered when I was with you folks were because of my own sin and my own ignorance, but now it's so different. And do you know what? I praise God that I am counted worthy to suffer for His sake. I praise Him for that! I think it's wonderful that He's counted me worthy to do that.

And He's answered so many of my prayers. I pray that He might answer the prayer that you'll come to the true knowledge of the truth, and that you will decide to walk in it. But that's something you have to decide.

My prayer is that you will see the truth and that you make your decision from there as to what you are going to do. If you don't want the things of God, if you don't want to walk in truth, then I really can't do anything for you, and neither can God. And I can tell you that if you do decide to walk with Him, you won't be disappointed.

Heed the Call

And that's all I have to say for right now. And please consider what the Lord is speaking to your heart. It might be your last chance. And like I asked the Rabbi, "What if you're wrong?"[37]

{End of tape to Candy}

Ira, you know that I am very willing to be used by the Lord in whatever manner He chooses. And contrary to what you believe, I don't have to be used by Him in any obvious way. Just the fact of being a Christian makes an impact on this evil world system we live in.

I know you and Candy think I have some great desire to be used by God in a major way, and that is really not that important to me. I know I've stated to you in the past that I truly would like to be able to reach lost people for Christ, but beyond that I am perfectly content in just getting to know my Lord and Master.

It would be a lot easier if I just pretended like I never knew you and just quietly moved away, never to be seen or heard from again. But that is obviously not in the Lord's plan for our lives. After all, He is the One who's in control. Praise God! Knowing that is what keeps me going every day.

I really don't take pleasure in creating a scene in public, but if the Lord so desires for that to happen, who am I to say no? I feel like if I was to try to just walk away from all this that the Lord just wouldn't let me.

I have been a changed person ever since 28 February 1993. The Lord God Almighty poured Himself into me on that night in a very mighty and supernatural way. I don't even want to imply that I fully understand it, but I know that I am different in a very wonderful way.

I don't have any need to convince you or any other person that it was of God. In your heart you know it's true if the Spirit of

Christ resides with you, and if you don't know the truth, then you will. But it will be too late if you wait for the "great and dreadful day of the LORD" to reveal it to you.

Ira, at this point, I don't know if you are truly deceived or if you are actually aware of all that is going on. But until the Lord confirms to me and establishes it in my heart, I will continue to hope and pray that you are deceived and that you really don't know what you are doing and saying.

I pray that you are genuinely misguided in your thinking when you say that what took place on the night of 28 February 1993 was under the power and control of demonic spirits. And I pray that the Lord will have mercy on both you and Candy for blasphemy against His Holy Spirit,[38] if you truly did it out of ignorance. God knows if you truly meant it in your heart, and depending on your heart motives, *that will* determine your outcome.

And I know if you continue to ignore His pleadings with you, your worst fear will come true, Ira. You remember you used to tell me that sometimes you were so afraid that when you stand before the Lord, that He wouldn't say, "Well done, My good and faithful servant?"

Ira, if you truly mean your statement that you have no doubt I am a servant of the Lord, then I pray that you will take heed and seriously consider these words of warning to you. You are walking with the enemy! At least he's my enemy, who is Satan, the Deceiver, the Father of all Lies.

I have many other things I would like to go into detail with you about, but I don't have the liberty to do that at this time, so I will close for now.

I would like to explain some of the accusations I made concerning you and Bill, but I would really like to hear Bill's stand on all this. Is it the same as yours? I won't assume that just because you said something, that it goes for him too. And I hope he doesn't have the same opinion that you and Candy have concerning the night of 28 February 1993.

I still have hope, and I will continue to pray for you as the Lord directs me. I hope one day we can look behind all this and be thankful to one another, and especially to the Lord, for delivering us from the power of darkness.

Sincerely,

C. Read

As signed by me in the presence of a witness
on the 14th Day of July in the year of our Lord,
One Thousand Nine Hundred and Ninety-Three.

TO THOSE WHO RESPONDED to my 5 June 1993 letter favorably, the Lord led me to send them a prophecy, dated 27 August 1992, which God had given me six months prior to leading me out of Bill's Bible study group.

Most people did not respond to that particular message, but I did receive two completely opposing views. The first letter that I received, dated 12 July 1993, was from a man who came to one of our Bible study meetings. He pretty much demanded that I stop what I was doing, and said I should submit to my husband, live a quiet life, do my housework, and teach my children at home, all of which I did, but he was very hostile toward the prophecy God gave me.

The second letter, dated 15 July 1993, was from a stranger, and her reaction was the exact opposite. She started out her letter by saying, "I bring you glad tidings in the name of our Lord and Savior Jesus Christ, the unspotted Lamb of God, to Whom all praises are due Him! For He is worthy to be praised! For truly He is Alpha and Omega, the beginning and the end…"

She went on to say, "You have sown abundantly, my dear sister; you shall reap abundantly. Well, I have something to share with you, my sister, being led of the precious Holy Spirit." Then she quoted the following passages:

Jeremiah 1:5–10 "Before I formed thee in the belly I knew thee; and before thou camest forth out of the womb I sanctified thee, [and] I ordained thee a prophet unto the nations.

Then said I, Ah, Lord God! behold, I cannot speak: for I [am] a child. But the Lord said unto me, Say not, I [am] a child: for thou shalt go to all that I shall send thee, and whatsoever I command thee thou shalt speak. Be not afraid of their faces: for I [Am] with thee to deliver thee, saith the Lord.

Then the Lord put forth His hand, and touched my mouth. And the Lord said unto me, Behold, I have put My Words in thy mouth. See, I have this day set thee over the nations and over the kingdoms, to root out, and to pull down, and to destroy, and to throw down, to build, and to plant."

Jeremiah 1:17–19 "Thou therefore gird up thy loins, and arise, and speak unto them all that I command thee: be not dismayed at their faces, lest I confound thee before them.

For, behold, I have made thee this day a defenced city, and an iron pillar, and brasen walls against the whole land, against the kings of Judah, against the princes thereof, against the priests thereof, and against the people of the land. And they shall fight against thee; but they shall not prevail against thee; for I [Am] with thee, saith the Lord, to deliver thee."

Ezekiel 2:1–9 "And He said unto me, Son of man, stand upon thy feet, and I will speak unto thee. And the Spirit entered into me when He spake unto me, and set me upon my feet, that I heard Him that spake unto me.

And He said unto me, Son of man, I send thee to the children of Israel, to a rebellious nation that hath rebelled against Me: they and their fathers have transgressed against Me, [even] unto this very day. For [they are] impudent children and stiffhearted.

I do send thee unto them; and thou shalt say unto them, Thus saith the Lord God. And they, whether they will hear, or whether they will forbear,

HEED THE CALL

(for they [are] a rebellious house,) yet shall know that there hath been a prophet among them.

And thou, son of man, be not afraid of them, neither be afraid of their words, though briers and thorns [be] with thee, and thou dost dwell among scorpions: be not afraid of their words, nor be dismayed at their looks, though they [be] a rebellious house.

And thou shalt speak My Words unto them, whether they will hear, or whether they will forbear: for they [are] most rebellious.

But thou, son of man, hear what I say unto thee; Be not thou rebellious like that rebellious house: open thy mouth, and eat that I give thee.

And when I looked, behold, an hand [was] sent unto me; and, lo, a roll of a book [was] therein;"

Ezekiel 3:1–27 "Moreover He said unto me, Son of man, eat that thou findest; eat this roll, and go speak unto the house of Israel. So I opened my mouth, and He caused me to eat that roll. And He said unto me, Son of man, cause thy belly to eat, and fill thy bowels with this roll that I give thee. Then did I eat [it]; and it was in my mouth as honey for sweetness.

And He said unto me, Son of man, go, get thee unto the house of Israel, and speak with My Words unto them. For thou art not sent to a people of a strange speech and of an hard language, [but] to the house of Israel; not to many people of a strange speech and of an hard language, whose words thou canst not understand.

Surely, had I sent thee to them, they would have hearkened unto thee. But the house of Israel will not hearken unto thee; for they will not hearken unto Me: for all the house of Israel [are] impudent and hardhearted.

Behold, I have made thy face strong against their faces, and thy forehead strong against their foreheads. As an adamant harder than flint have I made thy forehead: fear them not, neither be dismayed at their looks, though they [be] a rebellious house.

Moreover He said unto me, Son of man, all My Words that I shall speak unto thee receive in thine heart, and hear with thine ears. And go, get thee to them of the captivity, unto the children of thy people, and speak unto them, and tell them, Thus saith the Lord God; whether they will hear, or whether they will forbear.

Then the Spirit took me up, and I heard behind me a voice of a great rushing, [saying], Blessed [be] the glory of the Lord from His place. I [heard] also the noise of the wings of the living creatures that touched one another, and the noise of the wheels over against them, and a noise of a great rushing.

So the Spirit lifted me up, and took me away, and I went in bitterness, in the heat of my spirit; but the hand of the Lord was strong upon me.

Then I came to them of the captivity at Telabib, that dwelt by the river of Chebar, and I sat where they sat, and remained there astonished among them seven days. And it came to pass at the end of seven days, that the Word of the Lord came unto me, saying, Son of man, I have made thee a watchman unto the house of Israel: therefore hear the Word at My mouth, and give them warning from Me.

When I say unto the wicked, Thou shalt surely die; and thou givest him not warning, nor speakest to warn the wicked from his wicked way, to save his life; the same wicked [man] shall die in his iniquity; but his blood will I require at thine hand. Yet if thou warn the wicked, and he turn not from his wickedness, nor from his wicked way, he shall die in his iniquity; but thou hast delivered thy soul.

Again, When a righteous [man] doth turn from his righteousness, and commit iniquity, and I lay a stumblingblock before him, he shall die: because thou hast not given him warning, he shall die in his sin, and his righteousness which he hath done shall not be remembered; but his blood will I require at thine hand. Nevertheless if thou warn the righteous [man], that the righteous sin not, and he doth not sin, he shall surely live, because he is warned; also thou hast delivered thy soul.

And the hand of the Lord was there upon me; and He said unto me, Arise, go forth into the plain, and I will there talk with thee. Then I arose, and went forth into the plain: and, behold, the glory of the Lord stood there, as the glory which I saw by the river of Chebar: and I fell on my face.

Then the Spirit entered into me, and set me upon my feet, and spake with me, and said unto me, Go, shut thyself within thine house. But thou, O son of man, behold, they shall put bands upon thee, and shall bind thee with them, and thou shalt not go out among them: And I will make

ℋEED THE CALL

thy tongue cleave to the roof of thy mouth, that thou shalt be dumb, and shalt not be to them a reprover: for they [are] a rebellious house.

But when I speak with thee, I will open thy mouth, and thou shalt say unto them, Thus saith the LORD GOD; He that heareth, let him hear; and he that forbeareth, let him forbear: for they [are] a rebellious house."

She ended her letter by saying, "May the peace of God forever keep you and strengthen you always," and said she would be praying for me.

The man that was so adamantly opposed to the prophecy that God gave me suggested that I contact some of the "established body of Christ ministries," but considering what many of the popular Christian teachers and preachers stand for these days, they remind me of the Laodicean church.[39]

He did not respond to my follow-up letter, but a few years later, he replied to a letter I had sent to several Christian leaders and individuals asking about a revival that took place in Pensacola, Florida, on Father's Day 1995.[40]

It was called the "Pensacola Revival," which he happened to be in favor of. My second book[41] goes into detail about this disturbing event, but it is very similar to what took place at Bill's ministry, although on a much wider scale.

That "movement" is rooted in everything that is wicked and evil, and it is adversely affecting all the different churches, including Southern Baptists![42] For those who know the truth about the demonic practices relating to these so-called revivals, and have chosen not to warn God's people about it, they are actually furthering the agenda of the Devil by their silence.

I have since addressed these and other issues with several Christian leaders, and even though I was somewhat hesitant to confront them with what God had said to me, I could remain silent and do nothing or I could *heed the call*.

Walking with the Enemy

The following is one such letter that God led me to send out in response to this man's rejection of the prophecy that God gave me on 27 August 1992. ∽

25 July 1993

Dear Devin,[43]

I received your letter of 12 July 1993, and I would like to take this time to respond to it. First, I would like to thank you for the concern that you expressed for me, and I do appreciate that very much. I would also like to state that boldness is a very needed quality in a Christian if they are going to be able to stand against this present evil world system.

Devin, I do feel that you are truly concerned about me and my family, and I did prayerfully go before the Lord with your concerns, but the words in your letter did not bear witness with the Holy Spirit inside my heart and with the truth of the Word of God.

I shared your letter with my husband, and he was not in agreement with some of the statements you made, of which I will quote:

"I charge you, in Jesus's name, to leave this stuff alone now! If you feel God is giving you a prophecy, write it down and leave it there, between you and God. You can also neglect my words, but your blood is on your own hands because I have given you warning and a sure 'charge' in the Holy Spirit."

{End of Devin's statement}

My husband's response to your letter was that I must continue doing what the Lord has called me to do regardless of what other men might say. I also shared your letter with one of my daughters, and after reading it to her, she said, "It sounds like he's on their side." (Referring to Bill's ministry.)

HEED THE CALL

This Scripture came to me concerning your letter.

Matthew 16:21–23 "From that time forth began Jesus to shew unto His disciples, how that He must go unto Jerusalem, and suffer many things of the elders and chief priests and scribes, and be killed, and be raised again the third day.

Then Peter took Him, and began to rebuke Him, saying, Be it far from Thee, Lord: this shall not be unto Thee. But He turned, and said unto Peter, Get thee behind Me, Satan: thou art an offence unto Me: for thou savourest not the things that be of God, but those that be of men."

One of the most important lessons I have learned from my experience with Bill's ministry is that I can trust the Holy Spirit to lead and guide me into all truth, and I have no need for any man to teach me. And the Spirit will only speak what He hears the Father say, which will *always* bear witness with the Word of God.

John 16:12–13 "I have yet many things to say unto you, but ye cannot bear them now. Howbeit when He, the Spirit of truth, is come, He will guide you into all truth: for He shall not speak of Himself; but whatsoever He shall hear, [that] shall He speak: and He will shew you things to come."

1 John 2:26–28 "These [things] have I written unto you concerning them that seduce you. But the anointing which ye have received of Him abideth in you, and ye need not that any man teach you: but as the same anointing teacheth you of all things, and is truth, and is no lie, and even as it hath taught you, ye shall abide in Him.

And now, little children, abide in Him; that, when He shall appear, we may have confidence, and not be ashamed before Him at His coming."

I would like to share a letter that my husband wrote to me. (Please note that it was written almost two weeks before I received your letter.) It states many things that I feel are very prevalent to your concerns of whether I am in the will of God or not. And Devin, that is truly my only desire, to be in the perfect will of Almighty God for my life!

29 June 1993[44]

My dear sister in the Lord,

C., I pray the words I write to you, that you will hear them in your heart and not your mind, as I like to do. For He has laid it on my heart to write these words to you now.

C., I am truly sorry for my selfish attitudes and emotions that have come forth from my mind and heart. For they have not been of the Lord our God.

For I have been in this earth, as swine in a pool of mud. I do seek your forgiveness in all areas of my life, where my lack of sensitivity to the Lord has resulted in causing pain and grief in your life. I will not accept the excuse that I am just a man trapped in a sinful world. For that would be the easy way out, the earthly way out, and it would not be the truth.

C., these things were laid on my heart concerning myself. I do seek your love and understanding as I continue to grow in the truth of our Father's love. I don't seek to drive a wedge between us, or anything that cuts against the grain of your spirit. However, I do realize that is what I have been doing, and I am truly sorry.

Now more than ever, is it time to wake up and pay attention to what is going on in this world. Ever mindful to the presence of the Lord in our daily life, always being sensitive to the gentle and loving guidance of the Holy Spirit, that our God in Heaven has provided us with.

But C., in my ignorance I have allowed myself to give in to the ways of this world. These very words were spoken by you to

ℋeed the Call

me. I did not accept them then, for my pride would not let me hear, but I do now. Thank God!

C., we have to be strong for the causes of God. It would please Satan just fine for you to be defeated and to quit pursuing the mission God has called you to do. For divorce and separation to move into our lives would only enhance Satan and answer the prayers of those who curse and hate our Lord God Almighty.

C., Satan will use whatever means possible to accomplish his goals: your children, your husband, your church, your community, and the law of the land. So continue to be cautious of others and always to be sensitive to the Holy Spirit and the will of God, ever mindful of your responsibility to reprove those things that are not of the Lord.

I truly thank God for His faithful servant placed in my path, that He so graciously gave to me as my wife. I thank God for using you as an instrument to bring His Word into my heart. Praise God!

I didn't fully tell you just how beautiful and touching the card was that you gave me on Father's Day. It really meant a lot to me. It was one of the most touching things that I have ever received. The words you spoke through that card were filled with your love for me and the sweet fragrance of our Lord.

I am truly sorry that I have questioned your love or motivations. C., I do love you and I ask you for your patience and understanding in all things.

God Almighty and all-powerful will lead us through all of our tribulations. Praise God, for He is so wonderful!

Your friend in the Lord,

Your Husband

{End of letter from my Husband}

Devin, I would like you to know that I respect my husband as the authority God has put over me. And I trust the Lord completely for him. He has been very much a protection for me, and at times a comfort. The Lord has used my husband in many ways to confirm what He has spoken to my heart.

My husband has been in agreement with every letter that I have sent out. And if he opposes anything that I feel the Lord is leading me to do, I very prayerfully go before my heavenly Father in His Word and prayer, and seek His counsel on it. I trust the Lord to either work in my heart or in my husband's for His will to be accomplished.

God also knew I would continue to have much opposition to what He has called me to do, so He used my husband's letter to help strengthen me. And it most certainly did! His letter does take precedence over yours, especially since it's in accordance with God's Word. Note the following Scripture:

1 Peter 3:1–2 "Likewise, ye wives, [be] in subjection to your own husbands; that, if any obey not the Word, they also may without the Word be won by the conversation of the wives; while they behold your chaste conversation [coupled] with fear."

However, if you can believe it, your letter was also very encouraging for me. It shows me even more that Satan is very upset about the stand I have made and what I am doing. He's trying very hard to get to me by using a brother in the Lord, who I care about and respect, to try to place doubt in my heart.

My concern at this time is for you. I pray that you will go before the Lord and sincerely ask Him about me and the prophecy that I sent you. And the most important question I have for you is: How much time do you take to plant the good seed of His Word into a sincere and humble heart, so that He can make it grow up into His thoughts and His ways?

ℋEED THE CALL

I have many Scriptures I would like to share with you, but I don't feel now is the time. I have chosen a few that I pray you will consider and meditate on.

John 1:1, 14 "In the beginning was the Word, and the Word was with God, and the Word was God. [...] And the Word was made flesh, and dwelt among us, (and we beheld His glory, the glory as of the only begotten of the Father), full of grace and truth."

Revelation 19:7–13 "Let us be glad and rejoice, and give honour to Him: for the marriage of the Lamb is come, and His wife hath made herself ready. And to her was granted that she should be arrayed in fine linen, clean and white: for the fine linen is the righteousness of saints.

And he saith unto me, Write, Blessed [are] they which are called unto the marriage supper of the Lamb. And he saith unto me, These are the true sayings of God. And I fell at his feet to worship him.

And he said unto me, See [thou do it] not: I am thy fellowservant, and of thy brethren that have the testimony of Jesus: worship God: for the testimony of Jesus is the spirit of prophecy.

And I saw Heaven opened, and behold a white horse; and He that sat upon him [was] called Faithful and True, and in righteousness He doth judge and make war. His eyes [were] as a flame of fire, and on His head [were] many crowns; and He had a name written, that no man knew, but He Himself. And He [was] clothed with a vesture dipped in blood: and His name is called The Word of God."

Devin, I am sorry if I seem prideful or arrogant, because that is truly not my intention. If I am wrong in my perceptions, I ask for your forgiveness for not being sensitive enough to the Holy Spirit, but if I am correct, I pray that you will do something about it.

I know that righteousness and truth will prevail! And I pray that you will be found walking in truth. If you are not, you will be so ashamed when you stand before the Lord Jesus one day.

Walking with the Enemy

I am sorry if you were offended by anything I had to say, but if I feel the Lord is leading me to say something, I must say it, whether it pleases men or not. But I do welcome and encourage you to bring anything to my attention where you feel I am wrong.

I know that I am not beyond being deceived, but because of my experiences with Bill's ministry, I am very much on guard. After walking with the enemy for three years, I am very aware of many of his deceptive tactics to worm his way into my thoughts to try to affect my actions.

I do appreciate your boldness, and I pray that you will continue in that boldness under the direction of the Holy Spirit, as you submit yourself to God with your whole heart, soul, and mind.

I will always prayerfully consider anything you have to say, but the Lord Jesus Christ is my Master, my Redeemer, and my Judge! And the Lord God Almighty is my final authority! Praise the Holy precious name of Jesus!

Blessing, and honor, and glory, and power be unto Him that sitteth upon the Throne, and unto the Lamb, forever and ever. Amen!

Revelation 22:17 "And the Spirit and the bride say, come. And let him that heareth say, come. And let him that is athirst come. And whosoever will, let him take the water of life freely."

May the grace of our Lord Jesus Christ be with you.

Sincerely,
A servant of the Most High God,

C. Read

As signed by me in the presence of a witness
on the 27th Day of July in the year of our Lord,
One Thousand Nine Hundred and Ninety-Three.

Heed the Call

I SENT THE FOLLOWING LETTER to another member of the Bible Study group with the sincere desire that it would truly make a difference in his life. I don't know his outcome, but I still have hope.

2 August 1993

Dear Thomas,

The Lord has led me to write you this letter, and I pray you will listen with your heart and not with your mind. Just from past experience, I know my mind has lied to me and led me to believe many things that were not of God.

It all started in my mind, and once I gave into the lie, my heart was darkened through the deceitfulness of sin. And if someone were to have spoken truth to me, I couldn't hear it, so I continued to believe the lies. When I was finally broken enough by the effects of my sin, the Lord was able to get through to my unbelieving heart.

And I praise God Almighty for His mercy and His grace! Because His grace is truly the only thing that saved me! The Scripture that says, "By grace are ye saved through faith; and that not of yourselves, it is the gift of God. Not of works, lest any man should boast—" has become so real for my life in a way that I could have never imagined. (Ephesians 2:8)

I have always desired to walk with the Lord in truth, with all sincerity and honesty, and I believe you know that. I truly love the Lord Jesus Christ immensely, not because of anything I have done, but because of Him and everything He has done.

I've begun to realize more every day what He has done for me, what God is still doing for me, and what He will do for me in the future. There's such thankfulness in my heart for all that He is. And the main reason that I am writing to you is because He wants to do for you what He's done for me—namely, to set you free to serve and worship only Him.

Thomas, I am not really sure what your feelings are about me, or what you think about the stand that I have made against Satan. You have not made any attempts to contact me, so I will only assume you are of the same opinion as Ira, especially since you still support her and Bill's ministry.

I am going to share an excerpt from a letter that Ira sent me, which explains what she thinks about the night of 28 February 1993. [There is quite a gap between when it was written and the postmarked date of 13 May 1993.]

Letter to C. Read from Ira / 9 April 1993

When the message in tongues came forth that night, I was awestruck! I have heard demonic tongues before, but never in such intensity!

When you stood up and came to the front, I saw something in you that absolutely made me shudder—I saw Ruby.[45] *There she was, in living color! At that particular moment, there was such a fear that ripped through me. I was already furious at myself for not doing what God had specifically told me to do earlier—to stand up in front of you and command in Jesus's name by what spirit you spoke. At this point, however, I must confess, I was curious!*

All during the "prophecy" you gave—I say "prophecy" because God's Word says that tongues plus interpretation equals prophecy—the Word of God kept rising up inside my heart. I knew there was no stopping you, no way at that particular moment that you would listen to reason.

You were under the control of the same demonic spirit that has oppressed you all your life, the same spirit that held you captive that night at Dairy Queen.[46] *All this was nothing more than a continuation of the same events that had occurred all weekend.*

Heed the Call

God specifically warned us to be on guard against the tactics of our enemy, as we were under direct attack.

C., as soon as you believed you had a word from God, you were not even open to reason. During your walk with Jesus, you have so greatly desired the spiritual gifts, the things of the spirit, that the affection and desire for spiritual things has been the very thing that Satan has always used to deceive you.

{End of excerpt from Ira's letter}

Just in case you don't fully understand the statements she made in this letter, I will make it a little clearer for you. She attributed what took place on the night of 28 February 1993 as being from Satan and not from Almighty God.

Tom, you were there that night, and I pray that you will be very careful about what you say took place. I am sure you know that blasphemy against the Holy Spirit is the only unforgivable sin in this world *and* the world to come.

I really don't have to convince you or anyone else that what took place that night was of God, because I *know* that it was. It really doesn't matter whether anyone believes me or not; God knows, and that's all that really matters as far as I am concerned.

But as for you, it is a different matter altogether. If you believe in your heart the lie that Ira stated in her letter concerning the night of 28 February 1993, then you are in danger of being separated from the One, True, and Living God for eternity! And Tom, I truly don't desire that for you, or for any man. And neither does God.

I would like to, at this time, bring back to your memory what was spoken that night during Bible study, so it will be fresh in your mind. And here is the prophecy that went forth that night in my home.

Walking with the Enemy

Prophecy of 28 February 1993

"Many things you have been taught here have been done in secrecy and in darkness." I said this as I was looking at the congregation. *"You have been taught truth mixed with lies, and the* Lord *says it will go on no longer!"*

I looked at Bill and said, "And you are the one who has taught the lies, and the Lord *says it will go on no longer in this home. And the* Lord *is giving you a chance to turn from your sin. And He is so forgiving that He will not hold your sin against you if you repent. And if you do not, you will die!"*

While pointing at my husband, I said, "He is my husband." Then I looked at my husband and said, "I love him with a love that cannot be broken." Looking back at Bill, I said, "I love you too, but with a brotherly love. And I beg you to repent!"

Then I looked back at everyone and said, "Everything you have learned here has been tainted with evil, and you can't hold on to any of it. The only thing that you can hold on to is the fact that Jesus Christ died for you, and by His mighty power, God raised Him from the dead. And if you believe that in your heart and claim Him as Lord*, He will put the same Spirit that raised Jesus from the dead inside of you to lead you and guide you into the truth!*

Light will overshadow darkness, and darkness will not be able to stand in the presence of God!"

{End of prophecy}

Let the Word of God be the light that you use to judge all things to see whether they are of Almighty God or not. Please don't let a man come and steal what the Lord has spoken to your heart.

Heed the Call

Because Jesus came to this earth to reveal our innermost sin, all men will be without excuse on the day they stand before Him. This is the most important moment of your life. Please seriously consider what I am saying to you.

The prophet Jeremiah spoke of the new covenant that Jesus Christ established through His death on the cross at Calvary. And it is so important for all God's people to understand that this Scripture has been fulfilled because of the obedience of Jesus Christ to the will of God.

And I will ever be thankful to my Lord, my Master, and my Savior, for His demonstration of love by laying down His life so that I might live.

Blessing, and honor, and glory, and power, be unto Him that sitteth upon the Throne, and unto the Lamb, forever and ever. Amen!

The Scripture I referenced was from Jeremiah 31.

Jeremiah 31:31–34 "Behold, the days come, saith the LORD, that I will make a new covenant with the house of Israel, and with the house of Judah: Not according to the covenant that I made with their fathers in the day [that] I took them by the hand to bring them out of the land of Egypt; which My covenant they brake, although I was an husband unto them, saith the Lord:

But this [shall] be the covenant that I will make with the house of Israel; After those days, saith the LORD, I will put My law in their inward parts, and write it in their hearts; and will be their God, and they shall be My people.

And they shall teach no more every man his neighbour, and every man his brother, saying, Know the LORD: For they shall all know Me, from the least of them unto the greatest of them, saith the LORD: for I will forgive their iniquity, and I will remember their sin no more."

Walking with the Enemy

You know that I have always sincerely loved you with a brotherly love. And I still do. That is the reason I am earnestly appealing to you right now. I truly care about you, and I don't want to see Satan drag you to Hell with him.

He has lied to you so much and deceived you for so long, but it doesn't have to continue that way. I am pleading with you to submit yourself to God with your whole heart, soul, and mind. And if you do, Satan *must* relinquish his control over you. The sin that you are allowing to remain in your life is what's blinding your eyes to the real truth. And it will only get worse.

Please read the book of Romans to see an example, from God's Word, of what happens to those who claim to be walking in the truth but are actually submitting themselves to the desires of their own lust. And if you ever see this happen in your life, where God just turns you over to a reprobate mind, it can be a sign that you are, without a doubt, walking with the enemy!

The wages of sin is death! No matter whether you are deceived or not. Death tried to get its hold on me while I was walking with the enemy, but praise God, greater is He who is in me than he that is in the world! And it's only by the power of God that I was able to be delivered from the power of darkness.

Tom, I would love to talk to you about all the ways Satan tried to steal, kill, and destroy my life, but as long as you are submitting yourself to him, you won't really understand anything I have to say. In fact, you will think I am the one who is walking with the enemy, and that I am the one who is deceived, and that I am the one who is in danger of going to Hell.[47]

But one thing that is very certain: We will all stand before the Judgment Seat of Christ on that Day of the Lord and be required to give an account of ourselves to Him.[48] And it will be such a terrible day for many people. But the most important question we need to ask ourselves is: Whose side will we be standing on? And will the LORD be able to say to you or to me, "Well done, [thou] good and faithful servant?" (Matthew 25:21).

Ecclesiastes 12:13–14 "Let us hear the conclusion of the whole matter: Fear God, and keep His commandments: for this [is] the whole [duty] of man. For God shall bring every work into judgment, with every secret thing, whether [it be] good, or whether [it be] evil."

Satan will not go unhindered any longer! In the Lord's timing, Jesus will crush Satan beneath His feet, and if you are walking with the enemy, you will get crushed too!

The battle lines are being drawn in this war for the saints. The Lord is asking His people to make a stand for Him without compromise.

Tom, the Lord is giving you a chance to see the error of your ways so you can turn from your sin. Consider this verse that pertains to God's people.

2 Chronicles 7:14 "If My people, which are called by My name, shall humble themselves, and pray, and seek My face, and turn from their wicked ways; then will I hear from Heaven, and will forgive their sin, and will heal their land."

I know you have been taught, just as I was for three years, that sin is not an act that we do or don't do, but sin is simply not believing God. And *that* is a lie from the father of all liars, Satan himself! The devils *believe* God, and they absolutely shudder with fear!

I really don't know what more I can say to you to make you understand that I am sincerely concerned about you, and everyone from the group for that matter. The Lord has been trying to warn all of you to have nothing to do with the works of darkness, but obviously Satan has a very strong hold on you. This is your chance to be set free; please don't pass it up!

I am begging you to repent of your sins and turn back to the Lord God Almighty! He so loves you and desires for you to walk with Him in righteousness and in peace and joy in the Holy Spirit. That's truly what the Kingdom of God is all about.

God's Word is true—If you submit yourself to the Lord God above and resist the Devil, Satan must leave you alone. Not that he won't try some other way to worm his way back into your life, but if you continually stay before the Lord God in His Word and in prayer, He will be your protection, your direction, and your support if you let Him.

Please give my God a try. I love you, and I really don't want you to die. If you truly put your trust in the Lord Jesus Christ, He will not disappoint you or let you down. And it's so exciting to worship the Lord God in Spirit and in truth. I thought I was when I was with Bill's ministry, but I was so wrong. *The difference is like night and day!*

One thing I want you to know, you will always have a friend in me if you ever need one. Thank you for reading this, and I hope you will take heed to my warnings. Your eternal life or your eternal death is dependent on it!

I have spoken what the Lord has laid on my heart to say to you, and I hope you sense the urgency with which I speak. Please listen to what the Lord God is speaking to your heart. And I am sorry if I seem prideful or arrogant, because that is truly not my intent. If I didn't care, I would just be silent and do nothing. But I do care very much for all of you.

I will continue to pray for you and the other members of Bill's Bible study group as the Lord God directs me.

Heed the Call

Sincerely,
A servant of the Most High God,

C. Read

As signed by me in the presence of a witness
on the 4th Day of August in the year of our Lord,
One Thousand Nine Hundred and Ninety-Three.

AFTER I FOUND OUT THE TRUTH about Bill and Ira, I had a great burden to warn others about what I had been involved with. The Devil has tried very hard to stand in my way, but I thank God that Satan has not succeeded.

The following letter was sent to a man who occasionally came to our Bible study meetings, and even though I really had no idea how to contact him, God amazingly allowed me to meet up with him.

10 August 1993

Dear Philip,

I want to thank you for calling me the other day. It was very encouraging to hear from you. I have had a lot of opposition to the stand that I have made against Satan, so it was very comforting to hear words of support.

I have prayed for you, especially since the Lord revealed the truth to me about Bill's ministry. I had such a strong desire to get in contact with you and I really didn't know how. I had gone through the phone book one day looking for your name, and after I couldn't find it, the Lord told me to just be patient and that He would put me in contact with you when it was time. So I didn't give it another thought.

While looking through the tapes at the Baptist Book Store, I had already decided I wasn't going to get one, but for some reason,

I kept looking.[49] Then when I heard your voice behind me, and saw who you were, I knew exactly why I was delayed there.

God is so neat! He arranged that meeting. And I know that without a doubt. I was so excited when I went out to my car to get the letter for you. And I was thanking God the whole way. It's been so fascinating to watch the Lord work! He is so amazing!

I mentioned to you on the phone, when you called me last Friday, that I sensed you were a little apprehensive about running into me; and I just want to emphasize to you that I understand more than you might realize. I hope that you are always very cautious with all men. And I pray that you will be ever mindful of the presence of the Holy Spirit.

Philip, one thing I realize: Even the most sincere person can be deceived into believing a lie, and walk in that lie, professing and really believing that it's the truth. I know firsthand, because I did it for three years.

I was blind to the truth because of the sin in my own life. And because of my personal experiences, I understand the dangers of sin in a very real way. But I also know the saving grace of my Lord Jesus! I know that God will deliver *anyone* that calls upon Him from a sincere and repentant heart.

Whether you can believe it or not, I am very thankful for all that I went through. My faith in the Lord is so much stronger because of the trials that I endured. He's the only reason I was able to bear the emotional and spiritual pain that I experienced.

It's also because of Him that I am even able to discuss any of this with you now. I praise Him every day for the safety and protection that He allowed me to walk in, even though I was walking with the enemy!

HEED THE CALL

And because I sincerely love the Lord God Almighty and truly want to worship Him in Spirit and in truth, in His perfect timing He delivered me from the power that darkness had over me.

Praise the mighty name of Jesus Christ, the perfect Lamb of God, who came to take away the sin of the world![50]

God is all-powerful! God is in control! And it doesn't matter whether men believe it or not. The truth will prevail! Light will overpower darkness!

It has been really exciting since I have been walking in the True Light! As the Lord reveals Himself to me, and I gain more wisdom and understanding of Him, I just adore Him more every day. My relationship with the Lord is so different since the night of 28 February 1993. The Word of God has become so real for my life in a way that I could have never imagined.

I would like to share with you an excerpt from my journal. I wrote this exactly two weeks before the confrontation we had on 2 March 1993 with Bill and Ira.

Excerpt From Journal / 16 February 1993

I had asked the Lord, at the request of Elisha (Ira), to tell me if I could trust the people He'd placed around me. And she said that when things get crazy all around here, I can go back to this book and read what the Lord said.

The Lord is so neat! He didn't even address anyone else. He said to look at me and take notice of my behavior. He brought up two Scriptures. And I'll write them both down.

2 Timothy 1:7 "For God hath not given us a spirit of fear; but of power, and of love, and of a sound mind."

1 Corinthians 13:1–13 "Though I speak with the tongues of men and of angels, and have not charity, I am become [as] sounding brass, or a tinkling cymbal.

And though I have [the gift of] prophecy, and understand all mysteries, and all knowledge; and though I have all faith, so that I could remove mountains, and have not charity, I am nothing.

And though I bestow all my goods to feed [the poor], and though I give my body to be burned, and have not charity, it profiteth me nothing.

Charity suffereth long, [and] is kind; charity envieth not; charity vaunteth not itself, is not puffed up; doth not behave itself unseemly, seeketh not her own, is not easily provoked, thinketh no evil; rejoiceth not in iniquity, but rejoiceth in the truth; beareth all things, believeth all things, hopeth all things, endureth all things.

Charity never faileth: but whether [there be] prophecies, they shall fail; whether [there be] tongues, they shall cease; whether [there be] knowledge, it shall vanish away.

For we know in part, and we prophesy in part. But when that which is perfect is come, then that which is in part shall be done away.

When I was a child, I spake as a child, I understood as a child, I thought as a child: but when I became a man, I put away childish things.

For now we see through a glass, darkly; but then face to face: now I know in part; but then shall I know even as also I am known.

And now abideth faith, hope, charity, these three; but the greatest of these [is] charity."

The Lord told me if I don't see these things happening in my life that the enemy is attacking me and I must put on my armor. He then led me to the following Scripture.

Ephesians 6:10–20 "Finally, my brethren, be strong in the Lord, and in the power of His might. Put on the whole armour of God, that ye may be able to stand against the wiles of the Devil.

For we wrestle not against flesh and blood, but against principalities, against powers, against the rulers of the darkness of this world, against spiritual wickedness in high [places].

ℋeed the Call

Wherefore take unto you the whole armour of God, that ye may be able to withstand in the evil day, and having done all, to stand.

Stand therefore, having your loins girt about with truth, and having on the breastplate of righteousness; and your feet shod with the preparation of the gospel of peace; above all, taking the shield of faith, wherewith ye shall be able to quench all the fiery darts of the wicked. And take the helmet of salvation, and the sword of the Spirit, which is the Word of God.

Praying always with all prayer and supplication in the Spirit, and watching thereunto with all perseverance and supplication for all saints;

And for me, that utterance may be given unto me, that I may open my mouth boldly, to make known the mystery of the gospel, for which I am an ambassador in bonds: that therein I may speak boldly, as I ought to speak."

Dear Father, there is one thing I want to state here and that is this: I thank You for Your love and the wonderful gift of Your Holy Spirit. I know this is a real battle that we are in, and it's a matter of life and death.

Elisha (Ira) warned me yesterday that I was the one wanting to get into this, so I better get ready for the suffering part. But Lord, it's not that I want to get into all this junk. I just realize that, for right now, it comes along with getting to know You and Your Kingdom. And I would never, ever want to give back what I know about You.

I know because I chose to walk this path, I will get to know You in a more real way. The evil junk I could do without, and one day we will, but all I ask of You is that You will keep pouring out Your mercy and grace and truth on all of us, and give us Your strength to endure whatever is ahead. I am learning to totally depend on You, and I know if I am going to survive all this, I must depend on You! Help us, Lord, because we so need You!

C.

P.S. I will never forget what my Lord Jesus did on that cross, and I will always be indebted to Him for that display of love for me and for the whole world."

{End of excerpt from journal}

On the second of March 1993, my husband and I got together with selected members of the Bible study group to discuss what took place on 28 February 1993. I really had no idea what would transpire during that meeting. I just knew Ira stated that she had some very important things she needed to share with me and my husband. She had wanted to discuss it privately, but in light of what happened that night, I felt it was no longer a private matter.

I asked her, since the Lord had told her that He required her presence when Bill ministered to another person, if the same applied to her. She said she didn't have a problem with that, but she was still very persistent in trying to discuss the situation.

Finally, I had to insist that I was not going to talk about any of it with her until Bill was present. That particular evening (1 March 1993), Bill was working with Ira's father, so we couldn't get together then.

We got together the following night, and they brought Candy with them. I was hoping they would have invited Tom to come along, but they did not.

I called Wendell to see if he would be interested in coming over because we were going to have a meeting concerning Sunday

ℋeed the Call

night (28 February 1993). He was eager to come, but he was disappointed that they had not invited him.

I told him I had a feeling they preferred him not to be there, but I wanted him there, and so did the Lord. I asked him not to come until he saw their car, because I felt they would not have showed up if they knew he was coming.

We usually taped all of our meetings, except on Wednesday night, but I was very doubtful that Bill would want any of our discussion on tape. But due to the prompting of the Lord, I set up the tape player anyway. And this is what I recorded on that remarkable night.

Transcript of 2 March 1993

C. I know when I first came to this group that I was crying out to the Lord to relieve me of some of the burdens that were in my heart. And I know I gave you a letter— [I was speaking to Bill.]

Ira I would like to stop you here.

H. Let her talk, please. [H. is my husband.]

C. Could you at least—

Ira No, I'd like to stop here because I have an objection to the taping.

H. Why?

C. Why? Is there anything you have to hide, Elisha, as to the reason why you don't want anything on this tape? [I called her Elisha, but everyone else called her Ira.]

Ira No, there is not, but everyone in our church is here.

H. No, they're not.

C. Not everybody. I wish everybody was here, but they're not. And I wish you had addressed this issue Sunday night [28 February 1993], but you didn't. And that's because you do have something to hide.

Ira No, I don't.

C. Then let's tape it.

Ira No, I'm not in agreement with the taping.

C. Could you state why?

Ira Yes, because unless this is for this church, which is present here—

C. Why the secrecy? Why can't the church know exactly—you told me that—

Ira The church *is* here, C.

C. No, you told me—

Ira God's Word is specific here—

C. No, you told me that anything that you say to me, anything you say to her [referring to Candy], could be preached on the house, uh, mountaintops![51]

Ira Yes, it can.

C. So then, what's the problem?

Ira Because the only reason you are making this tape is not for this church, but for the members outside of this church.

C. That's a lie!

Ira And God—

C. I am not—I am not that type of person! And you have known me for three years…

Ira Church affairs out of the church…[Both of us were talking at the same time.]

C. That's crazy! You're lying! I'm sorry. That is not what I—how can you judge the intents of my heart?

Ira I'm not judging the intents of your heart.

C. You're saying this is for outside purposes. If there's anything that happened, why would you care? You said the mountaintops! The mountaintops are everywhere!

Ira Well, what does *God's* Word say, C.?

C. It says that anything, that *any* secret thing, will be revealed! *Every* secret thing! Thank God!

Ira It says that things will be taken care of in the church. That's what it says.

C. All right.

Ira It says we're not a part of the world.

C. Thank the Lord, I am *not* a part of this world!

Ira And it says that if things cannot be judged, that is to our shame.

C. And you know what? In the body of Christ, anybody is welcome. In the body of Christ, anybody is welcome to come into this house.

Ira But the *world* is not the body of Christ, C.

C. God wants them to be, though! He loved us so much—He loved the world so much that He gave His only begotten Son that whosoever believeth in Him will not perish, but have everlasting life! And how will the world hear, but we tell them! May I ask you that?

Bill Is this going to be telling the *world* about Jesus Christ?

C. I am not going to broadcast this to the world. And if what you're saying, if it's for the church's sake, that's exactly who it will be for. If you want the *whole* body to hear it, I don't have any problem with that at all.

Ira I think you made every effort to be sure that everyone that's within this body that you said God said should be here, is here.

C. No, there's some other people I wish were here, but God's our witness, and so it really doesn't matter.

Ira Then why do we need the tape?

C. Because you got something to hide, and we don't have to have the tape. I don't want to get into an arguing match. And it doesn't matter.

{End of 2 March 1993 transcript}

At the onset of this meeting, I had truly hoped we would be able to work out our differences and that Bill would repent of the sin that the Lord addressed on the night of 28 February 1993 during Bible study, but that was not to be.

At first he tried to deny the accusations that were made, but when he saw that he was losing my support completely, he admitted to everything and apologized to each person in the room, including me and my husband.

My husband asked him if he was truly sorry, why the secrecy? And under his breath, he made the statement, "I'm already dead."

About that time, Ira asked me to make a determination as to whether or not the Holy Spirit resided in Bill. I said, "I won't make that kind of judgment. God knows, and that's all that matters."

Then Bill presented this question to me: "Well, which *god* do you serve?" I got really excited when he said that, and I said, "By your words, you are condemned! If you have to ask me which *god* I serve, you don't serve the same one that I do! You serve Satan! And you are of the spirit of antichrist!" (Neither Bill nor Ira denied those accusations.)

At that point, my focus turned to Wendell, and I started pleading with him that this was a battle for his very soul. But because of everything that was revealed this night, he was just an emotional wreck. Candy, on the other hand, seemed like she was in some kind of trance. She was so different than I had ever seen her before.

And Ira, except for the initial dialogue and her question about the Holy Spirit, was unusually silent. At one point during the meeting, I got a little facetious and said to her, "What's the matter, *cat* got your tongue?"

Needless to say, in light of all that was revealed, I could no longer support Bill's ministry. I didn't realize until later that everyone in the Bible study group would be rejecting me because of my stand against Satan.

ℋeed the Call

Even though I had sincerely grown to love these people, I could no longer have any associations with them as long as they were walking with the enemy of my God.

I want to thank you again for your encouragement, and I would like to encourage you with this Scripture.

2 Corinthians 10:4–6 "(For the weapons of our warfare [are] not carnal, but mighty through God to the pulling down of strong holds;) casting down imaginations, and every high thing that exalteth itself against the knowledge of God, and bringing into captivity every thought to the obedience of Christ; and having in a readiness to revenge all disobedience, when your obedience is fulfilled."

Thank you for taking the time to read this, and I welcome any response you might have. I pray that God will continue to bless you and your ministry as you submit yourself to Him with your whole heart, soul, and mind. May He pour out His abundant love, mercy, and grace to overflowing.

Blessing, and honor, and glory, and power be unto Him that sitteth upon the Throne, and unto the Lamb, for ever and ever! Amen!

A fellow servant of the Lord Jesus Christ,
and the Most High God,

C. Read

As signed by me in the presence of a witness
on the 13th Day of August in the year of our Lord,
One Thousand Nine Hundred and Ninety-Three.

I never heard back from Philip, but I hope that he believed my testimony. I was prompted to write the following letter after I was questioned by a neighbor as to why I was taking my children out of the public school.

Walking with the Enemy

17 August 1993

Dear Becky,

I feel very compelled to explain to you why my husband and I have decided to start homeschooling our children again. I know when you came over yesterday you seemed very concerned about them not going to the public school this year, even to the degree that you felt they would be deprived of many opportunities they will need to be prepared for life.

In this letter, I would like to hopefully calm your fears and concerns and give you my perspective on the matter. I do want you to know that my desire to homeschool my children and keep them at home is in no way meant to condemn you for what you or other Christian women have chosen to do.

I know that I am completely responsible to God for the children He has given me, and I have always taken that responsibility very seriously. Not that I've done it perfectly, but I thank God that He has been so patient with me as I learn how to bring them up in the way they should go, so that when they are old they will not depart from the ways of God.

My greatest desire for my children is that they learn to love the Lord God with their whole heart, soul, and mind and to love their neighbor as themselves. And I am sorry to say that the atmosphere of public education does not promote the values that I have tried to instill in my children. In fact, it tears them down instead of building them up. And this is a reflection of the society we live in, not necessarily on the individual teachers or staff.

It would be so different if our society was based on godly principles, and you know, as well as I do, that it is not. With the leadership that this country is under, it will only get worse, especially since Satan has a hand in every segment of our society, including our public schools.

In light of the times that we are living in, I feel the most important job I have as a mother is to prepare my children to be in this world, but not to be a part of it. And in order to equip them for life, I feel God's wisdom is so much more important than man's wisdom or the wisdom of this world.

I want to teach my children to truly worship God in Spirit and in truth and to learn to trust and rely on the Lord Jesus Christ for all their needs.

I am not sure if I have discussed this with you or not, but it was because of Bill and Ira that I quit homeschooling in the first place. Because of the control they had over me, they were able to influence my thoughts and ideas about every aspect of my life. And they always used Scripture to establish their philosophies with me.

Because of what I went through with them, I see how easy it is to be deceived if you are not truly grounded in your faith. I feel in my heart that God expects me to protect and guard my children from the evils of this world until they can stand on their own. They are just not mature enough or strong enough in the Lord to be able to recognize the many different ways that Satan uses to get into our heart and mind.

The night of 28 February 1993 was the beginning of the first day of my life as far as I am concerned. The Lord called me out of darkness into His glorious light, and I see things with such a completely different perspective than I have ever seen before. Praise the Lord God Almighty!

I would like to take this opportunity to show you how I was able to be deceived by the enemy so easily when I first came to Bill's Bible study group. You have stated to me that you were also very deceived by Bill, so I feel it's important for you to understand what I went through, so that maybe you can learn from my error.

It started when Bill quit going to the Baptist church. I was concerned about him walking away from God, so I gave him a letter that was initially written to my brother-in-law after he had gone to the front of the church during a revival service. I liked the letter so much that I changed the salutation, and I started sending it out to other people that I cared about.

This is the first of many letters that I had given to Bill.

Fall of 1989

To Whom It May Concern,

I was just wanting to write a few of my thoughts about being a Christian. I know how hard it is with all the pressures of life, especially today. I wouldn't be so worried about you if I knew God was the center of your life. It's so important to have Him in you.

It's quite a challenge to be a Christian in today's world because the Devil has such a strong influence in every sector of society, but God is stronger! And it's so important to be on His side.

It's gotten to the point that riding the fence doesn't get it anymore. You have to make a stand one way or the other. And if you decide to live your life truly for God, the Devil will try to stand in your way every time, but you just have to pray for God to help you.

Just remember it's a gradual process and a learning experience to become Christ-like. You need to read the Bible to know what God wants you to do and how to live. He talks to you through His Word; you just have to be open to receive what

ℋEED THE CALL

He is saying. Don't worry that you won't always understand everything in the Bible; that comes with time and wisdom.

You also need to go to church. But wherever you're at, you just need to look for a preacher that preaches from the Bible, whether you want to hear what he's saying or not. If he starts talking about things that make you think you ought to change something in your life, then he's probably speaking the truth. Just pray for God's guidance, and He will help you in whatever endeavor you need to follow.

I hope you don't think I am preaching at you, but I guess I am. The only reason I am saying anything is because I love and care about you. And I want you to go to Heaven. You can be a good person, but unless you make a stand for God, you'll spend eternity in Hell.

I just want you to know that it's such a joy to be a true Christian, not just in name, but by example and attitude. I'll be praying for you. Take care and may God bless you and your family!

{End of Fall of 1989 letter}

I was very sincere when I wrote that letter, but I had no idea of the disgusting, self-righteous attitude that I had. It was that prideful arrogance that blinded my eyes to what was truly going on with Bill and his ministry. And it's only by the grace of God that I am now able to see. Praise His Holy Name!

One thing I want to make very clear: I am not judging the intentions of their hearts. That is only for God to do. Both Ira and Bill profess to be walking with God and that everything they do is ordained of God. But because of what the Lord revealed to me on the night of 28 February 1993 and the subsequent confrontational meeting we had on 2 March, I see that they are *not* walking with God, but they are walking with *the enemy* of God.

My involvement with Bill's ministry was an extremely humbling experience, and looking back, I see the "flesh nature" as the main way that Satan is able to get a "strong hold" in people's lives so that he can gain an influence over them. As John states:

1 John 2:15–21 "Love not the world, neither the things [that are] in the world. If any man love the world, the love of the Father is not in him.

For all that [is] in the world, the lust of the flesh, and the lust of the eyes, and the pride of life, is not of the Father, but is of the world.

And the world passeth away, and the lust thereof: but he that doeth the will of God abideth for ever.

Little children, it is the last time: and as ye have heard that Antichrist shall come, even now are there many antichrists; whereby we know that it is the last time. They went out from us, but they were not of us; for if they had been of us, they would [no doubt] have continued with us: but [they went out], that they might be made manifest that they were not all of us.

But ye have an unction from the Holy One, and ye know all things. I have not written unto you because ye know not the truth, but because ye know it, and that no lie is of the truth."

Due to my affiliation with that group, it established an even greater need for me to make sure my children have the proper training while they are young. And I know God will enable me to accomplish whatever He calls me to do.

Nevertheless, I thank you for your concern. I pray that the Lord's peace and blessings will be with you and your family as you submit yourselves to Him. And I will continue to pray for you as the Lord directs me.

Heed the Call

The greatest hope I have for Bill is that he will see the truth and truly desire to walk in it. He will have to turn from all the lies and the deceptions, though. And I hope that he will make that decision very soon, because time is running out!

        Sincerely,

        C. Read

*For You are
exalted King
of all the earth!*

chapter three

The Devil

"These are spots in your feasts of charity,
when they feast with you, feeding themselves without fear:
clouds [they are] without water, carried about of winds;
trees whose fruit withereth, without fruit,
twice dead, plucked up by the roots;"

Jude 1:12

My husband personally handed Bill the following letter, and as you continue reading, you will see that it was given to him at the perfect time. And even though I have no doubt that this man was led by the Devil, and his purpose was to destroy me, I take no great pleasure in knowing what his end will be.

24 August 1993

Dear Bill,

I have struggled with the idea of writing this letter to you, but the Lord has now given me a sign that it is time. I pray that I will be sensitive to His leadership as to what He would have me say to you, and I hope He will forgive me if I am not.

I know with all certainty that what God thinks about us is really the most important thing to consider in this world, *and* the world to come.

My motive for writing this letter is to hopefully convince you to turn from your sin and turn back to the Lord God Almighty, the One, True, and Living God, and persuade you to choose life instead of death, Heaven instead of Hell.

At this point, there is still a lot of pain and sorrow in my heart concerning you and those of the Bible study group, which I would think I could get over by now, but I still care about whether you live or die.

I know it might seem by the outward appearance of things that I have completely rejected all of you, but because of what the Lord has revealed to me in the last six months, I have no choice but to continue to stand apart from you until you repent.

I still have hope for you, though, and I believe I always will until you die. One thing I know for certain: If you die in your sin, still pretending that what you do is ordained of God, and you are a minister of Christ in righteousness, then you will be so ashamed on that Day when you stand before Him!

Reality will slap you in the face! And there will be no turning back then! Everything I have been trying to convince you of will become truth for you, and you will no longer be able to hide behind your pride.

I told someone that my greatest hope for you is that you will see the truth and desire to walk in it. But you will have to acknowledge the lies and deception that you have walked in and turn from all your wicked ways and do them no more. It's the first step toward true repentance. And it's the most important step you could ever take. Please seriously consider what I am saying to you.

I know because of everything that has transpired in your life, you must feel that there is no hope and no turning back. That you have just gone too far, and that God could never forgive

The Devil

you for all the things you have done against Him and other people. But God is so merciful and forgiving, and His grace is truly amazing. And I know if you ever truly experience God's forgiveness, your love for Him would be so great!

I hope as you read this letter that you will read it with an open heart that's willing to believe that I might be right. Please try to trust me just for this moment in time and give me the same benefit of the doubt that I gave you for the three years that I walked with you.

I really have no idea what I can say that will convince you to see the error of your ways, so I am just going to trust the Holy Spirit to do that. He is One that fully understands what is in your heart and mind, and I sincerely pray that He will lead me in this attempt to free you from the bondage of your sin.

I am going to assume you are as deceived as I was. I truly hope that you have sinned out of ignorance, instead of purposefully going against the commands of Almighty God. I know firsthand how easy it is to be deceived, and it was because of the sin in my own heart as to why my eyes were blind to the truth of what was going on when I first came to your Bible study group.

I now understand in a very real way why the Lord constantly warns us throughout His Word to obey Him and keep His commandments. It's not to deprive us of anything; it's to protect us from the dangers of sin.

Because of what the Lord did on the night of 28 February 1993, I see clearly now! And I attribute it all to the Lord Jesus Christ! I will forever be grateful to Him for giving me eyes that can truly see and ears that can truly hear. And I desire that for you and anybody else who is sincerely seeking with all their heart to serve and worship the Lord God Almighty in truth.

I am writing to you because I truly care about all God's people that may also be walking with the enemy unawares. And in this "little book," I will show you how I was blind to the real truth, held captive by the enemy, brokenhearted by my sin, and bruised because of the death process going on inside of me; and in so doing, I will reveal that this is also the condition of many of God's people.

I have learned many things about Satan's tactics that I would like to share with you so that hopefully you will see how you have come to be enslaved by sin and truly need to be saved. I sincerely desire for you to be delivered from all that is evil, and I hope you believe that.

Like I always used to say: I will love you no matter what you do or don't do, and that holds true even now, in spite of all that has happened. But I will not stand with you and support you in your sin and iniquity. God has called us to stand apart from sin and rebuke all wickedness. And I will do that.

My desire for you and your wife is that you live up to the commitment you made to her over twenty-five years ago and love her in the manner that God has ordained that a man love his *own* wife and children. If she was to ever accept you back, you would have to know that God intervened.

But whether she accepts you back or not, I pray that you will humble yourself before the Lord God and ask Him to forgive you and turn from all your sin. Only when you truly repent of the evil in your heart will you ever experience the cleansing forgiveness of the Lord God Almighty.

Do you remember that Scripture passage from Luke that I always used to think was for you? I never even once applied it to myself while I was with you. But since I am now walking in

The Devil

the True Light, the Lord has shown me that He *was* speaking to me back then; I just couldn't hear Him very clearly.

Luke 22:31–32 "And the Lord said, Simon, Simon, behold, Satan hath desired [to have] you, that he may sift [you] as wheat: But I have prayed for thee, that thy faith fail not: and when thou art converted, strengthen thy brethren."

That Scripture is the very essence of this letter, and because of what the Lord has revealed to me concerning my walk with the enemy, my primary purpose in this life is to share what the Lord God has revealed to me.

In order to establish what was in my heart and mind while I was walking with the enemy, the Lord has impressed upon me to use various letters and excerpts from my journal so that you can see how I was able to be deceived by Satan for the three years that I walked with you. Then maybe you will see how you have been deceived into thinking that you are walking with God, but in reality you have been walking with the enemy of God.

These first two letters are addressed to my husband. I feel it's important for you to understand what kind of relationship my husband and I had together prior to my joining your group. They will show why I was very vulnerable to the tactics of the Devil.

By sharing this letter with you, I want you to realize that it is in no way meant to condemn my husband or even imply that the sin I walked in was his fault, but I do feel my relationship with him is one of many reasons why I was so susceptible to being deceived by Satan.

18 June 1989

To My Husband,

Today is Father's Day, and since I can't talk to you, I guess I'll write down my thoughts to you. You not being here for the girls today goes along with the way things are the rest of the year. I am not wanting to be negative, but I can't help how I feel about our relationship and the relationship you have with the girls.

I was watching a preacher from the First Baptist Church on TV today. He spoke about several different types of fathers, and how important it is for the father to be the spiritual leader in the family, and that a father needs to be there for quality and quantity time.

He told a story about a couple who went to a nice restaurant and the man ordered the best steak on the menu. Well, when he got his steak, it was just a tiny piece of meat, along with some nice-looking vegetables. He asked the waiter about such a small piece of meat, and the waiter said it may be small, but the quality of that one piece of meat is the best you'll find.

But you know, just eating that made him want more. It's the same with the kids. If you give them bits of quality time too little and far between, it just leaves them feeling hungry and needing more.

He was also talking about the type of father that's at home a lot, but he might as well not even be there, because he doesn't ever really take time with anybody. He's just a fixture in the house.

I know you have other interests and obligations, but it would be nice if you made us feel like we're important too. You know, you give your work 101 percent of your effort. You give the National Guard 101 percent. You would drop anything to go to your shooting matches, but I don't think you can honestly say you'd do the same for your family. You might tell yourself that you do those other things for us, but all those things just contribute to the financial support of our family, nothing else. Do you think that a man's responsibility

The Devil

to his family is only paying the bills? That isn't my expectation of a father and a husband.

I just wish you would show as much enthusiasm to be around us as you do to go shooting or watching a war movie. You make me feel like being with us is the last place you want to be. I know it's not as exciting as work and Guard, but they do need you, and I do too, but you have gotten me where I really don't want to need you.

{End of letter to my husband}

I didn't finish that letter, and I am not sure if he even read that one, but I have written others very similar that I have given to him. Here's a letter that I feel is more in line with the attitude the Lord would desire that I have toward my husband, but I don't want to imply that he won't be held accountable for what he does with what the Lord has given him.

However, for my peace of mind and heart, I really needed to start seeing things from quite a different perspective, instead of focusing on how discontented I was with our relationship. I realize now that the only way to true peace is when you can look at this world from God's perspective.

And praise God, I was going to be embarking on a journey that would teach me how to do just that. As you should well know, it has been a very bittersweet journey. And I might add, it's not over yet. Here's the letter.

28 November 1989

My Dear Husband,

I just want you to know that I love you, no matter what. And I really wouldn't want to ever leave you. I guess I say that out of desperation or frustration. I really need to be more grateful for what I have instead of getting upset about what I don't have. And I guess your presence or time is what I've been upset about not having.

I am sorry about the way I make you feel sometimes, and I'll try not to be so emotional about things. I know you have other interests, and I'll try to be more understanding about that. I just really wanted to let you know a few of my feelings. With God's help, I can become a better wife and mother.

I love you,

C.

That letter was written four months before I started your Bible study group. We were just completing a course in MasterLife at the Baptist church when I was led to your group.[52] That was to be the beginning of my journey of walking with the enemy.

29 March 1990 was the first night I showed up at one of your meetings. I remember so clearly the astonished look on your faces when I walked through your door the following Thursday night. It was like you were so surprised that I even came back. But to your utter amazement, I did come back and hardly missed a night for the next three years.

Since Jesus is our example, we should expect to experience many things that He went through during His time on earth, and I do consider my time with your ministry as a wilderness experience where I was tempted by the Devil. Please note the following Scripture, and I encourage you to go back and read the entire chapter.

Matthew 4:1 "Then was Jesus led up of the Spirit into the wilderness to be tempted of the Devil."

Because Jesus is the perfect one, He knew the truth of the Scriptures, and He was able to refute anything Satan had to say. I wasn't even close to having a real understanding of the

The Devil

Lord Jesus Christ and His Word, but because I imagined that I did, that would be the cause of my fall.

Because I truly wanted to worship the Lord in Spirit and in truth and know the Lord Jesus Christ in a very personal way, He had a plan to get me there. He knew my sin of pride and self-righteousness had to be dealt with. And to accomplish that, I would have to be broken in my spirit and humbled in my soul before I could ever receive the truth about Him.

I praise God that I was led by His Spirit through this time of temptation. Like Jesus says, "I will never leave you or forsake you. I Am with you alway, *even* to the end of the world." (See Matthew 28:20 and Hebrews 13:5.)

This next letter shows how Satan was initially able to gain control over me, but keep in mind, it would only be to the extent that the Lord would allow. You probably remember this. It's pertaining to the night you "laid hands" on me and prayed that I would be "filled with the Spirit."

20 April 1990

Dearest Bill and Ira,

I just felt compelled to write you a letter expressing some of my thoughts and feelings. I really would like to thank you for the gift of your friendship and trust.

I've been praying for a while now that I could truly know Him and live my life centered around Jesus Christ. I feel God led me to you all. And I know you have much more knowledge and wisdom than I do, and if I can learn from you how to truly come to know Christ in the Spirit, then my prayers have been answered.

I know what I saw in your eyes last night was the Spirit of truth and love; and you passed some of it over to me through the grace of God; and I love you for that. Please know you can depend on me for any help I can give.

Yours truly through Christ,

C.

The Scripture that comes to mind, which I now understand the significance of:

1 Timothy 5:22 "Lay hands suddenly on no man, neither be partaker of other men's sins: keep thyself pure."

Because of my lack of knowledge, I allowed you to do something that God specifically warns us not to do, and thus you were able to gain an advantage over me. Had I not allowed you to lay hands on me, I would not have been able to be deceived to the degree that I was.

I would like you to keep in mind as you read this account that this was to be a learning experience that the Lord was leading me through. At the time, I had no idea that I was about to fall, but praise God, He would be there to pick me back up! This is a Scripture that comes to mind concerning this.

Romans 8:27–28 "And He that searcheth the hearts knoweth what [is] the mind of the Spirit, because He maketh intercession for the saints according to [the will of] God. And we know that all things work together for good to them that love God, to them who are the called according to [His] purpose."

That Scripture, along with many others, has become so real for me. The Lord has proved Himself to me in so many wonderful ways. But one thing I want you to understand is that I didn't see the truth of it all until I was delivered from the power that darkness had over me. And Jesus Christ is my deliverer! Praise His Holy Name!

Only because of the grace of God am I now walking in the True Light, and He has given me the understanding of what was really going on. You didn't fill me with the Spirit of God! What I saw in your eyes that night wasn't the spirit of truth and love; it was a demonic, seducing spirit!

And because of the blindness of my eyes due to my own sin, I allowed your sin to become a part of my life. I actually trusted and believed that what you did when you prayed for me was ordained of my God. Just as God warns us in His Word: "My people are destroyed for lack of knowledge."[53] I know if I had not truly loved the Lord God with all my heart, I would be walking with the enemy even still.

This next excerpt is from my journal and was written exactly a month and a half after I joined your group.

11 May 1990

My Dear Lord,

I have always addressed my words and thoughts to "my little book," but I am going to start addressing all my thoughts and words to "my Dear Lord."

I just want You to know what's been going on in my life lately. First off, I've been blessed and filled with that wonderful Holy Spirit. And I don't really know exactly how to describe the joy of it. It's like I met up with someone that I've always been looking for and finally found Him.

There's a completeness in me that didn't used to be there. My eyes see more clearly. I am starting to know what I've been sensing all along, but just didn't know what it was.

I know, dear Lord, that You have been watching over me. I can feel Your presence and Your love. And it's so beautiful! And I am so thankful for the people You've given me to learn from and be able to see You in them.

I just figured out what draws me to them, and it's You, Lord. The love they have for You is just flowing out of them, and I just can't help but to be attracted to it because I truly love You with my whole heart, mind, and strength, and no man can take that away from me.

I am starting to see the joy that Paul speaks of. And it's so wonderful! I really want to know You fully! I know You are guiding my steps, and I will go wherever You lead me. Thank You for choosing me.

Until later,

C. Read

As you noticed at this point, I was very attracted to both of you. It's because of the seducing spirit[54] I received when I allowed you to lay hands on me that night of 19 April 1990 as to why I had this extraordinary attraction to you, which I wrongly presumed was the love of God.

Nothing seemingly terrible happened that night, but because I didn't understand the ramifications of what took place, I would become more influenced by demonic thoughts, instead of God's Word.

When I look back on my feelings, it was so strange because I was willing to forget everything I had ever learned and fully trust both you and Ira, to the extent that your opinion was all that mattered.

This next letter was concerning my reaction to my youngest daughter being under a demonic attack, which you and Ira had informed me was going on. I now realize that this was all a tactic of the enemy to gain more control over me by increasing my dependence on you.

The Devil

It also established in me more of a respect for you due to your ability to fight off demons. In my eyes, you had to be of God if you could cast out devils. You always used to make reference to this particular passage, which gave credence to many of your claims.

Mark 16:15–18 "And He said unto them, Go ye into all the world, and preach the gospel to every creature. He that believeth and is baptized shall be saved; but he that believeth not shall be damned.

And these signs shall follow them that believe; In My name shall they cast out devils; they shall speak with new tongues; they shall take up serpents; and if they drink any deadly thing, it shall not hurt them; they shall lay hands on the sick, and they shall recover."

12 May 1990

My Dear Lord,

Last night sure was a night to remember! It was my first real confrontation with the other side. They were very persistent, but thank you, Jesus, for being who You are, and I am so glad that I am on the winning side.

This is really going to be a totally different kind of life. Living totally for the Lord Jesus and really knowing who He is, is really something! This really puts new meaning and purpose in one's life.

I am part of God's family now. I feel like I really understand what Paul went through. I haven't experienced the kind of persecution as him, of course, but I understand the spiritual side much more. I really see things in a different light. I just pray that I won't ever let God down. I will try with all my strength to please Him.

Until later,

C.

Walking with the Enemy

I saw things in a different light all right! I was walking in darkness, and I didn't know where I was going! By my words, you can see I was fully convinced that I was finally walking in the truth for the first time in my life.

I didn't go into what took place that night, so I will here. I am not really sure why you two were there, but I know I was glad because of what was going on with my youngest daughter. Earlier that day, I had rushed her to the doctor's office because she was having trouble breathing, and I had no idea why. The doctor took x-rays of her chest and then all of a sudden she coughed up pieces of a banana that were stuck in her throat, so to my relief, she was going to be fine. That night was a completely different story.

Later that evening, my little girl began screaming as if in excruciating pain. I became very worried that it was because of what had taken place earlier that day as to why she seemed to be hurting.

At the prompting of Ira, I called the doctor at his home. He was extremely impatient with me and said she shouldn't be having any problems. Ira informed me that she knew that would be his response, and based on what I know now, I feel she may have had something to do with why he was so short with me.

She went on to tell me that this was a demonic attack against my daughter and proceeded to pray for her in "other tongues" while she held my screaming little daughter. As Ira was praying for her, she appeared to be casting out demons and demanding they leave my home.[55] My daughter eventually calmed down, but what I didn't realize was that she was actually cursing my little girl under the authority of Satan.

I also understand that when you and Ira pray with other tongues, it is not inspired by the Holy Spirit but by demonic

The Devil

spirits. Just because someone can speak in other tongues doesn't mean they are praying the will of God. Paul warns us about this in his letter to the Corinthians.

1 Corinthians 14:27–28 "If any man speak in an [unknown] tongue, [let it be] by two, or at the most [by] three, and [that] by course; and let one interpret. But if there be no interpreter, let him keep silence in the church; and let him speak to himself, and to God."

On 14 May 1990,[56] I was given the gift of speaking in other tongues, and I marked it on my calendar because I was so excited about being able to finally speak in God's language. I truly considered it to be a gift from Him.

Do you remember how frustrated you used to get when I wouldn't be able to speak in other tongues when you would lay hands on me and pray for me to receive the gift of tongues? In light of what I know now, I am so thankful that you were nowhere around when the Lord gave me that gift.

The following is an excerpt from a letter dated 15 May 1990 that I had sent to some friends.

Speaking of God, I have really been learning a lot about Him these days. He's so much more than churches claim Him to be. They put too many limits on His power and abilities.

I've really grown to love the Lord, and I hope someday I can share with you some of my experiences. Of course, I'll always be learning, but the more I learn, the closer I get to Him. And you know what? God doesn't really mind you drinking that beer of yours unless you make it an idol.

The main thing you have to do is read that Bible and ask God to help you to understand what He's saying and invite Jesus Christ into your heart and go from there. And then learn how to listen to God.

I've been finding that a lot of what God has been telling me doesn't match up with what I've learned in all the churches. Just ask Him, and He'll lead you to the right church or group of people.

That neighbor I mentioned who stayed with the girls while I took my daughter to the doctor is a minister. But not your typical one. He looks like the rest of us, and he even smokes occasionally and drinks wine every now and then. And he's the godliest man I've ever met.

You might think I am crazy for saying this, but he acts like you think Jesus would when He was here. He's also very loving. Not in a lustful way, but very loving, and he makes you feel loved. But all that is not because of him, but because of that Holy Spirit inside of him. It's really neat to learn about the real truth of God, and I pray that you all do if you haven't already.

{End of letter to my friends}

Through the twisting of the Scriptures, Satan was able to plant some very radical thoughts in my head about the love of God and His truth.

I am going to take this time to state many of those ideas to help you, and myself included, to try to understand how I was able to succumb to the more obvious transgressions against God's commands.

Through seducing spirits and witchcraft, I was led to believe that you and Ira were "spiritual mates" and that your adulterous affair was ordained of God, even though both of you were married to different people.

I was also led to believe that the children you conceived together were sanctified by Almighty God. Ira even told me

The Devil

that the Lord revealed to her right after the act that she had conceived a child in both cases.

I was also led to believe that God said you would be like a husband to me until my husband started living up to that responsibility as revealed in God's Word. Here's the Scripture you used to reference.

Ephesians 5:24–27 "Therefore as the church is subject unto Christ, so [let] the wives [be] to their own husbands in every thing. Husbands, love your wives, even as Christ also loved the church, and gave Himself for it; that He might sanctify and cleanse it with the washing of water by the Word, that He might present it to Himself a glorious church, not having spot, or wrinkle, or any such thing; but that it should be holy and without blemish."

I remember the night all three of us were sitting out by Ira's pool when we had the conversation concerning who my *own husband* was as established by God's Word.[57] Prior to this you had requested that I go pray and ask God who you were to me. So I did.

The night we discussed it, you had asked if God had told me anything, and I told you He said, "You will learn a lot from this man." You agreed and said, "Yes, the Lord has appointed me as your teacher."

Then you asked me, "What else did He say?" I was a little reluctant to tell you what else I had heard because there was some confusion, mixed with fear, concerning the other things. So after rationalizing what I thought I'd heard, I stated, "He said you would be like a father to me."

I believe you sensed my hesitancy, and you said, "No, that's not what He said." And I said, "Well, I did hear a little something else." And you said, "Well, what is it?" I said, "I think

He told me you would be like a husband to me." And you agreed that that's exactly what God had said.

You stated that He had appointed you as my spiritual head, and that you would be like a husband to me, and both you and Ira would be my teachers. I didn't really know what to do with this conversation, or really understand what you meant, so I just put it in the back of my mind.

I now realize that part of Satan's tactics is to use Scripture to establish his lies, which he did very effectively with me, due to my lack of knowledge and experience. Bear in mind, I am just trying to establish the framework of what led up to some of the other things Satan misled me into believing was truth, as you will see as this letter progresses.

As I reread that letter to my friends, I now see how blind I was to the real truth. Because of the demonic control in my life, I attributed all my feelings for you as being from God and not from the lust that was within me. Because of my strong desire to be loved and to love, I allowed the lies of Satan to become truth for me. James addresses this issue.

James 1:12–16 "Blessed [is] the man that endureth temptation: for when he is tried, he shall receive the crown of life, which the Lord hath promised to them that love Him.

Let no man say when he is tempted, I am tempted of God: for God cannot be tempted with evil, neither tempteth He any man: But every man is tempted, when he is drawn away of his own lust, and enticed. Then when lust hath conceived, it bringeth forth sin: and sin, when it is finished, bringeth forth death. Do not err, my beloved brethren."

I hope you see this, because this is how it starts with all of us. And it gets progressively worse if we continue in our sin and

The Devil

don't allow the Lord to reveal it to us. I now understand why pride is so dangerous. Pride will keep you blind to the truth and never allow you to acknowledge your sin.

1 John 1:9 "If we confess our sins, He is faithful and just to forgive us [our] sins, and to cleanse us from all unrighteousness."

On the other hand, if we don't confess our sins, God will not forgive us and cleanse us of the unrighteousness that sin produces in our heart. And if we continue in "pride, and arrogancy, and the evil way," the end result will be death and separation from God forever. I thank God He is so longsuffering!

2 Peter 3:9 "The Lord is not slack concerning His promise, as some men count slackness; but is longsuffering to us-ward, not willing that any should perish, but that all should come to repentance."

Since I was walking in darkness, it was reflected in my words and thoughts. Even though my intentions were good, I was still walking with the enemy and under his influence. Because I was convinced that I had finally found the long-lost truth, I was even trying to get others to come to our meetings. I just thank God He didn't allow many people to be persuaded by my invitations.

One point I would like to make very clear: If I had known how to allow the Holy Spirit to bear witness to the truth of God's Word, instead of depending on you and my abilities, I would not have fallen for the lies of the enemy.

Since the Lord knew what it would take to break me of the pride in my heart and my self-righteous attitude, He would be using what Satan intended for evil and turn it around for His will to be accomplished. Praise God!

Continuing with excerpts from my journal:

18 May 1990

My Dear Lord,

You asked me to write some of my experiences down in the last month or so, and I will. First of all, Satan has really been trying hard to keep me from getting closer to God. He's tried a lot of different things to accomplish that, but he has not succeeded. Thank you, Jesus!

At first he put an idea in my husband's head that I shouldn't join Bill's Bible study group, but he let me go the next week. Then Satan realizes I've really found something meaningful in this group of people, which is You Lord, so he steps up his attack. He makes our financial situation look worse and feel more pressure from them, so my husband is ready to file for bankruptcy. After about a week, I am able to convince him that it's just not the way to go and he needs to put his faith in our dear Lord.

Then Satan really gets nasty! He attacks my beautiful daughter.... That was a very rough night, but Bill and Alisha (Ira) were here and they really helped. My husband had gone on a shooting match. It was Mother's Day weekend. And you know, even though all this was going on, Christ has put such an inner peace in me that is hard to put into words.

I just know that He has His hand on me, and He has chosen me for a task that I am very willing to carry out. I just want to please Him and get closer to Him. And I am really learning to listen to that wonderful Holy Spirit inside of me. It might not always seem logical, but I will do whatever is required of me. I am really starting to understand what Bill means when he says we must die to ourselves. And I am very willing to do that.

Until later,

C.

The Devil

You know the reason why Satan was able to get such a strong hold is because he gave you the ability to speak some very profound truth, and when the deception came, I didn't recognize it because I was already so trusting of you. Truth mixed with lies! Just like in the garden of Eden! The Devil hasn't had to change his tactics because men are still so ignorant of the truth. This Scripture would have been my salvation if I had known how to apply it to my life.

1 John 2:26–29 "These [things] have I written unto you concerning them that seduce you. But the anointing which ye have received of Him abideth in you, and ye need not that any man teach you: but as the same anointing teacheth you of all things, and is truth, and is no lie, and even as it hath taught you, ye shall abide in Him.

And now, little children, abide in Him; that, when He shall appear, we may have confidence, and not be ashamed before Him at His coming.

If ye know that He is righteous, ye know that every one that doeth righteousness is born of Him."

I am going to make a very bold statement that may be hard for you to accept, but that I feel you already know in your heart. You have *never* been born again to the Spirit of God, and neither have a lot of other professing Christians.

Reread that Scripture I just quoted: "If ye know that He is righteous, ye know that every one that doeth righteousness is born of Him." If you will be completely honest with yourself, *and* with God, you know that your conduct has been an abomination before the Lord! And your actions most certainly do not line up with the fruit of the Holy Spirit!

Had I been walking in the True Light, I would have recognized all this, thus not putting myself in the position to be led into deception and be a partaker of another man's sin. But I also want you to realize that the Lord has a plan that has not been completely revealed as of yet.

Walking with the Enemy

I have come to understand that many professing Christians are under the misguided belief that just because they make an altar call, or make a public profession of faith in Jesus Christ, that they have earned the right to enter into the Kingdom of God. One of the Devil's tactics is to deceive people into believing that they are born again when in reality they are not.

I realize this could be a hard pill for you to swallow if you've been living your life under the impression that you're going to Heaven just because you or someone else says that you are, but keep in mind that the purpose of this letter is to show you that you need to be saved from your sin—not to condemn you. You are already condemned if you do not truly know God.

After all, Jesus came to save sinners from death and destroy the power that sin has over us. Try to remember that as you read this. Please listen with your heart, and don't let your pride keep you from hearing what I am saying. The truth of all this will truly set you free. You'll wish you had listened if you find yourself barred from the Holy City on that Day.[58]

Here are more excerpts from my journal that will help to explain what was going on in my heart and mind as I was walking with the enemy.

22 May 1990

My Dear Lord,

Today I've been trying to get depressed and upset about the things I've been going through, and the changes that have been going on and will continue to go on in my life.

First off, I have had a problem with the fact that so many people that I've learned about God from, and that I thought were such godly people, really aren't as close to God as I thought.

The Devil

It's just hard for me to accept that all these people are wrong and only a few are right.[59] *But, dear Lord, in Your wonderful way, You led me to a passage that helped explain it to me.*

1 Peter 4:18 "And if the righteous scarcely be saved, where shall the ungodly and the sinner appear?"

I guess what that means to me is that just because you claim to be godly, doesn't mean you are, and even if you aren't but claim you are, God can still use you to get to the people that He knows will come to Him.

My husband leaving for military training has me feeling very lonely even though he hasn't left yet.[60] *But I am learning to put my faith in God and what He has for me to do while I am here on earth, and I'll try to not let the things and the cares of this world get to me.*

I talked with Alisha (Ira) a little while ago, and it really helps to talk to her about things that go on. She can really help put it in perspective. I really care about Bill and Alisha and the group. They are really very special people to me, and I am very thankful to God for the people He's led me to.

I'll write You again soon.

As you can tell by this letter, it was really starting to bother me that we were supposedly the only ones in town that were really worshipping the Lord in Spirit and in truth. And even though I believed you, it was very disturbing for me. The good part about it was that it encouraged me to pray for the people of this town even more.

Another reason why I was so taken with you all is because of this inward desire to be accepted by a group of people that I could call my friends. Since I grew up in the military, I never had the opportunity to establish lasting friendships; and Satan was aware of this, so he took advantage of that desire within me to lure me into being a part of your group.

I would like you to note the statement that I made in that letter: "Just because you claim to be godly, doesn't mean you are, and even if you aren't but claim you are, God can still use you to get to the people that He knows will come to Him."

I would like you to realize that, even though I was walking with the enemy in darkness, the Lord was still establishing His truth inside my heart, because He knew my desire was completely for Him.

This next excerpt was in response to the book by Frank Peretti that you two had encouraged me to read.[61]

4 July 1990

My Dear Lord,

I feel compelled to write to You. I just finished a book called This Present Darkness *by Frank Peretti. It was a very enlightening book on the power of prayer and of the spiritual warfare going on around us. I can now see and understand the many ways Satan has control of people. I just pray that I can be a source of power in Christ Jesus to deter Satan's demons.*

I love You, Lord, and I ask You to keep revealing things to me and give me the strength and desire to carry out Your will. Thank You for all that You do and will do and have done. Praise Your Holy Name!

C.

In light of what I know about your ministry, I feel the only accomplishment of that book was to prepare me for the demonic activity that followed you around. I praise God that

The Devil

He never allowed me to see the things that you said you saw, or be tormented by them the way Ira said she was.

I do remember one experience back in January 1991 that I'll never forget, though. You and Ira had gone to California to visit your birth mother. The Bible study group was gathered together to pray when all of a sudden I heard this terrifying scream that seemed to be circling the outside of my house. The first thought that came to me was that it was one of the kids.

Both Sue[62] and I heard it, and we went running upstairs. Every child was sound asleep and there was just this dead silence. For a moment, a fear came all over me, but then it was replaced with excitement at the thought that our prayers were able to chase demons away from my house screaming in terror!

I was so excited that I even called you and Ira in California. Do you remember? I always used to wonder why that occurred in your absence. I now understand that because of the demonic power given to you by Satan, when you and Ira left, the demonic spirits had no authority to stay either. Praise God!

God is in control, and Satan has no authority over anyone that is completely submitted to Him. I could look at my journey of walking with the enemy as a time that the Lord just gave me over to Satan, but because I desire to see things from God's perspective, He has shown me how He was working in all of us to have His will accomplished in spite of what Satan planned.

I realize you have a lot of knowledge concerning the Bible and that you have been to seminary and pastored some churches, but I hope you will not allow all that to stop you from hearing the truth when it's presented to you.

I also realize the fact of me being a woman might cause a little problem, but I hope you are beginning to see things from

God's perspective, instead of men's thinking. Here's what God thinks about it.

Galatians 3:27–28 "For as many of you as have been baptized into Christ have put on Christ. There is neither Jew nor Greek, there is neither bond nor free, there is neither male nor female: for ye are all one in Christ Jesus."

On 28 February 1993, I was baptized into Christ! Praise His Holy Name! And you were a witness to it! God has actually anointed me to speak His Word as He gives me understanding, and that's all I am doing here. If you do not agree, I hope that would encourage you to submit to God, through His Word and by prayer, and allow His Spirit to reveal the truth to you.

This next letter is from my heart to God's heart. One thing I want you to realize, even though I wasn't walking in the complete truth, my relationship with the Lord was growing and becoming more beautiful every day because He knew that my heart's desire was to know the truth and walk in it.

11 July 1990

My Dear Lord,

I would just like You to know that I truly love You, and I pray that I can be worthy of the love You have for me. You are so wonderful, and I praise Your Holy Name—Jesus!

I really want to have the mind of Christ, and I hope and pray that I will attain it. I know the more I read Your Word and pray, I will one day. And by Your grace, I will fully know You, because I really want to know You as much as is possible while on this earth.

You are my life, and without You, I am nothing. Nothing on this earth can fulfill me without You. And I thank You for leading me to the truth and giving me Your Holy Spirit.

The Devil

Until later,

C. Read

Here's a letter that reveals my feelings for you at that time. I would like to note that Alisha, Elisha, and Ira are all one and the same person. Everyone else called her Ira, but I felt God said her name as given by Him was to be Alisha. However, Ira informed me the correct spelling was Elisha. I now realize that it wasn't just God's voice speaking to me back then.

16 July 1990

Dearest Bill and Alisha,

I feel compelled to write you a letter today. The neat thing about it is I know God is prompting me to do it. I just want you to know that in the three and a half months since I've been coming to your Bible study, I've learned more about God than I would have in a lifetime of going to the traditional churches.

Ever since I've accepted Christ into my heart, my desire has been to know Him; and truly have wisdom, knowledge, and understanding of Him; and to know what His purpose is for me. And I know He gave you to me to help me attain that. And I am so thankful for that.

I have my faith in Jesus Christ, and I believe His Word, and I know that He is all-powerful. I guess my main problem is confidence in myself to be able to carry out everything He asks me to do.

I just never want to fall into the trap of Satan. I was reading 2 Peter 3:17 and 2 Peter 2:20–21 last night, and those verses make one realize it is quite possible for that to happen, and I pray that it will never happen to any of us.

Walking with the Enemy

I love the Lord, and I love you all. No matter where I am, I pray that I will always have that love in my heart. I so want to have the mind of Christ, and when people look at me, I don't want them to see me—just Christ living in me and through me. My prayer is that I will have the courage to stand up for my Lord and to do the will of the Father.

With love in Christ,

C. Read

Verses referenced in the previous letter:

2 Peter 3:17 "Ye therefore, beloved, seeing ye know [these things] before, beware lest ye also, being led away with the error of the wicked, fall from your own stedfastness."

2 Peter 2:20–21 "For if after they have escaped the pollutions of the world through the knowledge of the Lord and Saviour Jesus Christ, they are again entangled therein, and overcome, the latter end is worse with them than the beginning. For it had been better for them not to have known the way of righteousness, than, after they have known [it], to turn from the holy commandment delivered unto them."

My walk with the enemy was *so* ironic! Here I am praying that I won't ever fall into his trap, and I was *already* in his trap! Do you remember when I first started coming to your Bible study group? On the very first night, as I was walking down my driveway to your house, I heard a small voice that said, "Turn around and never go back." Well, I just dismissed that voice, and I attributed it to the Devil. I just figured he didn't want me to study the Bible.

I continued to have nagging doubts as to whether you were truly of the Lord as you claimed, and my doubts were pretty much alleviated after I attended a seminar at the invitation of a friend.[63] I am not sure if you remember, but I had asked you

The Devil

to come with me. I really wanted you to go so that I could see the minister's reaction to you. Since you couldn't come, I went by myself.

After the meeting, they asked if anyone needed prayer or desired to be "filled with the Spirit." So I decided to go up front. When he came to me and asked what my need was, I said that I wanted to be filled with the Holy Spirit.

I would like to remind you that you had already prayed for me to receive the Spirit. I wanted to go to this meeting because I was worried that I had received another spirit besides the Holy Spirit on 19 April 1990, when you laid hands on me and prayed for me to be filled with the Spirit.

He proceeded to pray for me and his only comment was, "You have already been filled with the Spirit."[64] So, there was my confirmation! I could finally trust you, and I refused to entertain any more doubts that I had about you. So, as far as Satan was concerned, I was right where he wanted me. But I hope you are starting to see that I was also right where God wanted me to be.

Here's another account of my experiences while walking with you.

30 July 1990

My Dear Lord,

I was just wanting to write down a few things that have happened in the last few days. Last weekend, we went to visit my mom, and it was an interesting weekend. She didn't come out and say it, but I feel she is a little skeptical about my Bible study group. If she fully understood, I don't think she would have any problems with it, but she's not really hearing from God, but I pray that she will one day.

My husband is getting a better understanding about God and how He works, and I pray he will become the man God intended for him to be.

Yesterday (two of my young daughters), me, Alisha, and Sue were baptized by Bill. I really felt led to be baptized again, and especially by Bill. I really feel like he has some great things ahead that God will fulfill, and I am so glad to know him and be under his leadership.

I just pray that I will live up to the things God plans for me and that I will fulfill His purpose for me. I love the Lord Jesus and I believe Him. I just hope I won't allow the things of this world to get in the way. I know that Devil will be trying all he can to make me not believe God, but with God's help, Jesus will overcome.

Until later,

C.

That letter shows how prideful and arrogant I was. It was that very attitude, along with the demonic influence, that kept me blind to the truth of what was going on with my feelings and emotions.

I remember that I was so honored to know someone that loved Jesus the way that you said you did. But I now understand that Satan's intent was to lure me in with the truth so he could deceive me with the lies.

Colossians 2:4, 8 "And this I say, lest any man should beguile you with enticing words....

Beware lest any man spoil you through philosophy and vain deceit, after the tradition of men, after the rudiments of the world, and not after Christ."

I'd like to mention that I no longer underestimate the shrewdness and abilities of my enemy. Furthermore, I know it's only

The Devil

by the grace of Almighty God as to why I am even able to see and understand any of this, which is why I will forever be indebted to my Lord Jesus Christ for delivering me from the power of darkness!

Here's another letter that reveals my feelings toward you at that time.

6 November 1990

Dear Bill,

I would just like to express a few of my thoughts to you. Sometimes, I can write them better than I can say them. Initially, I was wanting to write a letter to my sister-in-law to straighten her out concerning you and my walk with the Lord, and send copies to several other people.

But the more I sought the Lord on it, He led me to these verses in 2 Corinthians 3:1–6. It was like He was telling me you don't need to write it down on paper, just let them see Jesus and His love in you, and if that's not enough, it's their decision to accept or reject Him.

It really bothers me sometimes when people speak of you and treat you in the manner in which they do. And I know that all these things have to be. It just doesn't make it any easier to watch what you go through. I just wish I could do something to make them understand and to know the truth about you and our Lord Jesus.

Bill, I want you to know I understand and know the truth. I know Jesus lives in you, and His Spirit flows out of you like a river. I know you will follow your Lord no matter what this world says or thinks.

I just want to thank you for the things you've taught me about that beautiful Lord Jesus, and most of all to our Father for leading my steps to you.

Our bond is Jesus Christ, and because of Him, this tremendous love is flowing out of me. And I know it's because of your desire to minister and teach the love of Christ that I've been able to understand the depth of His love. I appreciate you and am ever thankful. Bill, I truly love you!

Your friend,

C.

This next verse is one you quoted quite often, especially in the beginning. I now understand why Satan would prompt you to do so.

Philippians 3:10 "That I may know Him, and the power of His resurrection, and the fellowship of His sufferings, being made conformable unto His death."

You used to state that your life was going to be one of terrible suffering, and that eventually you would be put to death because of your stand for Jesus. As I now see it, you are a master at manipulating people emotionally, physically, and spiritually for your own personal gain. And if you don't wake up, you'll spend eternity in Hell with the one who has manipulated you into believing and carrying out his lies and deceptions.

Ephesians 5:14–16 "Wherefore he saith, Awake thou that sleepest, and arise from the dead, and Christ shall give thee light.

See then that ye walk circumspectly, not as fools, but as wise, redeeming the time, because the days are evil."

This next letter was written right before you and Ira went to California to see your mom. Remembering back, I was so happy for you to meet up with her because of the joy it

The Devil

brought you, especially because of the heartache you seemed to be having over your wife and children.[65]

15 January 1991

Dear Bill and Elisha,

I just wanted to let you know that you are very special people to me, and that I praise the Lord for your willingness to be used of Him to teach others about Him. I've learned some things about the love of God that just can't be put into words. He is my life, and I just want to please Him and to learn His ways and have His thoughts. And I am so thankful that He's given you to me to help teach me.

You will be very missed, but I am so glad that you have this time together. I pray that you will be strengthened in the Lord Jesus and be able to withstand whatever persecutions come your way. I know the enemy will try whatever means that he can to come between you. Just remember to keep the whole armor of God on. I love you both very much.

C.

As you can see from this letter, my love for you and Ira was very genuine. I was so trusting of both of you, even to the degree that I was willing to believe that your relationship with Ira was truly ordained of God.

I completely stood by both of you, regardless of what anyone else said or did. As far as I was concerned, I knew you were of God, and that's all that mattered. It still amazes me how I could believe some of the things you told me, even though it was so against the very precepts of God's Word!

I would like you to note the following statement: "And I've also learned from His Word that the only thing He really considers sin is unbelief." You made this statement quite often in your teachings, which I unknowingly accepted as truth, but I have since come to understand that it's a perversion and a lie from Hell!

It was because of that statement, among many others, that Satan was able to lead me into deception and entice me into doing things that were completely against the very commands of God.

I would like to note that the Jewish fellow[66] you used to compare yourself with also used to make the same statement that "the only thing God really considers sin is unbelief." So, needless to say, I have serious reservations about him too, especially since I became aware of his ministry through you.

From this point on, my letters will have somewhat of a different tone, mainly because of the very humbling experiences I had gone through thus far. I know at one point you said that I should destroy all the letters I had ever written to you. I did get rid of some of them, but the Lord led me to save the ones that I did, and I hope in sharing them with you again, you will see how both of us were used as instruments of unrighteousness.

[I am not sure of the date of this next letter, but I know it was after my husband went to military training. He was gone from 4 January 1991 through 18 June 1992, with a short leave in between.]

Winter of 1991

Dear Bill,

This is my attitude toward the Lord: That I want His will accomplished and not my own, and I know that some of the things He will lead me to do will mean forsaking the things I've acquired in this world in order to be able to put Him first.

The Devil

I know I don't understand or perceive things the way He does, but it is my desire to be able to do that. I do know He desires that I be very sincere, open, and honest to those He's given to me, and I've tried to do that.

Concerning my relationship with you—I know the Lord has put you in my life for a very specific purpose. I know that doubts have come from every angle to mistrust that feeling in my heart toward you.

The feelings that are there weren't something I set out to have for you; they just kind of happened, and I don't even know how. It would be much easier for everyone concerned if they weren't there. But if they were established by God, they aren't going to go away.

A verse that always comes up is, "That what God has joined together, let no man put asunder."

I do want to learn to trust the Lord and have the same confidence that you have. And the things that float around my heart and mind I do want settled. And I know it does hinder my walk with Him because they aren't.

There is still a fear in me concerning you, and I know it's because I have not matured in the knowledge of God's love and I don't fully understand how He thinks and what His ways are. But He knows I want to.

And I know that I have to purpose in my heart that I will trust God to work in me. But sometimes I feel so inadequate and I wonder who am I that He even bothers with me. Sometimes I even feel that way about you.

Why do you even bother with me? How come you care about me? I am not anybody. Just some girl that used to live across the street from you.

There are some things that come up in my mind that I am not really sure where they're from, and I am afraid to speak them, but you know, it doesn't really matter if they're true or not. I can wait until all things are revealed when the Lord comes back.

Concerning my relationship with the Lord: I just want to have the frame of mind that I will trust Him and live by faith in Him and His abilities, and no matter what I say and do that it will be to give Him the glory and not to appease my flesh or other people's. And one thing I am sure of is that I can learn from you and your example on how to trust Him.

I'd like to reserve comment on this letter except to say that I was under a lot of condemnation by both you and Ira because of many things that had taken place. The blame was always put on me, which I was willing to accept because I believed that everything you did was ordained of God for my benefit so as to reveal my sins and weaknesses. I truly felt God put you in my life to help teach me about Him and His Kingdom, so I fully trusted you.

This next letter expresses my feelings toward Ira at that time. By the way, I trusted her right up to 2 March 1993, when we had our major confrontation.

15 April 1991

My Dear Elisha,

I figure I should put this paper to use for a good reason. I just want to thank you for your thoughtfulness in giving me a baby shower.[67] *And I also want to thank you for being my friend.*

I also thank my Lord for bringing us together. Anything from Him is much more fulfilling and lasting than anything this world has to offer. I just pray that we won't ever allow Satan

The Devil

to steal away what God has given us. I am very aware that he's out there to do just that, but because you are so sensitive to the Spirit, you bring things to light so that they aren't able to get much of a stronghold.

And I am very grateful for your words of encouragement and correction, especially in my ways of treating my youngest daughter. One of my greatest desires is that all of my children follow after the Lord, and I want to do everything I can to encourage that. And I really don't mind if you bring it to my attention when I may be falling down in that area. I love those children that God gave me. As it says in Psalms 127:3, "Lo, children [are] an heritage of the Lord: [and] the fruit of the womb [is His] reward."

Elisha, I love you, and I pray that I can be a source of encouragement and joy in your life. I desire to have the spiritual insight that you have so that one day I can be for you what you are to me. Thank you again.

Your friend in the Lord,

C.

By this letter, you see my love for her was very genuine, even though I never felt it was mutual. She had won my favor and respect, and I allowed her to tell me how I should treat my children, even though I was never in agreement with the way she treated her own.

I now realize that, due to the strong demonic influence over me during my time with you, I submitted to many things that were contrary to God's Word. Had I been walking in the True Light, I would have seen the error. And even though I *was* walking with the enemy, the Lord has never forsaken me!

Walking with the Enemy

The following message is one I truly felt God gave me to write down, and I shared it with you privately and then during Bible study. Even though you were rather indifferent about it, you, or Ira, never denied it as being from the Lord.

9 June 1991[68]

From the Lord,

If it bears witness with you, fine, do something about it. If it doesn't, do something about that too.

I have called all of you to be My body, but there are some parts missing because I haven't added them yet. There is a very specific reason why I haven't. In fact, I've taken away that which you had. You may think it was the enemy, and to some degree it was, but I allowed it.

You say that I am your Lord with your mouth, but your actions don't match up to what you confess. Most of you only want Me, and allow Me, to demonstrate Myself in you when it's convenient for you or when you feel like it.

Separately, you all are planting seeds to some degree, but you would be much more effective if you work together like I intended for you to.

Look at your daily lives and see how you treat one another. I know you all love Me, but that wasn't My only commandment. You must love each other and not just whomever you choose.

All of you are very spiritually perceptive, and you can be a mighty force for My Kingdom, but only if you allow Me to demonstrate My Spirit in you.

I want to add more to you, but you haven't even used what I've given you in the manner that I've ordained for you to do.

You are My family, but I must be the head, and if I am not, you will continue as you are—each of you doing your own thing

The Devil

individually, and in the midst of it, I am still able to work, but I can be much more effective through you if you learn to deny yourself, take up your cross daily, and follow Me.

That's what you say you want to do. Well then, do it! You say you want people to see Me in you. Well, let Me come out!"

{End of message.}

(While I was walking with the enemy, I believed it was the Lord speaking to me, but I now see it was actually a demonic spirit.)

Here's another letter that sheds more light on the relationship I had with you. I wrote this after you came back from staying with an old girlfriend of Ira's.

28 July 1991

Dear Bill,

I have been wanting to write to you a few of my thoughts, but I just couldn't put them down on paper. In fact, I sat down a week or so ago to write you a letter, but I couldn't get past the first sentence.

I know you must think I am crazy because I write you so many letters, especially since I have the ability to just tell you what's on my mind. Most people write letters to those that live away from them, but I guess I am not most people. And I never really have been.

For some reason, I can put my thoughts to you down on paper better than speaking face to face. And you know, in a way, that kind of bothers me. I don't really understand why I get nervous around you at times. It's almost like my brain quits working.

I would like to understand why I react that way, and I am sure God will reveal it to me in due time. But for the time being, I hope you don't get bored with my letter writing.

Bill, I write these letters because I do want you to know what's going on and I do feel led to share it with you. I know you really care about me and everyone in our church and our walk with that dear Lord Jesus of ours.

And it's because of your teachings that I have learned how to really get to know Him. The verse that reminds me of you is in John 15:13, "Greater love hath no man than this, that a man lay down his life for his friends."

Bill, I know you have done that, and I thank you. I am just sorry because I am so stubborn, and because I don't always see things, you have to go to such extremes to get the point across to me. And I am sorry for any pain I have caused you because of my unbelief. You have enough pain in your life, and I hate to be the cause of more.

Bill, I know you are a man of God, and that you will follow Jesus no matter what you are required to do, and no matter how much it might hurt. It's because of your love for Jesus that I love and respect you so much. It's because of that attitude and your willingness to do that, that I have learned some very valuable lessons concerning my walk with God.

I have learned that my reliance and trust must be totally in the Lord and not men. I have learned that He can use all situations and turn them around for good to those that love Him, and I do love Him. And He uses those situations to show me where I need to work on my relationship with Him.

I do know that my love for you is a spiritual one. I just know that the only thing that is fulfilling and produces life—His life inside of me—is what God gives by His Spirit. And that's really all I seek. I want His life inside of me.

And I know because of His Word that He will continue to reveal Himself to me, and I will get to know Him more every day.

The Devil

I do thank the Lord for all the people He has given me and the love and friendships He has established between us. But I am very reluctant to admit that I need other people and that they might need me.

All my life, whenever I've grown close to someone, I've always had to say goodbye, and that was always very painful for me. So that might be the reason I seem to close myself off to others.

I do have a desire in my heart to act in a godly way in all situations, circumstances, and relationships with people. And I know God will work that out in me. But my dependence is on Him to do it and not myself or other people.

I really don't feel like I am very mature in the Word yet, but I truly desire to be. I know by your example and your willingness to teach and encourage us that we will be. I thank the Lord that He has gone to such lengths to reveal Himself to me. And I thank you and Elisha for being the vessels He has used to show me things.

I love you both very much. And I pray that one day I will be a comfort to both of you like He said I should be.

Your friend,

C.

I was extremely broken due to some of the experiences I had been through, and I was in a very confused state concerning our relationship. The following Scriptures will shed some light as to what God thinks about that.

1 Corinthians 14:33 "For God is not [the author] of confusion, but of peace, as in all churches of the saints."

James 3:13–16 "Who [is] a wise man and endued with knowledge among you? Let him shew out of a good conversation his works with meekness of wisdom.

But if ye have bitter envying and strife in your hearts, glory not, and lie not against the truth. This wisdom descendeth not from above, but [is] earthly, sensual, devilish. For where envying and strife [is], there [is] confusion and every evil work."

If I had been wise, I would have known that the strife and confusion in my heart was not of God, but of the Devil, and he was in a battle for my soul. I now see why it's so important to delight completely in the Word of God, because only obedience to the truth will set us free from the lies of Satan.

This next letter will show that I was still walking with the enemy, but praise God, I wouldn't be in the end!

16 September 1991

Dear Bill,

I wrote you a letter the other night, but I tore it up because after I read it a few times, I felt like it really wasn't what God would have me say to you. I really want to have His thoughts and His ways. That is truly my desire. And He has impressed upon me to give you some verses from His beautiful Word.

Philippians 3:13–15 "Brethren, I count not myself to have apprehended: but [this] one thing [I do], forgetting those things which are behind, and reaching forth unto those things which are before, I press toward the mark for the prize of the high calling of God in Christ Jesus. Let us therefore, as many as be perfect, be thus minded: and if any thing ye be otherwise minded, God shall reveal even this unto you."

Romans 10:11 "For the Scripture saith, Whosoever believeth on Him shall not be ashamed."

Bill, I love you! And it's not contingent on anything you do or don't do. I know the feelings and emotions toward you that were put there by God will always be there and anything else will fade away, because He knows that my heart is for Him.

The Devil

One of the hardest things that could happen to me in this lifetime would be if I thought you no longer wanted me as a friend. And I truly want to be called your friend. I am not ashamed in the least to be associated with you. And the feeling in my heart toward you and that beautiful wife of yours is that I would and will lay down my life for you.

You two are the most special people I have ever been acquainted with in all my years of meeting people. And I've met plenty. But nobody like you. I pray that we will always walk together in like-mindedness. But if we don't, I won't worry about it, because sooner or later, God will reveal it to us.

C.

I don't know if you can tell by that letter, but my emotions were being pulled in many directions at this point in my walk with the enemy. The only peace I could get was from God's Word. If you recall, I used to share the Scriptures with you hoping that they would give you as much comfort as they gave me.

As I said in that letter, one of the hardest things for me in this lifetime is if I thought you no longer wanted me as a friend, but because you are an enemy of my God, I can no longer befriend you, despite the feelings I had for you. This Scripture will show why this is true.

1 John 2:18–19 "Little children, it is the last time: and as ye have heard that Antichrist shall come, even now are there many antichrists; whereby we know that it is the last time.

They went out from us, but they were not of us; for if they had been of us, they would [no doubt] have continued with us: but [they went out], that they might be made manifest that they were not all of us."

I hope by now you can see that you do not minister by the Spirit of Christ, but by the spirit of antichrist. I didn't see and understand all this until the night of 2 March 1993. Please pay very close attention to this passage.

Ezekiel 18:20–32 "The soul that sinneth, it shall die. The son shall not bear the iniquity of the father, neither shall the father bear the iniquity of the son: the righteousness of the righteous shall be upon him, and the wickedness of the wicked shall be upon him.

But if the wicked will turn from all his sins that he hath committed, and keep all My statutes, and do that which is lawful and right, he shall surely live, he shall not die. All his transgressions that he hath committed, they shall not be mentioned unto him: in his righteousness that he hath done he shall live. Have I any pleasure at all that the wicked should die? saith the LORD GOD: [and] not that he should return from his ways, and live?

But when the righteous turneth away from his righteousness, and committeth iniquity, [and] doeth according to all the abominations that the wicked [man] doeth, shall he live? All his righteousness that he hath done shall not be mentioned: in his trespass that he hath trespassed, and in his sin that he hath sinned, in them shall he die.

Yet ye say, The way of the Lord is not equal. Hear now, O house of Israel; Is not My way equal (or fair)? Are not your ways unequal (or unfair)? When a righteous [man] turneth away from his righteousness, and committeth iniquity, and dieth in them; for his iniquity that he hath done shall he die.

Again, when the wicked [man] turneth away from his wickedness that he hath committed, and doeth that which is lawful and right, he shall save his soul alive. Because he considereth, and turneth away from all his transgressions that he hath committed, he shall surely live, he shall not die.

Yet saith the house of Israel, The way of the Lord is not equal. O house of Israel, are not My ways equal? are not your ways unequal? Therefore I will judge you, O house of Israel, every one according to

The Devil

his ways, saith the Lord God. Repent, and turn [yourselves] from all your transgressions; so iniquity shall not be your ruin.

Cast away from you all your transgressions, whereby ye have transgressed; and make you a new heart and a new spirit: for why will ye die, O house of Israel? For I have no pleasure in the death of him that dieth, saith the Lord God: wherefore turn [yourselves], and live ye."

In case you have a problem with this Scripture passage because it's from the Old Testament, I will reference a few passages from the New Testament so the truth will be established in your heart. In so doing, I realize that all of this will refute the "once saved, always saved" theory, which I understand is a lie from the very depths of Hell![69]

Romans 15:4 "For whatsoever things were written aforetime were written for our learning, that we through patience and comfort of the Scriptures might have hope."

1 Corinthians 10:9–12 "Neither let us tempt Christ, as some of them also tempted, and were destroyed of serpents. Neither murmur ye, as some of them also murmured, and were destroyed of the destroyer.

Now all these things happened unto them for ensamples: and they are written for our admonition, upon whom the ends of the world are come. Wherefore let him that thinketh he standeth take heed lest he fall."

Hebrews 3:12–13 "Take heed, brethren, lest there be in any of you an evil heart of unbelief, in departing from the living God. But exhort one another daily, while it is called To day; lest any of you be hardened through the deceitfulness of sin."

Hebrews 10:26–27 "For if we sin willfully after that we have received the knowledge of the truth, there remaineth no more sacrifice for sins, but a certain fearful looking for of judgment and fiery indignation, which shall devour the adversaries."

Walking with the Enemy

Romans 16:25–27 "Now to Him that is of power to stablish you according to my gospel, and the preaching of Jesus Christ, according to the revelation of the mystery, which was kept secret since the world began, but now is made manifest, and by the Scriptures of the prophets, according to the commandment of the everlasting God, made known to all nations for the obedience of faith: to God only wise, [be] glory through Jesus Christ for ever. Amen."

This next letter is one I put in your Christmas card that year.

21 December 1991

Dear Bill and Elisha,

I would like to address something that has been on my heart for a while now. If I am being presumptuous or out of line or incorrect in my assumptions, I certainly don't mind if you bring it up. I am sure I'll find out where I may have been led astray in my thinking, and my dear Elisha, I thank the Lord for that.

You know, at first when you're being corrected, it's not so enjoyable, but later on, I praise God for showing me the truth. I desire to know the truth, and I know God will get it to me in whatever means I can receive it. Oh well, back to the reason I am writing this letter.

When I wrote Christmas cards, I contemplated whether I should address yours to both of you or separately. It used to be where I wouldn't even question something like that. I would automatically figure what I said to one of you would apply to the other one. I think of you two as one, but I don't sense the unity or oneness that used to be there. I remember when I met you and Elisha when I first started coming to Bible study, there was a very special bond between both of you that was very evident. I don't see that anymore.

The Devil

I know in the spirit you are one, as we all are one in Christ, but we certainly have an enemy who would like to destroy that unity or at least lie to us and make us think it's not there.

You two remind me of me and my husband before I started putting my total expectations in the Lord Jesus. I used to have so many expectations of my husband, and since I don't anymore, or at least I try not to, just in Jesus, he can't let me down. Not that he doesn't sadden me and frustrate me at times, but he's not able to take my peace away because of what he does or doesn't do.

Now I am not saying that Jesus isn't enough for you, but I hope you will examine your hearts and see if there are any areas in your relationship with each other that don't line up with God's will for your lives. That has been a prayer of mine for you two, that you will be everything to each other that God has ordained for you to be according to the truth of His Word.

I desire that all of us walk together in oneness, and I know the only way we can do that is if our total expectations are in Jesus and His Word. If Jesus wasn't our bond, I really don't believe any of us would be together. I love both of you very much, but I feel almost afraid to show it at times.

Elisha, I know you feel I favor Bill, and that I love him more than you, but that's so untrue. If you're one, you can't be separated. So if I love one of you, I have to love both of you. And I do! It wasn't put there by my desires; God has established the love I have for you both.

I would like to close this letter with a verse from Philippians. This is a prayer that I pray for all of us, but especially for you two. You are our spiritual leaders, and I look up to and trust both of you. And I know Satan would love to get to you any way he can, but I pray you will keep on guard and keep on trusting the Lord in everything.

Philippians 1:9–11 "And this I pray, that your love may abound yet more and more in knowledge and [in] all judgment; that ye may approve things that are excellent; that ye may be sincere and without offence till the day of Christ; being filled with the fruits of righteousness, which are by Jesus Christ, unto the glory and praise of God."[70]

Your friend in Christ,

C.

So at this point, I finally got up the courage to address your relationship. For the most part, I was very intimidated by both of you, so it took a lot for me to address this issue with you. Candy and I had expressed concerns about this to one another, but we were still willing to give you the benefit of the doubt. But when Ira started getting more and more discontented and frustrated with you, it just gave room for more doubt.

This next letter is not actually a letter; it's a message I felt the Lord had spoken to me. These words came to my heart at a time when I was in an extremely confused state about our relationship, even to the point that I was ready to just cut ties with all of you. I shared this with you, and you said it was from the Lord. I also shared it with Ira, but she said it wasn't, so that added to my confusion since you two weren't in agreement. Here it is.

27 February 1992

Word from the Lord,

This is my word to you. All that you feel in your heart was put there by me, to have my will accomplished. Your love for him is genuine, and it will always be there and it will not fade away. He is my gift to you and you to him. I told you long ago

The Devil

that you'll be a comfort to him, and right now is the time my servant needs your comfort.

He is a very special, called, chosen, and set-apart man with a very specific purpose I have called him to do on this earth. And all the feelings you have for him are put there by me. You have submitted yourself to me with your whole heart and soul, and thus I am able to use you. Don't fight what you feel in your heart toward him because if you do, it'll affect how you feel about me.

Just remember you only know in part and you will prophecy in part, but on that day, you will fully understand all things. The truth will prevail! Now quit being affected by what other people think and give no thought for tomorrow and stand on my word to you. And if you know with all certainty that I have called, chosen, and set you apart also, which I have, then you will never fall.[71]

{End of "Word from the Lord"}

At the time I heard this, there was a lot of uncertainty as to whether or not this was from the Lord. Considering the confusion, I should have realized that something just wasn't right.

Looking back, I have more reason to praise God that I am able to see where *my* Lord can, and will, use anything the Devil intends for evil and turn it around for my good and the good of others.

These Scriptures came to mind concerning the previous message:

2 Peter 1:10–12 "Wherefore the rather, brethren, give diligence to make your calling and election sure: for if ye do these things, ye shall never fall: For so an entrance shall be ministered unto you abundantly into the everlasting Kingdom of our Lord and Saviour Jesus Christ. Wherefore I will not be negligent to put you always in remembrance of these things, though ye know [them], and be established in the present truth." ∽

Jude 1:24–25 "Now unto Him that is able to keep you from falling, and to present [you] faultless before the presence of His glory with exceeding joy, to the only wise God our Saviour, [be] glory and majesty, dominion and power, both now and ever. Amen." ∽

Since my heart's desire is to live "by every word that proceedeth out of the mouth of God," my enemy had to use the Scriptures to try to establish his lies in my heart and mind. That message was filled with several references to God's Word in order to persuade me that it was of the Lord, but because God has opened my eyes, I now see that what I heard was truth mixed with lies! Furthermore, it was not given by the Spirit of Christ, but by the spirit of antichrist!

The following is a letter I wrote to you right after I received that message.

27 February 1992

Dear Bill,

I am writing down my thoughts concerning that letter because, sometimes when I am alone, I can see what's in my heart better, and I want you to know what's there concerning my relationship with you.

I feel like those words came from my spirit instead of my mind. It was just very different than the regular junk that goes on. Regardless of all that, I tried to discern every line that I read to see if it would line up in the Word based on my understanding on how to do that.

The questions that remain are what is in my heart for you and what really is God's idea of comfort. This is very hard to express, but I pray the Lord will give me the words to say it. There is this closeness and unity that I feel deep inside of me

The Devil

toward you that I know was put there because of our union with the Lord Jesus.

There's such a caring in my heart for what you go through. Whether it's good or bad, it's almost like that doesn't matter. I just want to share it with you. I really want to be a friend you can really trust and know that it doesn't matter what you do or don't do as to whether I am going to keep being your friend or not.

I just have such a desire in me to be involved in your life; not to where I am controlling your life, but being someone that God has given you to help you, and encourage and comfort and be with in the midst of this awful world we live in that really does hate us.

And the encouragement and comfort I am talking about is that God would lead me by His Spirit to say and do what He would have me do, so that it would strengthen you in Him and push you closer to Him. Because I know that He's the only reason worth living for. I know if I didn't have Jesus in my heart I would be so ugly and there would be nothing in me worth loving.

My desire is not to tear you down, but to build you up, so that you can endure the things that happen to you with confidence and patience and assurance that you're doing what the Lord has called you to do, and you know with certainty that He has called you and chosen you and set you apart to do a very special task.

I know in my heart that you are a very special man to Him. And you have been called to do something that's going to require His Word to be so grounded and rooted and established in your spirit that whenever you speak, it will only be the Word of God, so that it will either kill people or give them *life. And I really feel that what you are going through with all of us is your training ground to get it established in your heart.*

Bill, all these desires and feelings of comfort and encouragement that I have inside of me, I also have for Elisha. But it's almost like she doesn't want it from me. I am not really one she cares to be around, only when she really feels the Lord is leading her to talk to me, or many times when she just wants to see what's going on in my head lately.

But you know, I still have this overwhelming love for her, and it feels the same way as I feel in my heart about you. The only difference is that you make me feel so loved and cared about, but it's almost as if she can't receive anything from me.

You sometimes wonder whether I trust you or not, and the fact is that I do very much, because my Lord said I can—it's me that I don't trust. And when I express doubt about things, it's because I know that I am not perfect and that I have a sinful nature that I really don't fully understand. But the thing about it is that I have told God I want Him to change me and make me the way He wants me to be and not the way the world or even I expect me to be.

Bill, I love you and Elisha so very much. And I know that because of our relationships, our time together has been some of the most painful, but also the most joyful. And if all the things I have gone through with you produces godliness, then it's really worth it.

My biggest fear concerning my relationship with you is that, because of my actions, I might encourage ungodliness instead of the thing I so desire, and that's for all of us to walk in perfect unity in love toward one another and not allow the world or what people think to affect how we respond to each other. Because I know they won't ever understand us and won't ever

The Devil

desire to understand unless they really want to understand our Lord and Savior.

I'll always pray for you,

C. Read

By the way, I am still praying for you, even though you were one of the instruments Satan used to try to drag me to Hell with him. And you have to know it's only because of God's love in my heart that I have no ill feelings for you or for any of the other members of the Bible study group.

For your own good, I truly hope you did not purposefully seek to turn me away from my God. Here are some Scriptures to let you know what God thinks about the person that does that.

Proverbs 28:10 "Whoso causeth the righteous to go astray in an evil way, he shall fall himself into his own pit: but the upright shall have good [things] in possession."

Deuteronomy 13:1–11 "If there arise among you a prophet, or a dreamer of dreams, and giveth thee a sign or a wonder, and the sign or the wonder come to pass, whereof he spake unto thee, saying, Let us go after other gods, which thou hast not known, and let us serve them; thou shalt not hearken unto the words of that prophet, or that dreamer of dreams: for the LORD your God proveth you, to know whether ye love the LORD your God with all your heart and with all your soul. Ye shall walk after the LORD your God, and fear Him, and keep His commandments, and obey His voice, and ye shall serve Him, and cleave unto Him.

And that prophet, or that dreamer of dreams, shall be put to death; because he hath spoken to turn [you] away from the LORD your God, which brought you out of the land of Egypt, and redeemed you out of the house of bondage, to thrust thee out of the way which the LORD thy God commanded thee to walk in. So shalt thou put the evil away from the midst of thee.

If thy brother, the son of thy mother, or thy son, or thy daughter, or the wife of thy bosom, or thy friend, which [is] as thine own soul, entice thee secretly, saying, Let us go and serve other gods, which thou hast not known, thou, nor thy fathers; [namely], of the gods of the people which [are] round about you, nigh unto thee, or far off from thee, from the [one] end of the earth even unto the [other] end of the earth; thou shalt not consent unto him, nor hearken unto him; neither shall thine eye pity him, neither shalt thou spare, neither shalt thou conceal him:

But thou shalt surely kill him; thine hand shall be first upon him to put him to death, and afterwards the hand of all the people. And thou shalt stone him with stones, that he die; because he hath sought to thrust thee away from the LORD thy God, which brought thee out of the land of Egypt, from the house of bondage. And all Israel shall hear, and fear, and shall do no more any such wickedness as this is among you."

I am certain your false teachings resulted in causing me to walk in ways that were quite contrary to the Scriptures, and based on this passage, it would seem that God expects me to bring it to the attention of others so as to hinder this type of wickedness.

I just hope you did not purposely try to pull me away from God. On the other hand, I have serious doubts about Ira. Based on her actions, it would seem that her intent *is* to separate me from my God!

I don't know if she has ever mentioned it to you, but due to a conversation that I had with her right before we broke up, I now realize that Satan has given her power to control demonic spirits through witchcraft and sorcery.

One morning when she called me, I mentioned that I had a dream about you, and she was very interested to hear about it. I told her it was a pretty weird dream, but that just made her

The Devil

even more curious. Finally, she became extremely impatient and said, "Well, tell me about it!"

Bill, I dreamed that you were fixing to bow your knee to Satan! And when I said that, she freaked out! She said you would let them skin you alive before you would ever do that! And I said, "Well, it seemed pretty real."

Then I proceeded to tell her more about it, and right in the middle of my sentence, my mind went completely blank! I couldn't even remember what I was talking about. Then after a long pause, I finally said, "Ira, I really don't know where I am going with this."

She said, "I guess not! I had to ask God to intervene!" I said, "You mean God can just take something right out of your mind like that?" And she said, "Yeah, if he doesn't like what you're talking about." I got so excited to think that He could stop me from talking about junk that I had no business saying.

That night, I even mentioned to Candy what the Lord had done for me. She didn't have much of a comment, though. I was *terribly* naive back then, but I am so thankful to God that I can finally see the truth!

In this next letter, you'll see how you were still capable of manipulating me, which is what prompted this letter. But praise God, it wouldn't be long before Satan's hold on me would be released and he'd be running scared.

22 May 1992

Dear Bill,

Since you obviously don't want to speak to me, and I can understand why, I hope you will at least read this letter. I just want you to know that what I did the other night was extremely hard for me to do, and the last thing in the world

I would ever want to do is humiliate you in front of other people. But I had to do it because I know the Lord said to do it that way. But that didn't mean it didn't kill me inside to do it.

Bill, I love you, and if you can believe it, I did it because I love you. I want to know you in eternity with our Father in Heaven. And if I thought that I had a part in causing a man to walk away from the Lord and what He has called him to do on this earth, I don't think I could bear that.

Please don't do that to me, and more importantly, don't do that to Elisha. That woman is such a special person to me, and I can't really express in words how I feel about her. And her love for you is like no other love that I've ever seen from a woman to a man.

But my greatest desire for us, and Jesus states it better than I ever could:

John 17:22–23 "And the glory which Thou gavest Me I have given them; that they may be one, even as We are one: I in them, and Thou in Me, that they may be made perfect in one; and that the world may know that Thou hast sent Me, and hast loved them, as Thou hast loved Me."

My prayer for you, Bill, is that you will let Jesus be your strength and your support and accept the love of the people that He has placed around you. Whether or not you ever speak to me again, I hope you always know deep down in your heart that my love for you is genuine and will always be there.

Thank you for at least reading this.

C.

I wrote that after the confrontation we had over at your place. I had invited Candy as a third witness, and of course, Ira was also there. I will never forget that night because I was so nervous, and it was very obvious as the meeting progressed that I did not come in the boldness or strength of the Lord, even though I felt He prompted me to confront you in this way.

And because I was still walking in darkness and not completely free of the demonic influence, I was still very intimidated by both you and Ira. But on 17 June 1992, the day before my husband came home, I finally came to terms with the sin that was killing me, and I experienced His forgiveness and cleansing power. Praise God, the stronghold Satan had on me would soon be broken! Remember that verse from Luke I mentioned earlier?

Luke 22:31–34 "And the Lord said, Simon, Simon, behold, Satan hath desired [to have] you, that he may sift [you] as wheat: but I have prayed for thee, that thy faith fail not: and when thou art converted, strengthen thy brethren.

Especially notice what the overconfident Peter said next.

And he said unto Him, Lord, I am ready to go with Thee, both into prison, and to death. And He said, I tell thee, Peter, the cock shall not crow this day, before that thou shalt thrice deny that thou knowest Me."

Bill, if someone had told me when I first started coming to your Bible study group that I would actually commit the act of adultery, not once but on three separate occasions, I would never have believed I would be capable of doing something as terrible as that. But that is, in fact, exactly what happened!

Of course, it was Satan's plan right from the beginning to lure me into sexual sin, because that's the kind of sin that would keep me in darkness and eventually kill me. It was because of my ignorance of the enemy's tactics, and my complete lack of understanding of God's Word, as to why Satan was able to deceive me into believing all the lies that were put into my mind by you, Ira, and the demonic voices that were sent to me.

I must remind you that God knew what would happen from the beginning, and He also knew what would happen in the end. He knew I had to be humbled in order to break that prideful, self-righteous attitude, and due to that very humbling and tremendously shameful experience, I have more understanding and compassion for someone that has been manipulated by another person whose intent is to seduce them into sexual sin.

And because of my *falling away* from the ways of the Most High God, I am much more aware of the extreme danger of this sin if it's allowed to take place, much less continue. Please note the following Scripture.

1 Corinthians 6:18 "Flee fornication. Every sin that a man doeth is without the body; but he that committeth fornication sinneth against his own body."

The problem that Satan had with me is that I couldn't keep quiet about my sin because of the devastating effect it had on me emotionally, spiritually, and physically. You know, I never blamed you for what happened with me, and I still don't. I just see you as someone that is deceived, and is deceiving others, unto your own destruction!

I just praise the Lord God that He saw fit to deliver me! And He will do it for you, too, if you are willing to delight completely in the Word of God and take a hold of the Tree of Life and eat! Blessing, glory, and honor unto Him that sitteth upon the Throne, and unto the Lamb, forever and ever! Amen.

I realize that most people cannot even begin to understand how a true Christian could do such a thing as I did, but the

The Devil

Lord led me to this Scripture, which will shed some light on the evil and deception behind this sin.

Revelation 2:20–23 "Notwithstanding I have a few things against thee, because thou sufferest that woman Jezebel, which calleth herself a prophetess, to teach and to seduce My servants to commit fornication, and to eat things sacrificed unto idols.

And I gave her space to repent of her fornication; and she repented not. Behold, I will cast her into a bed, and them that commit adultery with her into great tribulation, except they repent of their deeds.

And I will kill her children with death; and all the churches shall know that I am He which searcheth the reins and hearts: and I will give unto every one of you according to your works."

Ira told me that she took great pleasure in seducing men into sexual sin, especially married Christian men. Of course, she said this was *before* she started walking with the Lord, but I have since found out that the truth is not in her. She is a liar and has been lying from the very beginning! And for those who have "ears to hear," she is that woman Jezebel!

When you let her read this, please tell her to take heed to that Scripture I just referenced, because the Lord has put her on notice. It's time to repent and turn from all your transgressions, so iniquity shall not be your ruin! And God is so merciful that He gives all men, *and women*, space to repent.

I don't know if you are aware of it, but the final straw came when Ira told me about you and Kim. When she informed me that you had also seduced her into believing that you were her husband, I just broke down.

All the emotional pain, grief, and heartache that I went through came flooding back, and I couldn't handle the thought of her going through what had happened with me, especially since she was so young and vulnerable.

I had hoped you had repented and that it had stopped with me, but obviously based on what Ira just told me, it had not. She realized she had made a grave mistake by mentioning this to me, because at that point, I was ready to throw you out of my house right then.

I told her I thought it was such an honor to have the truth taught in my home, but after this, any trust or respect I had for you was completely gone. She tried to calm me down and convince me I was wrong. She said you were our pastor as appointed by God, and I needed to respect His "anointed one."

At that point, I said, "God never told me you were my pastor; that's what *you* said!" The only thing I was sure that God had said to me is that I would learn a lot from that man. Boy, was He ever right!

She said this was an area you were weak in and that you needed our prayers. She used to compare you with King Saul and referenced the Scripture where David wouldn't kill him because he was anointed by God to be king.

She went on to say that since you were "God's anointed," I needed to let God handle this; otherwise, I would be in sin.[72] She was able to persuade me to see it her way after that statement. So at that point, I just handed all of my concerns about this to my heavenly Father, and I was going to trust Him.

He knew how I felt about it and how I could not support you any longer after I found out that you had not repented of that detestable evil. I had faith that God would deal with this problem in His way and at the proper time, so I decided to just wait on Him. And He handled it wonderfully!

On 28 February 1993, He made His presence known in our midst, in such a supernatural way that there's no doubt as to

The Devil

what He thought. I'll repeat what God spoke through me that night so it will be fresh in your mind.

Prophecy of 28 February 1993

"Many things you have been taught here have been done in secrecy and in darkness. You have been taught truth mixed with lies, and the Lord says it will go on no longer!

And you are the one who has taught the lies, and the Lord says it will go on no longer in this home. And the Lord is giving you a chance to turn from your sin. And He is so forgiving that He will not hold your sin against you if you repent. And if you do not, you will die!

He is my husband. I love him with a love that cannot be broken. I love you too, but with a brotherly love. And I beg you to repent!

Everything you have learned here has been tainted with evil, and you can't hold on to any of it. The only thing that you can hold on to is the fact that Jesus Christ died for you, and by His mighty power, God raised Him from the dead. And if you believe that in your heart, and claim Him as Lord, He will put the same Spirit that raised Jesus from the dead inside of you to lead you and guide you into the truth!

Light will overshadow darkness, and darkness will not be able to stand in the presence of God!"

{End of prophecy}

I hope because of this letter that you will come to terms with your sin and not deny it any longer, because if you don't ever face up to the truth, you will die in your sin. Please consider what I am saying to you.

Walking with the Enemy

I am a disciple of the Lord Jesus Christ, and He has given me the authority to speak His Word as He gives me understanding, so please do not reject what the Lord is speaking to your heart!

This next letter is one I never finished, but I feel led to share what I have. I wrote it exactly three weeks after we broke up.

21 March 1993

Dear Bill and Ira,

I am not really sure why I am even writing this letter, but I feel compelled to write to you. It's not like you aren't used to it, but I am sure you didn't really expect me to write to you about anything ever again, especially in light of everything that has transpired in the last few weeks.

The whole time I've known you two, excuse me, the whole time I've walked with you would be much more accurate, I've written you letters, which seems really foolish, and I am sure you have gotten a good laugh at my stupidity.

And from this side of it, I realize just how naive and ignorant I was. Oh well, I guess you live and learn.

You know, I had no idea things would ever turn out this way, that I would be the one standing up for the truth and all of you rejecting me. It still kind of blows my mind.

I am sure this bit of information will give you great comfort to know that you have been the cause of such great pain, sorrow, and grief in my heart that I can't really even put it into words how I feel.

Our whole walk together has been a most painful one, and I guess now I understand what the Lord meant when He said I would be a comfort to you.[73] *At the time I didn't realize that you got your comfort out of destroying people's lives in whatever way you possibly could.*

The Devil

I know one thing that you must really hate about me is my desire to know the truth and walk in it and to be perfectly honest with all people. That desire hasn't changed at all, and I will continue to be that way.

Even though I have found out that your greatest desire was to drag me to Hell, I am very surprised that I don't have any real feelings of resentment and anger or hatred toward either of you. Actually, the love that I had for you two is still there, but it's almost like it is a futile effort.

I just feel a lot of pain at the thought of someone I used to have such deep respect and even honor for, and knowing that you're going to burn in Hell is really hard for me to understand and grasp right at this moment. I don't desire that for you or anybody, and I know in my heart that in your present condition that's exactly where you both will spend eternity. And whoever else you happen to grab ahold of will go with you.

I just thank my Holy Lord God Almighty that He intervened and revealed the truth to me, and He will do the same for whoever else truly desires it.

Ira, you really had me fooled for the whole time. Not until that Tuesday night (2 March 1993) did I realize just who you actually served. You're really a sly one. You're a real good hypocrite. You can pretend so very well, especially to idiots like me.

But you know what, Bill? For some reason, I still feel like you've been ensnared in a trap, and you have just walked in such sin, and have transgressed God's laws so much and for so long, that He's just given you over to a reprobate mind and has sent you a strong delusion to believe the lies that come to your mind from yourself, your sin, and other men.

And Ira does have a lot of power over you. I don't really understand much about witchcraft, but I know she doesn't have power over me anymore because I have finally found out the truth about you two through the revelation of God Almighty! Thank God!

The hardest part of all of this is coming to terms with the fact that we don't serve the same God, and all along I believed we did. But all you have to do is look at the fruits in your life—they aren't of the Holy Spirit at all.

One thing I do want you to know, which I am sure you already know, is that my God is very upset with you two. And I happen to be His vessel, and I don't really question as to how He uses me. Like, for instance, the other day when you came to get the piano,[74] I really didn't plan on that outburst of anger toward you, but when the Holy Spirit came over me and started quoting that Scripture, I just couldn't contain myself. I'll quote it for you.

Galatians 1:9b "If any [man] preach any other gospel unto you than that ye have received, let him be accursed."

My neighbor said she even heard me in her house all the way from across the street. And my next-door neighbor and her whole family came running out. Pretty wild, huh?

{End of letter to Bill and Ira}

That was the letter I was not able to finish because my husband had interrupted me, but I don't feel the Lord really wanted me to finish it or even send it to you then. I was very upset due to a program I had just watched by Ben Haden. It was very significant because it was an answer to a prayer.

God had spoken to my heart and told me that if any of you continued to deny that what took place on the evening of 28 February 1993 was from the Lord, then you would be in danger of blasphemy against the Holy Spirit.

The Devil

That was very troubling for me, because I know it is the only unforgivable sin. I don't really understand the ramifications of unforgivable sin, but I know it's something you will carry with you forever, and the burden and weight of that sin is something you will sense for eternity.

I asked the Lord to confirm that to me because I was very upset at the thought of any of you going to Hell; when just a few weeks before that, I felt like I would know you forever. And God is so great! In less than a week, He answered my prayer, and on national television even![75]

These are some of the Scriptures Reverend Haden referenced, which, by the way, were the very Scriptures the Lord had spoken to my heart days before this.

Matthew 12:31–32 "Wherefore I say unto you, All manner of sin and blasphemy shall be forgiven unto men: but the blasphemy [against] the [Holy] Ghost shall not be forgiven unto men.

And whosoever speaketh a word against the Son of man, it shall be forgiven him: but whosoever speaketh against the Holy Ghost, it shall not be forgiven him, neither in this world, neither in the [world] to come."

Hebrews 6:4–6 "For [it is] impossible for those who were once enlightened, and have tasted of the heavenly gift, and were made partakers of the Holy Ghost, and have tasted the good Word of God, and the powers of the world to come, if they shall fall away, to renew them again unto repentance; seeing they crucify to themselves the Son of God afresh, and put [Him] to an open shame."

Hebrews 10:30–31 "For we know Him that hath said, Vengeance [belongeth] unto Me, I will recompense, saith the Lord. And again, The Lord shall judge His people. [It is] a fearful thing to fall into the hands of the living God."

I even taped this program because I knew right from the start that it was what the Lord wanted me to hear to confirm what

He had spoken to my heart. And another amazing thing: I received the transcript of this show in the mail the exact day I sent out the "warning letter"[76] to the members of the Bible study group and your families, so I included it with that letter.

Bill, I would like to remind you of the main reason I am writing this. It is to hopefully convince you to turn from your sin and turn back to the Lord God Almighty. It is truly my hope that you will choose to walk with the Lord Jesus Christ, instead of with the enemy of my God.

I am going to share the cover letter that I sent to your parents, along with what I sent to you. Many of the Scriptures referenced in that warning letter are also mentioned in this letter, so I'll only repeat the last passage that I noted before I made the proclamation to you.

I would like you to especially note the day you received this letter, which was Friday, 16 April 1993, and on the following Monday, David Koresh and his remaining followers were destroyed by the fire for all the world to see on 19 April 1993.[77]

Just another interesting tidbit of information: 19 April 1990 was the day you laid hands on me to receive a demonic spirit, and exactly three years later is when many demonic spirits were cast out of those they had once possessed![78]

The following is the first and last page of the major warning letter that I sent to the members of the Bible study group and their families on 15 April 1993.

14 April 1993

Enclosed is a letter that I sent to your child that I would like for you to read and be aware of. It is very important that they read and take heed to the words in that letter because it is

The Devil

God's final word to them, and it may be their last chance to repent of their sin.

If you are truly a God-fearing person, I hope that you will pray for your child. It's a matter of eternal life and eternal death.

I had been involved with their Bible study group for over three years, and I am no longer! They have not been allowed to speak, preach, teach, or anything else in my home since the Lord God from above came down into my living room in a very mighty way on the night of 28 February 1993, during Bible study, to reveal the truth. (By the way, that was the same day the Waco cult was exposed.)

We had a subsequent confrontational meeting on the night of 2 March 1993, where more of the truth was revealed, and I have been walking in the True Light ever since. (This was also when David Koresh and the FBI officials met to discuss the situation.) I do not stand in agreement with them, and ever since that night, the whole group has rejected me. I actually love all of those people, and it hurts very deeply to think that they may spend eternity in Hell if they continue on their present course.

Many people have been deceived by them, and you may be one of them. I pray you are not, but I do have confidence in the Lord that if you truly want the truth, you will certainly find it.

Jesus is the door. Keep on seeking and you will find. Keep on knocking and the door will be opened up to you. Keep on asking and you will receive. He did it for me, and He will do it for you. I will pray for you and your child as the Lord directs me.

Please mention the enclosed letter to them just in case they didn't receive it or decided not to read it. This is a very important matter, and I pray that you or they will not take it lightly or just dismiss it. God has put them on notice, and they may say they are suffering for Jesus's sake, but in actuality, they are reaping what they have sown.

A servant of the Lord Jesus Christ, and the Most High God,

C. Read

14 APRIL 1993 [79]

TO WHOM IT MAY CONCERN,

THE GOD OF ABRAHAM, ISAAC, AND JACOB SAYS TO YOU, THIS IS YOUR FINAL WARNING! REPENT AND TURN FROM YOUR SIN! YOUR SIN HAS DARKENED YOUR EYES AND YOU KNOW NOT WHERE YOU ARE GOING OR WHERE YOU HAVE BEEN.

YOU MAY THINK YOU ARE WALKING WITH THE LORD GOD ALMIGHTY, BUT YOU HAVE BEEN DELUDED INTO BELIEVING A LIE.

YOUR LIVES ARE BASED ON LIES. AND WE ALL KNOW THAT SATAN IS THE FATHER OF LIES. ONLY TRUTH WILL SET YOU FREE FROM THE POWER OF DARKNESS!

I PRAY THAT YOU WILL HEED THESE WORDS OF WARNING AND HUMBLY CONSIDER WHAT THE LORD GOD ABOVE IS SPEAKING TO YOUR HEART. IT IS A MATTER OF YOUR ETERNAL LIFE OR ETERNAL DEATH.

WHETHER YOU BELIEVE IT OR NOT, I LOVE YOU ALL VERY, VERY MUCH AND SO DOES THE LORD. AFTER ALL, HE GAVE HIS LIFE FOR YOU SO THAT YOU MIGHT LIVE.

HE CAN FORGIVE YOU OF ALL YOUR SIN EXCEPT BLASPHEMY AGAINST HIS HOLY SPIRIT. SO PLEASE DO NOT DISREGARD WHAT HE DID ON THE NIGHT OF 28 FEBRUARY 1993, AND ALSO THE FOLLOWING SUNDAY NIGHT WHEN YOU CAME AND GOT THE PIANO. THAT WAS MOST CERTAINLY THE HOLY SPIRIT WORKING THROUGH ME, WHICH I HAD NO CONTROL OVER.

YOU ALL KNOW MY STAND WITH THE LORD HAS ALWAYS BEEN "HERE I AM LORD, SEND ME!" AND HE HAS DONE IT! PRAISE THE LORD GOD!

The Devil

IF YOU CONTINUE ON YOUR PRESENT COURSE, THE LORD WILL COME UPON YOU LIKE A THIEF IN THE NIGHT, AND WHEN YOU STAND BEFORE HIM, THERE WILL BE NO MORE EXCUSES OR JUSTIFICATIONS. YOU CANNOT DECEIVE THE PERFECT ONE!

BLESSING, AND GLORY, AND WISDOM, AND THANKSGIVING, AND HONOR, AND POWER, AND MIGHT UNTO MY GOD! FOREVER AND EVER. AMEN!

Ecclesiastes 12:13-14 "Let us hear the conclusion of the whole matter: Fear God, and keep His commandments: for this [is] the whole [duty] of man.

For God shall bring every work into judgment, with every secret thing, whether [it] be good, or whether [it] be evil."

{End of 14 April 1993 warning letter}

A servant of the Most High God,

C. Read

As signed by me in the presence of a witness on the 22nd Day of September in the year of our Lord, One Thousand Nine Hundred and Ninety-Three.

{End of 24 August 1993 letter to Bill}

ALMOST ONE YEAR FROM THE DAY that Bill received that letter, he left a message on my answering machine on 12 September 1994, during Rosh Hashanah, just three days before Yom Kippur—the holiest of all Jewish holidays.[80]

He requested that I pick up the phone and speak to him. It was ten o'clock at night, and as I was listening to his message, I had no inclination to pick up the phone, but I felt that I would be calling him back.

A week later, the Lord impressed upon me to return his phone call, and the following are excerpts from the taped conversation that I had with Bill. I wasn't sure why the Lord had me record our discussion.

I just know that God said to do it. So I did. Both of us were very nervous, so I left out some of the more obvious indications of that. Otherwise it is verbatim.

Transcript of Taped Recording Between Bill and C. 18 September 1994

C.   I got your message last week, and I was kind of waiting until I talked to my husband about calling you...

Bill   Well, thank you. I'm glad you returned my call...

C.   What did you need?

Bill   I just wanted to talk to you for a few minutes. And you know, first of all, again, I wanted to apologize to you for all the things that have happened here.

C.   Why is that?

Bill   Well, I mean, you know, C., I found that my own heart is not what I would want it to be. And as I presented it before the Lord over the last few months and years, ya know, I've just allowed the Lord to, or hopefully allowed the Lord to, do the work in my heart.

And reveal areas of weakness and sin and darkness that are there that stain our lives, or that stain my life, and cause me to be something that I don't want to be, or something that I don't choose to be. And ya know, the things that were there were not pleasing to me, and they're certainly not the things that I wanted to be.

So, as I've looked at—had those things exposed, and will have them exposed in the future, by the Lord; as they come up and as they are brought to my attention, I go back and I try to rectify, and correct, and do what the Scriptures talk about doing, which is seeking forgiveness and forgiving those around me and—

C.   Bill, let me interrupt you just for a minute, okay?

Bill   Okay.

C.   I do want you to know that my husband is listening on the other end. And that's one of the main reasons why I waited to call you, because he wasn't here last week. And anything that I do I will go through him before I even attempt to do it. So, I hope you know that.

Bill   That's great.

The Devil

C.   I really hope that what you're saying to me is genuine, but ya know, time will tell that too. Go ahead. I just wanted to let you know that.

Bill   Huh, well you know, it's *genuine* to me. Whether it is to anybody else or not—

C.   Well, it's between you and God. It's really—

Bill   Ya know, I agree with what you said that night, that things were out of order. I do not agree with the *spirit* by which you said it, nor do I agree with the spirit by which you've operated since that time.

C.   Oh, you don't?

Bill   No. Because that's, that is, it's, ya know, that's a personal thing. You know, you got to do what you got to do. And I'm not here to judge it. I'm not here to condemn it either.

I'm just telling you that things were out of order. Things were out of order in my heart; things were out of order in my life. I've not submitted some areas of my life to the Lord, that he had been wanting to deal with, and ya know, that has caused me to walk in sin. And I'm calling you tonight, not so much to—

Ya know, I'm not trying to get you to do anything here.

C.   Oh, I don't take it as that.

Bill   Ya know, I think that perhaps things are—Well, wherever they are, they are, but I am calling you, and one of the primary reasons that I am calling you is to ask you to very seriously and prayerfully consider being reconciled to both Ira and Candy.

I want to tell you that neither one of them are opposed to you. And that they very much sincerely love you. And that they do not agree with me on what happened. That they're not standing around here supporting me. And doing all kinds of things to, ya know, justify my position or anything else. Both of them have made it, and are still making it, very plain to me that those things were not right. That neither the things that I taught, and many of the things that I believed, many of the things that I perceived as far as being from the Lord, that they were not.

And ya know, there's no reason in the world for you to feel like they're your enemies, or that they're opposed to you.

And I guess if I had one primary purpose for calling you tonight, or calling you the other night, was to ask you to really prayerfully consider reestablishing lines of communication and friendship with those two sisters in the Lord of yours.

And I'm not telling you to do that. I'm not begging you to do it. I'm just asking you to prayerfully consider a reconciliation with them. And realizing that I'm not in the way here. I'm not asking you to be bosom buddies, and to start something, or have anything. Because I'm out of the picture.

C. Do you not live with her anymore?

Bill No. I haven't lived with her in a long time.

C. You haven't?

Bill No.

C. How come?

Bill When her husband left, I left.

C. How come? Her husband's not staying there either?

Bill Ira [and her husband] are divorced.

C. They are?

Bill Sure.

C. When did they get divorced?

Bill Last November.

C. Well, I know she's always wanted to.

Bill I'm not sure she would have preferred that, but that's what happened.

C. Oh, she didn't want to get divorced? I don't mean to get personal because I'm not—

Bill Ya know, you can talk to her about that, but it wasn't her that did it. No, her husband just left—

C. I do want you to know that I have been concerned about all of you. The love I had for any of you was not a pretense of any kind. But I do know—

Bill Well, I know that. And that's why I'm calling you now because I really want, and I desire, and I really honestly believe that the Lord does, but I'm not putting that kind of pressure on you. It was like I asked you before to prayerfully consider that matter of reconciliation with them. Realizing that as far as—

Ya know, for the most part, C., they agree with you. They agree with what you said. I don't know whether or not—

There may be differences of opinion, just like there are differences of opinion with me concerning the methods that you used since that time, or even that night, but regardless—

C.   What is it that you said, the *spirit* in which it was done? What do you mean by that? That you didn't agree with?

Bill   Well, you know the Bible is very clear, isn't it? You know that you walk in love towards your brother.

C.   Well, wouldn't exposing their sin when they wouldn't hear it any other way? I mean, and I don't want to get in an argument with you about Biblical things.

Bill   I'm not going to argue with you.

C.   But that really wasn't me speaking that night. I attribute that completely to the Holy Spirit, and I am really concerned, Bill, if you really think that that was a demonic spirit—

Bill   C., I just know this—okay, I just know this. I know that people that are led by the Spirit of the Lord—ya know, to—I can understand you coming against me, okay. I can.

C.   Well, it's more against your sin, not necessarily you as a person.

Bill   No, I can understand you coming against me. I can understand you coming against the message, and false teachings, and erroneous doctrine, and sin in my life—

C.   Well, you know what really got me, though, was with Kim. Ya know, when it happened to me—when Ira told me about you and Kim, how you seduced her to make her think that you were her husband too.

That is, it's like, when it happens to you, you can pretty much kind of overlook it, but when it happens to somebody else, it was different.

Bill   Well, C., I have taken all this before the Lord. These are the areas in my life that the Lord needed to deal with. And I've taken these areas before the Lord here. And you know, the Lord is dealing with my heart, and dealing with my attitude, and dealing with my whole being about some of these things. And you know, I didn't—

Ya know, I don't walk in justification for the things that I've done, whether they're right or whether they're wrong. If you believe sincerely, truthfully, and honestly in your own heart that you're led by the Spirit of the Lord—

C. Oh, I know I Am.

Bill —to do those things that you've done, then, you know, you stand on that. I'm not condemning you for that. And I'm not prejudging you for it. I'm just simply saying to you, C., and to your husband, that I regret these things that have happened.

It was my sin that caused it, not anybody else's. It was my attitude and the areas of my heart that I had refused to allow the Lord to deal with that led up to it. And that those areas are being dealt with very slowly, but very surely. And I called you tonight to, or last week—

C. Yeah, you're a little confused there, but—

Bill I'm talking to ya, anyway, tonight, to come to you and to say, look, these two women do not support me.

C. So, you don't preach over there anymore at all either?

Bill No. I don't preach anywhere at all anymore.

C. Do you go to church anywhere?[81]

Bill Oh yes, very much so. Ya know, the thing here is that these two women, Candy and Ira, you know they love you. And you love them. And ya know, you may have differences of opinion.

One of the hardest things that's ever been in a church is for people who even have doctrinal differences, that you can walk with somebody even though you—

You may have doctrinal differences, but you can still walk with them. You can still love them. And you can still have a friendship with them. And you can still even be challenged by them. Because nobody's arrived yet.

C. Oh no, but I am going. I can't wait. I'm getting there.

Bill But I called you because I want you, C.[82]

The Devil

You know, I don't have any visions that you're sitting over there all by yourself and locked away, and all this kind of stuff, but that's not what I'm talking about.

C.   What do you *mean?*

Bill   I'm talking about two women who love you. And who care about you. And you, who care about Ira and Candy. And you know, being friends with them. And reconciling yourselves, all three of you, to a point where you're able to communicate, where you're able to share things again.

Because you are all three sisters in the Lord. And there is no reason in the world for this thing that happened with me to be a guiding factor in the breakup of relationships and friendships between sisters in the Lord.

C.   Well, you know what? She does not agree with this, like you told me at the beginning here, that the spirit in which I've been operating in since I've left y'all. She doesn't agree with that either, so there's really no way that I could walk with somebody that thinks that I am listening to the Devil instead of to God.

Bill   All of us do that, C.

C.   Do what?

Bill   Anybody who believes that they cannot be influenced and deceived by satanic voices or demonic influences, you know, anybody who believes that they can't be has already become that way.

I don't say you are demonically possessed. I'm not trying to say anything like this.

Even if you have a difference of opinion, say between you and Ira, have a difference of opinion about whether or not what you heard was from Jesus Christ, or what you heard was not. If she thinks it wasn't, then you know, that's still—

The fact is that you profess Jesus Christ as your Lord and Savior. And the fact is that Ira and Candy both profess Jesus Christ, the *same* Jesus Christ, as their Lord and Savior. That does say something. That puts all three of you in one body.

And you're not going to get to unity in the faith in Jesus Christ by remaining at odds, or saying I can't, or I won't, or anything else that allows a continual valley to exist here.

I'm trying to tell you that these two women do—they may have differences of opinion with you. You're going to have differences of opinion with them.

C. Oh, I have differences of opinion with a lot of people. You know, that's really not the issue.

Bill Oh, yes it is! Because you can have a difference of opinion and still walk with somebody and love them.

C. Oh yeah, well look at my husband. I don't agree with him all the time. In fact, well, I don't want to go into any details, but I still love him, and I won't ever get rid of him. But it's not quite the same.

You know, with everything that was involved there—Bill, it would just be really hard to—

Ya know, once you've been really lied to, and lied about, that really puts, like, a bad taste in your mouth. And ya know, it's really hard to drink of that same cup again. And that's basically the situation here.

And not that I wouldn't forgive them. And if you are sincerely sorry for seducing me into having a sexual relationship with you, I hope that that is the truth. I hope that you are really sorry.

And I really hope that you didn't intentionally pull me away from walking with God. Because you know when I first came to your group, that was my heart's desire, is to walk in a deeper relationship with God. And you knew that. And God knew that.

[I became very emotional at this point in my conversation with Bill.]

And that sin that you seduced me into was about the worst thing that I could ever do in my life, is to commit adultery to the man that God joined me to. And that Scripture that used to come up all the time, that "Whatsoever God hath joined together, let no man put asunder," that Scripture didn't apply to you, it applied to my husband!

[I became extremely emotional at this point.]

And you were the man that was trying to take me away from my husband! And that really bothers me. And it really hurts. And I hope you're sorry. And you will have to answer to God for that.

And if you are sorry, I know He'll forgive you, but I can't come back to a group of people that sanctioned that. That agreed with it.

The Devil

You know, with their mouth they say I don't agree, but I know with their actions they do. Because Ira stood by and watched it happen. And I'm sorry, I can't be friends with her anymore, or Candy.

But I do hope—the only hope I have for all of you is that you will submit to God. Because He's the One who can put you into Hell or allow you to come into His Kingdom. And that's my concern for you.

That's the only reason why I've written you. That's the only reason why I have written anybody, is because I don't want you to die in Hell. I really don't. And I hope you know that.

Bill Yes, I know that. And I—

C. But you will be the one that places yourself there based on your heart decisions.

That's really all I have to say there for a moment.

Bill Well, let me just share this with you. Ira does not agree, neither does Candy, nor did they stand by and let this happen. There was a battle, and there was a fight, and they lost. But they weren't the big losers here. Ya know, *I* was the loser. And you were the loser. And ya know, I disgraced my father. I disgraced my Lord.

C. So did I.

Bill I disgraced them. And they did not stand there, and please do not believe that they did, and condone this, nor agree with it, nor push it to happen in any way. And there is absolutely no way in the world that Ira or Candy, either one, ever, there was no time, there was no way that they agreed with it.

They were brokenhearted over it before, they were brokenhearted during it, and they've been brokenhearted afterward.

Because of the destructive nature of it, and because of the sin and the evil that was there in it. And don't for a minute think that they stood there and supported me. They tried to love me through it as a brother in the Lord. They tried to help me to pick up the pieces. But even with that, the destructive nature of that sin in my own heart was so great that it destroyed a lot of things.

And it cost everybody. And don't think I don't know that. Don't think I don't know the price that you paid or the price that everybody else has paid that was involved with it.

So that's why I can come to you and say, look, they're not opposed to you. They're not in disagreement with you in that area. They do not condone, nor tolerate, nor accept what I did.

And you can call it your sin all you want to, C., but the bottom line is that I am the one who is held accountable for it. I am the one who will be standing before the Lord giving Him account for it. Not you, me. You are not the teacher. You are not the leader. You are not the one standing up professing yourself to be the spiritual leader. I was, and I'll be the one who's held accountable for it.

And I know the hurt is there. And I know the pain is still there. But I assure you that one of the ways that you can reconcile that pain, and reconcile the hurt that's in there, is by being reconciled to your sisters here.

I'm being reconciled to you in the only area that I know how to do, and that's by coming to you and speaking the truth to you and telling you that I am sorry for it and I regret it more than you will ever know.

I do not expect you to come back to any Bible study or teaching group, or even accept anything here from me. In fact, all I wanted to do was have the opportunity to share this with you. And to say again to you the things that I've said. But also to primarily say to you, yes, you can be reconciled to these two women. They're your sisters in the Lord. They love you. They do not agree with me. They do not stand beside me. They do not support me. Nor did they ever support me in the midst of all this. They tried to love me through it. They tried to help me through it. My own heart was hardened.

C.   Can I ask you a question? And you don't have to answer, but I just felt like asking, um, did you ever have sex with Candy?

Bill   Nope.

C.   She wouldn't ever let you?

Bill   (After a long delay) Never had sex with her.

C.   I know the other ladies, they used to tell me that you tried with them, and Candy said you had tried with her, but she never did, and I was just wondering if that's true or not. I am glad to hear that she wasn't lying to me.

The Devil

Bill, I am glad I called you tonight. I am glad to hear what you had to say. I will consider what you were saying. I had written Ira a letter, I think it was to Ira and Candy, I don't know if they shared it with you or not—but did you share that letter that I wrote you with Ira? You know, that one that I wrote a year ago?

Bill Oh, yes.

C. And it was real fascinating how it ended up. I had my husband give it to you, and it was the eve of Yom Kippur. And that was very fascinating to me. And ya know, I don't keep up with Jewish holidays, but that's like the final day to ask—

Bill It's the Day of Atonement.

C. Yeah, to ask the Lord to forgive you. And it was real neat that it ended up—And I don't know if you noticed that you called me during Rosh Hashanah. Did you notice that?

Bill Yeah, I knew what time of the year it was.

C. You did?

Bill Yeah.

C. To me it was just fascinating that it's kind of worked out that way. I do hope that you reconcile with God. That's the most important thing as far as I am concerned. And I hope you realize that, okay? And I guess I'll let you go...

{End of 18 September 1994 transcript}

As you can see, I didn't seek him out, but it was Bill that pursued me in order to request that I re-establish a line of communication with Ira and Candy. I had not spoken to him in over a year and a half, and he had not responded to any of my letters, so I was surprised to hear from him. I could sense that he was very uneasy, and at times, there was a desperation in his voice.

I really don't trust anything he said to me that day, and I feel the only reason he called me was as a last resort to try to persuade me to get back in with someone from the group, since nothing else had seemed to work.

Bill was very convincing, and if I were to allow pride to creep back into my life so as to blind my eyes to who they are, he could succeed in misleading me again. Should that ever happen, it would be much worse the next time.

I pray that I will never forget that it is only because of the Lord Jesus Christ that I have ears to hear the truth. I praise God that He has allowed me to discern the spirit behind his words, and it certainly is *not* the Spirit of Christ!

Because of everything I have been through, I am even more convinced of the importance to warn unsuspecting souls about this sort of evil. And after this conversation with Bill, I have no reservations whatsoever in allowing my testimony to be available for all to read if God desires for that to happen.

I know Satan must be very displeased that they allowed me to get out from under their control in the first place, and because of the mistakes they have made, I am certain that demonic spirits are tormenting them even more.

It really breaks my heart to think about what may befall these people that I grew to love, but I am much more concerned about the innocent souls being misled by ministers of Satan. May God use my testimony of *Walking With the Enemy* to uncover the truth behind many of the deceptions of the Devil!

John 3:17–21 "For God sent not His Son into the world to condemn the world; but that the world through Him might be saved.

He that believeth on Him is not condemned: but he that believeth not is condemned already, because he hath not believed in the name of the only begotten Son of God.

And this is the condemnation, that light is come into the world, and men loved darkness rather than light, because their deeds were evil.

For every one that doeth evil hateth the light, neither cometh to the light, lest his deeds should be reproved.

But he that doeth truth cometh to the light, that his deeds may be made manifest, that they are wrought in God."

chapter four

Exposed

> "For there is nothing covered, that shall not be revealed; neither hid, that shall not be known. Therefore whatsoever ye have spoken in darkness shall be heard in the light; and that which ye have spoken in the ear in closets shall be proclaimed upon the housetops."
>
> Luke 12:2–3

THE FOLLOWING LETTER WAS WRITTEN to the young girl that Bill had also seduced into believing that he was her "husband." After he was exposed, I had hoped she would be able to see the danger in associating with Bill, *or Ira*, but the last I heard she was still with them. And to my great dismay, she chose to dismiss the warnings!

28 October 1993

Dear Kim,

It has been exactly eight months to the day since the Lord revealed the truth about Bill and his ministry, of which you were a witness. Based on our conversation the other night, there seems to be a lot of confusion in your mind as to whether what took place that night was of the Holy Spirit or not.

When Candy's sister called last Sunday night to tell me that you had left Candy (and the group) and were staying with her, I was quite apprehensive, but I was equally excited at the thought of you finally seeing the truth.

Even though I really wanted to talk with you, I was somewhat reluctant when I asked if I could speak with you. As I spoke to you over the phone that night, it was so strange. The feeling I had was that this would be my last chance to convince you to see the error of your ways. I felt extremely desperate, and I was trying to think of anything I could say that would make you understand.

After we spoke, I got the impression you have no idea what you're involved with. I perceived that I did not get through to you at all. In this letter, I hope I will be able to impress upon you the urgency of the matter and help you see who you are walking with and what will happen if you continue.

My prayer is that I will be very sensitive to what the Lord would have me say to you, so that I might help clear up any doubts and confusion you may have. After all, God is the only one that truly knows all things, and only His truth will pierce your heart so as to reveal your true intentions.

You need to keep in mind that this is a battle for your soul, so please realize this is very serious and it will affect your eternal life or death. The most important decision you have before you right now is whether you are going to continue to believe the lies or embrace the truth. And you know in your heart what is right and what is wrong.

You have the truth written in your heart just like God's Word says, but Satan has been stealing it from you. By the same token, your own sin has been blinding you to the truth. This is why sin of any kind is so dangerous.

If sin goes unacknowledged and without repentance, it will only grow and become stronger and have more power over you. But Jesus Christ won the victory over sin and death and came to set you free from all that is evil if you will only believe His Word and walk in it.

Kim, the Lord is giving you another chance to walk with Him, and I just happen to be the one He has chosen to use to direct your way back to Him. I am nothing! He is everything! And I will only speak to you what I hear my Father say, so please seriously consider what I am saying to you now.

If you recall, during the Waco incident, several people were allowed to leave before David Koresh and his remaining followers were destroyed by the fire on 19 April 1993. I hope you realize that was most certainly by the Lord that those people were released.

The Lord will most definitely save those who truly love and belong to Him, and He will make a way out of every temptation if we are willing to take it. But you must be prepared to follow the truth and everything that is right.

There are many Scriptures I could share that will refute every single one of the lies Satan has spoken to you, but I don't feel this is the time for that. It's more important for you to know what it truly means to have eternal life. Please meditate on these Scriptures so the Lord can speak to your heart.

Genesis 3:22–24 "And the LORD GOD said, Behold, the man is become as one of us, to know good and evil: and now, lest he put forth his hand, and take also of the Tree of Life, and eat, and live for ever:

Therefore the LORD GOD sent him forth from the garden of Eden, to till the ground from whence he was taken.

So he drove out the man; and he placed at the east of the garden of Eden Cherubims, and a flaming sword which turned every way, to keep the way of the Tree of Life."

Psalms 119:92–93 "Unless thy law [had been] my delights, I should then have perished in mine affliction. I will never forget Thy precepts: for with them Thou hast quickened me."

John 1:1, 14 "In the beginning was the Word, and the Word was with God, and the Word was God…. And the Word was made flesh, and dwelt among us, (and we beheld His glory, the glory as of the only begotten of the Father,) full of grace and truth."

John 14:6 "Jesus saith unto him, I Am the way, the truth, and the life: no man cometh unto the Father, but by Me."

1 Corinthians 2:14 "But the natural man receiveth not the things of the Spirit of God: for they are foolishness unto him: neither can he know [them], because they are spiritually discerned."

Matthew 13:18–23 "Hear ye therefore the parable of the sower. When any one heareth the Word of the Kingdom, and understandeth [it] not, then cometh the wicked [one], and catcheth away that which was sown in his heart. This is he which received seed by the way side.

But he that received the seed into stony places, the same is he that heareth the Word, and anon with joy receiveth it; yet hath he not root in himself, but dureth for a while: for when tribulation or persecution ariseth because of the Word, by and by he is offended.

He also that received seed among the thorns is he that heareth the Word; and the care of this world, and the deceitfulness of riches, choke the Word, and he becometh unfruitful.

But he that received seed into the good ground is he that heareth the Word, and understandeth [it]; which also beareth fruit, and bringeth forth, some an hundredfold, some sixty, some thirty."

When I was with Bill's ministry, I did not understand that Satan could steal the truth right out of my heart. But because of my ignorance of his tactics, I put my complete trust in what another person said, instead of having my confidence totally in the Lord Jesus Christ and His Word.

Exposed

It's only because of Him that I am now walking in the True Light. It's only because of Him that I am now walking in the real truth. It's only because of Him that I have access to the way of the Tree of Life. And Jesus is the only one who deserves the honor and glory, because He is the One who gave His life so that I might live!

I am not asking you to believe me! I am asking you to put your trust, hope, and dependence completely on the Lord Jesus Christ, and Him *alone*. It's only through God that you get understanding. Men can deceive you, sometimes knowingly, and sometimes very innocently, which is why we need the Lord!

I truly desire that you and all God's people be saved, especially those who are deceived into thinking that they are walking with the Lord God Almighty in truth when in reality, they are walking with the Devil in deception.

Because of my experience of walking with the enemy, I am much more cautious about whom I put my trust in. Just because someone professes that they love and serve the Lord Jesus Christ doesn't mean they do. That's why it's so important to be in union with Christ Jesus by His Spirit, so that He can reveal what the truth is. These Scriptures will establish what I am saying.

2 Corinthians 11:13–15 "For such [are] false apostles, deceitful workers, transforming themselves into the apostles of Christ. And no marvel; for Satan himself is transformed into an angel of light. Therefore [it is] no great thing if his ministers also be transformed as the ministers of righteousness; whose end shall be according to their works."

1 John 2:26–29 "These [things] have I written unto you concerning them that seduce you. But the anointing which ye have received of Him abideth in you, and ye need not that any man teach you: but as the same anointing teacheth you of all things, and is truth, and is no lie, and even as it hath taught you, ye shall abide in Him.

And now, little children, abide in Him; that, when He shall appear, we may have confidence, and not be ashamed before Him at His coming.

If ye know that He is righteous, ye know that every one that doeth righteousness is born of Him."

If you have truly been anointed by God with His Spirit, then what John is saying here applies to you, but if you have never genuinely committed your heart, soul, and body to the Lord God above, then it's time that you did.

Salvation is certainly a free gift from God, and He will save those who sincerely call upon Him, but if you are to continue in that salvation, you *must* continue in His Word and allow God's love and life to grow up inside of you.

And if you have truly received Jesus Christ, the perfect gift, as Lord and Savior, then His seed has been planted in your heart. But because of sin, pride, and our lack of knowledge, we fall into the traps set by the enemy, which keep us from fully realizing the free gift we have received by faith in Christ.

1 Corinthians 15:1–4 "Moreover, brethren, I declare unto you the gospel which I preached unto you, which also ye have received, and wherein ye stand; by which also ye are saved, if ye keep in memory what I preached unto you, unless ye have believed in vain.

For I delivered unto you first of all that which I also received, how that Christ died for our sins according to the Scriptures; And that He was buried, and that He rose again the third day according to the Scriptures:"

It's so important to read the Scriptures in order to know the One who came and died for us. The One who was raised from the dead to give us eternal life. It's only through the true knowledge of the Lord Jesus that we can get the understanding we need so we can refute all the lies and deceptions of Satan.

Contrary to what you have learned, the Old Testament is just as important as the New Testament to gain an understanding of God and His Word. Here are some Scriptures to help establish what I am saying.

2 Peter 3:2 "That ye may be mindful of the words which were spoken before by the holy prophets, and of the commandment of us the apostles of the Lord and Saviour:"

Romans 15:4 "For whatsoever things were written aforetime were written for our learning, that we through patience and comfort of the Scriptures might have hope."

2 Peter 1:21 "For the prophecy came not in old time by the will of man: but holy men of God spake [as they were] moved by the Holy Ghost."

I realize that many people think I am being very presumptuous for claiming that God has spoken through me, and I admit I can understand why it bothers some people. But the fact remains, I know what God has said to me, and I will do what He says regardless of whether men agree with me or not.

My allegiance is to my God and Him alone, and if others want to stand with me, that's wonderful! But if they do not, then I will stand alone. But in essence I will never be alone, because my Lord is always with me.

This next letter is a personal excerpt from my journal. My hope in sharing this with you is that perhaps you'll come to understand what the Lord God Almighty has done for me, so you can truly realize what He's willing to do for you and for all those who call on Him from a sincere and contrite heart.

Walking with the Enemy

Wednesday / 12 May 1993

Dearest Lord God Almighty,

I found out from [Candy's former husband] yesterday that he got a court date. I am so excited at the thought of having the opportunity to stand before people and speak Your Word.

I know that time the Bible study group got called before [the] courtroom;[83] *I was a nervous wreck. I bet Ira must have been going nuts inside, hoping that I would contain myself. She seemed so calm and cool, along with Candy.*

I really had a very hard time that day. That was the first time I ever snapped at her and Candy, and I ran out of the room crying. They came back to my room to comfort me, and they were able to calm me down, but I know the reason I was so crazy is because I knew in my heart that there were many things in my life that I would be so ashamed of if I had to speak of them in public.

But Lord, those same things are in my past, and You have cleansed me of the unrighteousness that I was walking in, and now I can speak without being ashamed before You. I still feel a sense of shame at what I allowed myself to be a partaker of, and I have reaped what I have sown, but I see the truth now, where before I was walking with the enemy in deception.

I praise You, and I am ever thankful to You for coming down by Your mighty power to show the truth, and You did that during Bible study on the night of 28 February 1993. That date is a day I'll never ever forget!

You released the chains that bound me! You gave sight to my eyes! You unstopped my ears! And You released the power that darkness had over me! Praise the Mighty Name of my Lord and Savior Jesus Christ, the Anointed One!

Exposed

And now I can walk around with an ability, because of You, to see exactly what's in front of me. And I will take each day as it comes and not be concerned about what's up ahead, because I trust You completely!

You are a light unto my path! Thank You for the understanding that You have given me and the wisdom to apply what I know about You. I am still trying to learn how to be quick to listen and slow to speak. I truly want to guard what comes out of my mouth.

I now understand the verse that says, "Don't cast your pearls before swine because they will trample them under their feet and turn around and tear you to pieces." But praise God, You are able to heal my wounds.[84]

They most certainly did exactly what You said in Your Word that they would do, but the thing I was mistaken about was: I thought they served You. I thought they loved You. I thought they loved me.

But You shed Your glorious light on the situation because of Your love for me and the whole world. I say the world because I do realize the calling You have placed on my life from birth. And Father God, I accept that calling with no reservations whatsoever. I will forsake all to follow You and You alone.

And I know there are many people that won't understand. There are many people that will say bad things about me. There are many people that will hate me and lie about me and even give false testimony about me.

But you know what? Even if they try to imprison me for doing nothing wrong, I will count it a joy to suffer shame and disgrace for the Mighty Name of Jesus, my Lord! I fully accept the commission that You have called me to.

A servant of the Most High God! And the Jesus who came and died for me that I might have life forever with the Father, Creator of all things.
Praise the L*ORD* *God Jehovah!*

C. Read

Signed on this 12th Day of May in the year of our Lord, One Thousand Nine Hundred and Ninety-Three.[85]

{End of excerpt from journal}

Kim, in case there is any doubt in your heart as to Whom I serve, I will close with this excerpt from a letter I wrote to Candy that I did not finish. I hope if you share this with her that she realizes there is still time to come to the Lord Jesus, but please tell her to come quickly before They close the door!

Proclamation of Faith by C. Read
Dated 8 May 1993

At this time, I would like to clarify who my Lord and my God is, Whom I serve. He is the Lord God Almighty! Maker of Heaven and earth and everything that is made.

He is all-powerful! He is the Most High God! He has all authority! And He loved the world so much that He sent His only begotten Son to die for us so that we might live to serve and worship Him in Spirit and in truth.

And to prove to Satan that only the Lord God Jehovah is all-powerful, He raised Jesus from the dead. And death had no more power over Him.

And all who believe in their heart that God was able by His mighty power to do that and confess Him as Lord will be saved from the wrath that is to come on all the children of disobedience.

Jesus Christ won the victory! And He is my Master! And He is my Lord! And because I have been obedient to Him and to the testimony of Jesus Christ, He has anointed me with His Holy Spirit. Praise the Holy Name of Jesus!

I would also like to clarify who my God's adversary is: he's that old serpent, the Devil, and Satan who hates my God and His saints. He is a very powerful foe! He is the second-highest power! He has much authority here on earth. He can kill! He can steal! And he can destroy people's lives! And that is his primary objective. And his target is God's people!

You may not be able to see him, but he works in the children of disobedience. So don't underestimate his abilities. And don't think for a minute that he won't try any way he can to get to you. He is very sly, wily, crafty, and cunning. And he uses underhanded and calculated methods to secretly introduce his lies and deceptions. And he can only operate in darkness!

And for the most part, people don't give Satan credit for many of the things that he does. And he prefers it that way. He masquerades as a Christian. He pretends that he loves the Lord Jesus. He pretends that he serves the Lord Jesus. He claims that he would die for the Lord Jesus. And he uses men to make these proclamations through the spirit of antichrist!

And he has deceived many people! He's working very hard these days because he knows his time is coming to a close very soon. And you will know that's true because the world will get more and more wicked as you see the Day approaching.

Most people don't acknowledge God or give Him credit for what He does either. You may not be able to see Him, but He works in the children of obedience. So don't underestimate His power and abilities either. And don't think for a minute that He won't save those that truly love and belong to Him.

He is very loving, kind, gentle, compassionate, merciful, and so forgiving. He is truly an awesome God!

He uses honesty, sincerity, and truth to present Himself to us. And there is only one way that He can come into your life. That doorway is Jesus Christ! And He can only operate in the light!

{End of proclamation of faith}

I hope you know that my love has always been true.

*A servant of the Most High God,
and the Lord Jesus Christ,*

*As signed by me in the presence of a witness on
the 1st Day of November in the year of our Lord,
One Thousand Nine Hundred and Ninety-Three.*

{End of letter to Kim}

IRA WROTE ME MANY LETTERS attempting to get me back. I wrote the following letter just as I finished a three-day fast by direction of the Lord, and I am so amazed at what God reveals to me when I am attentive to His voice.

4 December 1993

Dear Ira,

I did receive your October letter, which I responded to, but the Lord said not to send it because He said you wouldn't receive it. Instead, He told me to start a new letter after I read through the entire Scriptures.[86]

I have done that, so in this letter, I will speak only what I feel the Lord would have me say to you. My hope is that I will not allow my feelings or emotions to get in the way of what He would have me put down on paper.

I believe you know me well enough to know that all I desire to proceed from my mouth is the truth of the Word of God. I have come to understand in a more intimate way exactly why it is so important to seek only His truth and wisdom and to live it out in our lives moment by moment, in every situation.

I have come to realize exactly how I came to be so deceived during my time with you and Bill, and after reading through the Scriptures, that fact has been even more established in my heart. Your recent letter confirms this further.

On the surface, there isn't really anything seemingly wrong or out of order with anything you said. Actually, it was a very kindly worded letter that I sincerely wished was the truth, but because I know better, I realize that it's just another attempt to try to manipulate me in order to make me think you have finally realized the truth. However, everything you stated in that letter is the exact position I presumed you held while I was with you. So I really don't understand what new truth you are talking about.

In other letters, you have also tried to appeal to my emotions in an attempt to persuade me that I am the one who is walking with the enemy and under demonic control. You have even accused me of lying, slander, and revenge; none of which are true.

Ira, in this letter, I am going to disregard the words you spoke to me and just confront you with what I know in my heart to be the truth behind your words. I do sense that the Lord has given me the responsibility of bringing some of these things to your attention, and whether you receive what I say or not is between you and God.

I contend that I have always been a child of the Lord God Almighty from the very beginning! On the other hand, I contend that you are a child of the Devil and have been from the very beginning! And I will explain why I know you are *not* of the Spirit of Christ, but are of the spirit of antichrist!

In order for you to understand why I have come to this conclusion about you, I feel it's necessary to bring up several incidents that I am aware of through my personal relationship with you and the other members of the group. The following evidence substantiates why we are so opposed to one another and reveals why I could never be a part of your and Bill's ministry ever again.

The most outrageous thing you ever told me about your past was when you used to pursue men with the intent of seducing them into a sexual encounter, whether they were married or not. You said that you preferred Christian men that were married because they were so much more of a challenge.

You stated that this was like a game with you, and you would tease and flirt with them until you were sure that you had won them over completely. Then, after you were able to seduce them into having a physical relationship, you would just cut all ties without any concern for the emotional damage that you had inflicted on these men. (Not to mention what it did to their families!)

As you told me about this, I just imagined you laughing in their faces, as if you took considerable pleasure and satisfaction in their pain. I remember asking if you were concerned about the hurt this must have caused them, and you said, "No, it was their problem, they should have known better." [87]

The following testimony will confirm why I am so opposed to you and Bill. This is a transcript from a sworn statement that

I had given to the attorney of Candy's former husband, and it was used as evidence in their custody battle.

Transcript of Sworn Statement of C. Read
25 March 1993

Q. I think this may be the easiest way to get into it. You mentioned earlier in your statement that you left the group recently, in early March, due to the fact that there was some allegations made to Bill of which he did not repent?

A. He didn't deny the allegations. He pretty much just sat there.

Q. Did he admit them?

A. The sexual allegations? Yes, he did.

Q. Now let's just take the sexual allegations first. And what were those allegations? And again, I'll caution you that it's really not necessary at this point in time for you to use names, but just, if you can, describe the situations.

A. He pursued the ladies in the group in a sexual way if they would have it. You know, I mean, it wasn't—it is really weird to try to explain it. Basically, he would lead you to believe that he was your "spiritual husband," and pretty much seduce you into having a relationship with him.

Q. Now of your own personal knowledge, are you aware, and remember you're under oath, of any actual sexual relations that he had with any members of the group?

A. That I'm actually aware of?

Q. Yes.

A. Yeah.

Q. And how many?

A. Where I actually saw or just knew from them telling me?

Q. Let's say where you actually witnessed.

A. Two.

Q. Now, what I really want to know, first of all, is the sexual acts that you witnessed…were those sexual acts in a group situation?

A. No, they were not, at all.

Q. Was Bill and the other individual who was having sex aware of your presence?

A. Very much.

Q. And would you describe, without names, how that occurred?

A. Well, it was after a Bible study meeting.

Q. At your home?

A. This was when it was at Ira's.

Q. Across the street?

A. No. We were just sitting there talking.

Q. Who's *we*? Bill and the other person and you? Is that correct?

A. Yes. And we were just—I was sitting in front of the couch and they were in their chairs. They were sitting there, and all of a sudden, they just started taking off their clothes and having sex right there on the floor in front of me. And that was basically it. And I was pretty shocked at it. It's a weird thing.

Q. Now let me ask you this. The three of you were sitting after a meeting. Who else was present in the house at the time this occurred?

A. The children were in the back.

Q. Rebecca[88] was not present?

A. No.

Q. Candy was not present?

A. No.

Q. And were you all in a locked room?

A. No. We were in the living room where the front door was still unlocked, or actually, the carport door.

Q. Did the children have access?

A. Sure, very much.

Q. Now the way you described it was that they just commenced to doing this?

A. No warning at all.

Q. Did they ask you to leave?

A. No. They took pleasure in me being right there.

Q. What did they say?
A. Nothing.
Q. I mean, the meeting was over, you were talking, and they—
A. I had asked them why they did it, and they said God told them to, and that was about it.
Q. And when you said they had sex, did they actually complete the sexual act? They completely disrobed?
A. Oh yeah.
Q. And how long did this take? I mean, was this—
A. It wasn't real long. Thank God.
Q. Did they invite you to participate?
A. No, they didn't.
Q. Why did they tell you that God told them to do it?
A. Because I was such a self-righteous Christian. God wanted to do shocking things to me.

Because they used to cuss in front of me and say such disgusting things in front of me. And then they did *that*. And they said it was to get me out of the mode of being self-righteous and being able to accept shocking things. Because when you go out in the world to witness, you're going to need to not be affected by what you see on the outside and be able to look at people on the inside.

That was mainly—it was like shock treatment for me, and it was very shocking, actually.

Q. Did Bill admit this allegation in front of other people that this occurred?
A. No.
Q. Now how many others? You said there was one other occasion you witnessed. Was that in the presence of anyone else?
A. No.
Q. Is anyone else aware that that occurred?
A. Yes.
Q. Is the group aware that that occurred?

A. At present, yes. Well, not actually the whole group. It was at our confrontation.

Q. Members of the group are aware?

A. Yes.

Q. Did that occur at one of the meetings that is taped?

A. No. It was after hours.

Q. Was there more than one occasion that you witnessed this?

A. Three.

Q. On these three occasions, were there any other people in the house?

A. Children.

Q. And did the children have access to the area where this took place?

A. Uh huh.

Q. Did any of the children witness any of this occurring?

A. No. I am so thankful.

Q. Was Rebecca one of those children?

A. I don't think she was there then. It's quite possible she was for the first time. I believe she was in the back room, yes. Because that's when they were living with me. So it's very likely she was there. I can't say yes, exactly, that I remember her being there, but it's very likely she was because Candy and Ira had just left for a moment, just for fifteen or twenty minutes.

Q. Now what other allegations were made? Sexual allegations have been made against him?

A. This isn't an allegation, but it's an actual personal experience that I saw him do during a meeting. And it was when he was ministering—and he was praying for him, laid hands on him, and then he started French kissing him.

Q. By French—

A. Just a real sexual kiss.

Q. What was the reaction of the group when this occurred?

A. I was kind of shocked myself, but I don't really—nobody spoke about it. It was not something we talked about.

Q. What was the purpose of the kiss?

A. I'm assuming this, because I didn't discuss it with Bill. [He] used to say that the reason—and he would kiss me that way when I initially came to the group, and he said that it was because he had the love of Jesus inside of him and that is how God had him demonstrate the love of Jesus.

Q. Did he kiss other people in the group the same way?

A. Yes.

Q. Did he kiss any of the children that way?

A. Not that I know of. I'm sure—is a seventeen-year-old a child?

Q. That's correct.

A. Yes, he did kiss her that way. She's the other allegation that was made that Tuesday night we had the confrontation. He actually had sex with her.

Q. And did he admit that?

A. He admitted that, and the adoptive mother was present, Candy.[89] She admitted it. And Ira is the one who told me about it.

Q. And how did this incident occur with the minor?

A. I don't know if he's gone into the details with you, but this is when the court was trying to get Kim to come back to her home. It's when she was seventeen. I even have a letter that she wrote me while she was away. It's when she just—this is based on what they told me after the fact. Bill was supposedly to have gone up there and seduced her and told her that she was his wife. And they—

Q. Had sex?

A. Yes.

Q. On one occasion?

A. Just from my knowledge of what they told me, it only happened once.

Q. In the presence of any other person?

A. I don't think so. I think it was just her and him.

Q. Does Candy approve of the actions of Bill having these relations with these women? French kissing the man? French kissing the women?

A. No, she doesn't.

Q.	She does not approve of that?
A.	She stated to me that she doesn't.
Q.	Has she attempted to stop Bill from doing that?
A.	No. Well, when he pursues her, she stops it, so she says.
Q.	Has she left the group?
A.	No.
Q.	She continues?
A.	She condones it by being a part of the group now.
Q.	It's wide open now, and she continues to be a part of the group?
A.	Sunday night not everything was divulged, but Tuesday night I went through everything that had ever taken place with me in the presence of Wendell, Candy, Bill, Ira, and my husband and made those allegations. And so, all of them are completely aware of everything that transpired, as far as that goes. And she's still part of the group. She condones that behavior, yes.

{End of C. Read's sworn statement of 25 March 1993}

On the morning of 17 May 1993, after I made my appearance in the courtroom, the attorneys and the judge went to the back.[90] Without calling any witnesses to the stand, the judge ruled that Candy had to relinquish all rights, and her former husband was granted full custody of their child. It seems that someone is afraid of the truth being brought out into the open.

God has said that there is nothing covered that shall not be revealed and nothing hid that shall not be made known. Because you have chosen to continue in the lies and deceptions and condone the sin of others, one day, God will expose your sins for all the world to see.

Ira, had you acknowledged and repented of your sin so that the Lord could forgive you and cleanse you of your unrighteousness, it would never have come to this. I take no great pleasure in causing pain in your life, but God will not allow you to blaspheme His name much longer.

*E*XPOSED

These Psalms indicate how the Lord God Almighty feels about wickedness and deception and what He plans to do about it.

Psalms 5:4–6 "For Thou [art] not a God that hath pleasure in wickedness: neither shall evil dwell with Thee. The foolish shall not stand in Thy sight: Thou hatest all workers of iniquity. Thou shalt destroy them that speak leasing (or falsehood): the LORD will abhor the bloody and deceitful man."

Psalms 145:20 "The LORD preserveth all them that love Him: but all the wicked will He destroy."

Psalms 21:8–11 "Thine hand shall find out all Thine enemies: Thy right hand shall find out those that hate Thee. Thou shalt make them as a fiery oven in the time of Thine anger: the LORD shall swallow them up in His wrath, and the fire shall devour them.

Their fruit shalt Thou destroy from the earth, and their seed from among the children of men. For they intended evil against Thee: they imagined a mischievous device [which] they are not able to [perform]."

Based on these Scriptures, those who do evil will not prosper. And those that lie and do wickedness will not stand. For you to say that you are Jewish and a prophet sent by God to proclaim His truth, when in actuality you are walking with the enemy in deception and deceiving others into believing your lies, is inexcusable and an abomination before the Lord God Almighty!

The apostle Paul encountered a very similar situation as ours, and I would like you to especially notice his response. Please read this very carefully and take heed to what God may be speaking to your heart.

Acts 13:6–11 "And when they had gone through the isle unto Paphos, they found a certain sorcerer, a false prophet, a Jew, whose name [was] Bar-jesus: Which was with the deputy of the country, Sergius Paulus, a prudent man; who called for Barnabas and Saul, and desired to hear the Word of God. But Elymas the sorcerer (for so is his name by interpretation) withstood them, seeking to turn away the deputy from the faith.

Then Saul, (who also [is called] Paul,) filled with the Holy Ghost, set his eyes on him, and said, O full of all subtilty and all mischief, [thou] child of the Devil, [thou] enemy of all righteousness, wilt thou not cease to pervert the right ways of the Lord? And now, behold, the hand of the Lord [is] upon thee, and thou shalt be blind, not seeing the sun for a season. And immediately there fell on him a mist and a darkness; and he went about seeking some to lead him by the hand."

Your sin will find you out and be your ruin. You will reap what you have sown. And you'll have no one to blame but yourself! Due to your disobedience and rebellion against God, He will not allow you, or any other workers of iniquity, to go unhindered any longer!

Of course, you have it all worked out in your mind that all is well with your soul, but that's a lie too! The Deceiver has been very successful if you truly believe that everything you do is ordained and sanctioned by God.

It's quite apparent, based on the fruits in your own life, that you follow that which is evil and wicked. I now understand why demonic spirits have the authority to torment you as they do, *because you belong to them!*

Even though you claim to be a servant of the Lord Jesus Christ, I know because of the Holy Spirit Who resides within me that you are most certainly not of the Lord God above.

1 John 4:1–6 "Beloved, believe not every spirit, but try the spirits whether they are of God: because many false prophets are gone out into the world.

Hereby know ye the Spirit of God: Every spirit that confesseth that Jesus Christ is come in the flesh is of God:

Exposed

And every spirit that confesseth not that Jesus Christ is come in the flesh is not of God: and this is that [spirit] of antichrist, whereof ye have heard that it should come; and even now already is it in the world.

Ye are of God, little children, and have overcome them: because greater is He that is in you, than he that is in the world. They are of the world: therefore speak they of the world, and the world heareth them. We are of God: he that knoweth God heareth us; he that is not of God heareth not us. Hereby know we the spirit of truth, and the spirit of error."

Because of my very humbling experience in connection with Bill's ministry, I have come to a greater dependence on the Lord God, instead of myself or other people. I have gained insight into the fact that only the Spirit of God can truly reveal what spirit another person is actually controlled by.

When you first met me, you were under the mistaken impression that I had not been a Christian very long. Had you been aware of the truth, you would have known that I had been a Christian for ten years and was extremely committed to the Lord. Not only did you not know me, but I did not know you, which is the very reason Satan was able to deceive me from the start.

Had I known that I would be enticed away from my church and family and committed to a false prophet, you would never have known me.

Had I known that Satan would attempt to seduce me away from my God by the use of witchcraft and sorcery, you would never have known me.

Had I known that you bow your knee to Satan while claiming your allegiance to the One, True, and Living God, you would never have known me.

But my God had different plans. He knew all these things, and He could have told me, but He wanted me to know you. And the Lord God Almighty, in His infinite wisdom, used this extremely naive and unsuspecting, non-conformist woman to expose the lies and deceptions of the Devil himself!

Had I taken pleasure in sin, I would be with you still. Had I been that newborn Christian you assumed I was, I probably would have been another statistic of those broken individuals you seem to leave in your path.[91]

Don't get me wrong, I was greatly affected by my association with you and Bill's ministry, and it's *only* by the grace of God that I am still standing! And I will continue to stand until He's ready to take me home! Praise the mighty, all-powerful, glorious name of Jesus Christ, the Son of the Most High God!

These Scriptures will show you exactly why I know that you are of the "synagogue of Satan" and that his purpose is to steal, to kill, and to destroy God's people. And he uses sinful, unholy men to carry out his evil deeds.

Matthew 13:24–30 "Another parable put He forth unto them, saying, The Kingdom of Heaven is likened unto a man which sowed good seed in his field: But while men slept, his enemy came and sowed tares among the wheat, and went his way. But when the blade was sprung up, and brought forth fruit, then appeared the tares also.

So the servants of the householder came and said unto him, Sir, didst not thou sow good seed in thy field? from whence then hath it tares? He said unto them, An enemy hath done this.

The servants said unto him, Wilt thou then that we go and gather them up? But he said, Nay; lest while ye gather up the tares, ye root up also the wheat with them. Let both grow together until the harvest: and in the time of harvest I will say to the reapers, Gather ye together first the tares, and bind them in bundles to burn them: but gather the wheat into my barn." ∽

Matthew 13:36–43 "Then Jesus sent the multitudes away, and went into the house: and His disciples came unto Him, saying, Declare unto us the parable of the tares of the field.

He answered and said unto them, He that soweth the good seed is the Son of Man; the field is the world; the good seed are the children of the Kingdom; but the tares are the children of the Wicked [One]; the enemy that sowed them is the Devil; the harvest is the end of the world; and the reapers are the angels. As therefore the tares are gathered and burned in the fire; so shall it be in the end of this world.

The Son of Man shall send forth His angels, and they shall gather out of His Kingdom all things that offend, and them which do iniquity; and shall cast them into a furnace of fire: there shall be wailing and gnashing of teeth.

Then shall the righteous shine forth as the sun in the Kingdom of their Father. Who hath ears to hear, let him hear." ∽

I am sure by now you are sorry you ever met me, and you're wishing that I would just go away. The hardest thing for me to accept with all this is that none of this would be necessary had you repented.

But because you contend that you have done no evil, God in His perfect justice cannot allow it to continue.[92] I don't know if you've noticed, but the Lord is exposing darkness all over the world.

I sincerely loved you, and there was never any pretense or hypocrisy on my part. And because I was so trusting of you and Bill, you were able to take advantage of me to the degree that you did. But God has a wonderful way of comforting me through His Word. Notice the situation David experienced.

Psalms 41:9–13 "Yea, mine own familiar friend, in whom I trusted, which did eat of my bread, hath lifted up [his] heel against me.

But Thou, O Lord, be merciful unto me, and raise me up, that I may requite them. By this I know that Thou favourest me, because my enemy doth not triumph over me.

And as for me, Thou upholdest me in mine integrity, and settest me before Thy face for ever. Blessed [be] the LORD GOD of Israel from everlasting, and to everlasting. Amen, and Amen."

I do realize you may not understand many things I've addressed in this letter, or know how I have come to the conclusions that I have, but these Scriptures will explain why you are not able to comprehend the truth.

Proverbs 4:14–19 "Enter not into the path of the wicked, and go not in the way of evil [men]. Avoid it, pass not by it, turn from it, and pass away. For they sleep not, except they have done mischief; and their sleep is taken away, unless they cause [some] to fall. For they eat the bread of wickedness, and drink the wine of violence.

But the path of the just [is] as the shining light, that shineth more and more unto the perfect day. The way of the wicked [is] as darkness: they know not at what they stumble."

Proverbs 28:4–5 "They that forsake the law praise the wicked: but such as keep the law contend with them. Evil men understand not judgment: but they that seek the Lord understand all [things]."

God's Word is true when He says:

Revelation 21:8 "But the fearful, and unbelieving, and the abominable, and murderers, and whoremongers, and sorcerers, and idolaters, and all liars, shall have their part in the lake which burneth with fire and brimstone: which is the second death."

Blessing, and honor, and glory, and power be unto Him that sitteth upon the Throne, and unto the Lamb, forever and ever! Amen!

*E*XPOSED

Sincerely,
A servant of the Lord Jesus Christ,
and the Most High God,

C. Read

P.S. I would like to share my first letter with you so you can compare the two and see the benefits of prayer, fasting, and the *Word of God*.

{End of second letter to Ira}

3 November 1993

Dear Ira,

Thank you for your letter. I hope you know that I am still very concerned about you and what might happen to you. Contrary to what you might think, I still love you very much and I truly hope the best for you.

The day I received your letter was so neat because earlier that morning you had really been on my heart. I had even thought about writing you a letter. I had been thanking the Lord, because everything I learned about Him during my "wilderness" experience caused me to have a deeper love, respect, and dependence on God than I have ever had before in my life.

Not only did I learn so much about God, but I learned so many things about the enemy of my God. Had I never known you, I would not have had the opportunity to have my senses exercised to discern both good and evil.[93]

I am very thankful that the Lord did not allow me to walk with the enemy long enough to experience the very depths of Satan, but just long enough for me to truly understand and know how extremely dangerous it is to walk in self-righteousness, pride, and sin of any kind.

I appreciate your letter because it's given me a little glimpse of what's going on in your own life right now. I can see from your letter that you still feel that I am wrong and you are right. You are still calling sweet for bitter, and bitter for sweet. In essence, you still profess to be in the light when in reality you are still in darkness. Please realize my main purpose in writing this letter to you is first of all because God said to, and second because I sincerely desire for you to see the truth.

I know Satan would much rather I write you guys off and just forget about you, but I just can't until I know for certain that you are fully aware of who and what you are involved with. And by the grace of God, I will do that.

I would first like to establish the purpose of God's Word in relation to those who desire to serve Him and contrast that with those who are against Him. Please allow God to speak to your heart as you read this.

2 Timothy 2:15, 3:16–17 "Study to shew thyself approved unto God, a workman that needeth not to be ashamed, rightly dividing the Word of truth....

All Scripture [is] given by inspiration of God, and [is] profitable for doctrine, for reproof, for correction, for instruction in righteousness: That the man of God may be perfect, thoroughly furnished unto all good works."

Before we can be equipped to do God's work, we must study the Scriptures to know the truth, but knowledge in itself is not enough; we must also have wisdom in applying that knowledge. And the only way you can have true wisdom is from God above. This next Scripture passage will confirm this.

Proverbs 2:6–7 "For the LORD giveth wisdom: out of His mouth [cometh] knowledge and understanding. He layeth up sound wisdom for the righteous: [He is] a buckler to them that walk uprightly."

That Scripture implies there are different types of wisdom, and I would like to share what the Lord has brought to my attention concerning this.

James 3:13–18 "Who [is] a wise man and endued with knowledge among you? Let him shew out of a good conversation his works with meekness of wisdom. But if ye have bitter envying and strife in your hearts, glory not, and lie not against the truth. This wisdom descendeth not from above, but [is] earthly, sensual, devilish. For where envying and strife [is], there [is] confusion and every evil work.

But the wisdom that is from above is first pure, then peaceable, gentle, [and] easy to be intreated, full of mercy and good fruits, without partiality, and without hypocrisy. And the fruit of righteousness is sown in peace of them that make peace."

1 Corinthians 2:4–5 "And my speech and my preaching [was] not with enticing words of man's wisdom, but in demonstration of the Spirit and of power: That your faith should not stand in the wisdom of men, but in the power of God."

1 Corinthians 3:18–20 "Let no man deceive himself. If any man among you seemeth to be wise in this world, let him become a fool, that he may be wise. For the wisdom of this world is foolishness with God. For it is written, He taketh the wise in their own craftiness. And again, The Lord knoweth the thoughts of the wise, that they are vain."

Those passages establish that there is wisdom from God, wisdom of man, wisdom of this world, and wisdom of the Devil. These next Scriptures will explain how to obtain God's wisdom and what the results will be.

Proverbs 2:1–5 "My son, if thou wilt receive My Words, and hide My commandments with thee; so that thou incline thine ear unto wisdom, [and] apply thine heart to understanding; yea, if thou criest after knowledge, [and] liftest up thy voice for understanding; if thou seekest her as silver, and searchest for her as [for] hid treasures; then shalt thou understand the fear of the LORD, and find the knowledge of God."

Proverbs 1:7 "The fear of the LORD [is] the beginning of knowledge: [but] fools despise wisdom and instruction."

Proverbs 8:13 "The fear of the LORD [is] to hate evil: pride, and arrogancy, and the evil way, and the froward mouth, do I hate."

Ira, I know that you have read all these Scriptures many times before, but I just feel a need to bring them to your attention so you can determine in your own heart whether your perspective is from the wisdom of this world, your own wisdom, or even worse, the wisdom of Satan.

I know with all certainty that your wisdom is not from God, because if it was, you would hear and understand everything I've been trying to say to you since the night of 28 February 1993. The following Scripture confirms this.

1 John 4:6 "We are of God: he that knoweth God heareth us; he that is not of God heareth not us. Hereby know we the spirit of truth, and the spirit of error."

I know in my heart that you are walking in error, and all I am trying to do is convince you of that fact before it's too late. Had you truly been walking with the Lord, then on the night of 2 March 1993, you would have stood by me, instead of coming against me. Here's a Scripture that will show exactly why I know you are not of the One, True, and Living God.

1 John 2:18–19 "Little children, it is the last time: and as ye have heard that Antichrist shall come, even now are there many antichrists; whereby we know that it is the last time.

They went out from us, but they were not of us; for if they had been of us, they would [no doubt] have continued with us: but [they went out], that they might be made manifest that they were not all of us."

Exposed

In case you have a problem with me trying to persuade you to accept what I am saying, I would like to give an example from the writings of Paul, to show why he tried to convince men to see things God's way too.

2 Corinthians 5:10–11 "For we must all appear before the judgment seat of Christ; that every one may receive the things [done] in [his] body, according to that he hath done, whether [it] be good or bad. Knowing therefore the terror of the Lord, we persuade men; but we are made manifest unto God; and I trust also are made manifest in your consciences."

I know it would be a very humbling experience for you to have to admit that you have been wrong all along, but please don't let your pride send you to Hell. God is such a merciful God, and He is giving you a chance to repent and turn from the error of your ways. Please don't let this opportunity pass you by.

You might feel like I totally despise you, but my love has always been true. I know when I was with you that I never felt there was a real unity between us, but I had always wanted there to be. And because I still do love you, I'll try to help you realize what you have been walking in all these years.

Proverbs 27:5–6 "Open rebuke [is] better than secret love. Faithful [are] the wounds of a friend; but the kisses of an enemy [are] deceitful."

You stated in one of your letters to me that Paul never exposed evil or spoke against those who opposed him. The following will prove that your opinion is completely unfounded and not based on the truth of God's Word.

2 Timothy 2:16–18 "But shun profane [and] vain babblings: for they will increase unto more ungodliness. And their word will eat as doth a canker: of whom is Hymenaeus and Philetus; who concerning the truth have erred, saying that the resurrection is past already; and overthrow the faith of some."

Notice that Paul specifically named the two people who departed from the faith and were causing others to follow them.

2 Timothy 4:10a, 14–15 "For Demas hath forsaken me, having loved this present world, and is departed unto Thessalonica....

Alexander the coppersmith did me much evil: the Lord reward him according to his works: Of whom be thou ware also; for he hath greatly withstood our words."

Not only did Paul make a point of mentioning their names, but also their exact whereabouts in certain instances. Here's another Scripture reference that will establish my point even more. And I want you to notice that this came from one of the disciples that had a very personal and intimate relationship with the Lord Jesus.

3 John 1:9–11 "I wrote unto the church: but Diotrephes, who loveth to have the preeminence among them, receiveth us not. Wherefore, if I come, I will remember his deeds which he doeth, prating against us with malicious words: and not content therewith, neither doth he himself receive the brethren, and forbiddeth them that would, and casteth [them] out of the church. Beloved, follow not that which is evil, but that which is good. He that doeth good is of God: but he that doeth evil hath not seen God."

This Scripture shows that even evil men can be in positions of leadership within the church, which John is warning about. This next verse shows an extreme case of what Paul did concerning two men that chose to continue to walk in sin to the point where they began to blaspheme God.

1 Timothy 1:19–20 "Holding faith, and a good conscience; which some having put away concerning faith have made shipwreck: Of whom is Hymenaeus and Alexander; whom I have delivered unto Satan, that they may learn not to blaspheme."

Exposed

I hope you are starting to see that the voices you listen to are not of the Spirit of Christ, since they completely contradict the very precepts of God's Word.

You have stated that when people walk away from you that they are rejecting Jesus and bad things come upon them because of their disobedience. But I hope you are beginning to realize by now that it's not because they necessarily walked away from the Lord; it was because they were tainted with the evil and wickedness that surrounds you and your ministry.

If you truly understood the Holy Scriptures you would see that God warns and instructs His people throughout the Bible about who we associate with, who we allow into our homes, and even who we should speak with. The following Scriptures will help establish the point I am trying to make.

2 Corinthians 6:14–18, 7:1 "Be ye not unequally yoked together with unbelievers: for what fellowship hath righteousness with unrighteousness? and what communion hath light with darkness? And what concord hath Christ with Belial? or what part hath he that believeth with an infidel? And what agreement hath the temple of God with idols? For ye are the temple of the living God; as God hath said, I will dwell in them, and walk in [them]; and I will be their God, and they shall be My people.

Wherefore come out from among them, and be ye separate, saith the Lord, and touch not the unclean [thing]; and I will receive you, and will be a Father unto you, and ye shall be My sons and daughters, saith the Lord Almighty. Having therefore these promises, dearly beloved, let us cleanse ourselves from all filthiness of the flesh and spirit, perfecting holiness in the fear of God."

I realize you contend that I am not able to discern God's Word accurately, and when I was with you, that was very true. But praise God, I am not the same as I was before! I see with different eyes! I hear with different ears! And I perceive from a completely different perspective!

The Lord has done a mighty work in me since 28 February 1993 when God poured His Spirit into me. I realize you don't believe that what happened that night was of the Holy Spirit, but that's quite understandable considering where you are and who you serve. Satan has to keep you believing the lies; otherwise, you would be forced to look at your own lifestyle.

I cannot emphasize to you enough that you are walking on shaky ground because of your contention that what took place on 28 February 1993 was of demonic spirits. Nevertheless, it reinforces the conviction in my heart that you are most certainly walking with the enemy of the LORD God Jehovah!

I know I am nothing without the Lord, and it's only by the grace of Almighty God that I am able to share any of this with you. It's all due to the fact that God delivered me from the power of darkness and has translated me "into the Kingdom of His dear Son." (See Colossians 1:13.) Praise the mighty name of Jesus Christ, my Lord, my Savior, and my Redeemer!

These next Scriptures will show you exactly why I have chosen to stand apart from you and Bill. It is not only because of what took place on the night of 28 February 1993, but everything that led up to that night, *and more importantly,* what has transpired *since* that night.

Please allow the Lord to speak to your heart. Let down your defenses and humble yourself before the Lord God Almighty. I pray you will listen to His Word as if your eternal life depends on it, because it does.

1 Corinthians 5:1–13 "It is reported commonly [that there is] fornication among you, and such fornication as is not so much as named among the Gentiles, that one should have his father's wife. And ye are puffed up, and have not rather mourned, that he that hath done this deed might be taken away from among you.

For I verily, as absent in body, but present in spirit, have judged already, as though I were present, [concerning] him that hath so done this deed, in the name of our Lord Jesus Christ, when ye are gathered together, and my spirit, with the power of our Lord Jesus Christ, to deliver such an one unto Satan for the destruction of the flesh, that the spirit may be saved in the day of the Lord Jesus.

Your glorying [is] not good. Know ye not that a little leaven leaveneth the whole lump? Purge out therefore the old leaven, that ye may be a new lump, as ye are unleavened. For even Christ our Passover is sacrificed for us: Therefore let us keep the feast, not with old leaven, neither with the leaven of malice and wickedness; but with the unleavened [bread] of sincerity and truth.

I wrote unto you in an epistle not to company with fornicators: Yet not altogether with the fornicators of this world, or with the covetous, or extortioners, or with idolaters; for then must ye needs go out of the world.

But now I have written unto you not to keep company, if any man that is called a brother be a fornicator, or covetous, or an idolater, or a railer, or a drunkard, or an extortioner; with such an one no not to eat.

For what have I to do to judge them also that are without? do not ye judge them that are within? But them that are without God judgeth. Therefore put away from among yourselves that wicked person."

The following is an excerpt from a lesson you wrote up. Listen very carefully to what you said and notice how the words you spoke here are so inconsistent with your actions.

Ira's Lesson: "Among you (within your body—among the parts of the body—there should be no mention of each other committing sexual sins of any kind). The outside world will persecute us, they will speak all manner of evil against us, but within our body, there should be no mention of misconduct.

If the body will respond to each other in a godly manner, no one could even misunderstand something that looked to be misconduct—nothing would look ungodly!"

{End of excerpt from Ira's lesson}

In light of these statements that you made, how can you support a man who seduces women into believing he is their "spiritual husband" as ordained of God? And more personally, how can you continue to condone your own adulterous relationship with him? You were always ready to condemn me, but you never applied the Word of God to yourself.

I know you have stated to me that your relationship with Bill is sanctioned by God, including the children that you have conceived together, but if you were to be totally honest with yourself, you would have to admit that you have always had lingering doubts in your heart and mind concerning all of it.

God will never allow you to have peace in that relationship because it's of the Devil! And if you keep rejecting the truth, you will continue in the lies and deceptions and lead others into it as well. Please don't allow Satan to deceive you anymore! I hope you can take hold of the truth and live.

However, you will never understand the truth or walk in the True Light until you acknowledge your sin, and in so doing you will see the sin of others so as to warn them. But because you are walking with the enemy, he will continue to control how you think, what you do, and how you perceive God's Word, regardless of how much you read it. Only truth will set you free!

Revelation 21:7–8 "He that overcometh shall inherit all things; and I will be his God, and he shall be My son. But the fearful, and unbelieving, and the abominable, and murderers, and whoremongers, and sorcerers, and idolaters, and all liars, shall have their part in the lake which burneth with fire and brimstone: which is the second death."

You have been used as a vessel unto dishonor and shame. You have been used as an instrument of unrighteousness and wickedness. You are walking with the enemy in darkness and it will only get darker!

You stated that Candy thought she was right when she was gone for those eight months, but all the while death was at work in her. That was very true, and the reason she didn't see the truth is because when she left you, she was still blinded by her own sin, and thus she continued walking with the enemy.

So you see, it doesn't matter where you are—you can walk with the enemy anywhere. If you are not willing to give up your sin and embrace the truth, Satan will have control and authority over your life regardless of where you are walking or who you are walking with. And realize, that your heart motives will determine to what degree God will allow Satan to affect you.

Nevertheless, I sincerely hope you will be one that overcomes. I know how faithful and committed you can be, and oh, what a wonderful thing if we were truly on the same side!

2 Timothy 2:19–26 "Nevertheless the foundation of God standeth sure, having this seal, The Lord knoweth them that are His. And, Let every one that nameth the name of Christ depart from iniquity.

But in a great house there are not only vessels of gold and of silver, but also of wood and of earth; and some to honour, and some to dishonour. If a man therefore purge himself from these, he shall be a vessel unto honour, sanctified, and meet for the master's use, [and] prepared unto every good work.

Flee also youthful lusts: but follow righteousness, faith, charity, peace, with them that call on the Lord out of a pure heart. But foolish and unlearned questions avoid, knowing that they do gender strifes.

And the servant of the Lord must not strive; but be gentle unto all [men], apt to teach, patient; in meekness instructing those that oppose themselves; if God peradventure will give them repentance to the acknowledging of the truth; and [that] they may recover themselves out of the snare of the Devil, who are taken captive by him at his will."

Revelation 22:13–15 "I am Alpha and Omega, the beginning and the end, the first and the last. Blessed [are] they that do His commandments, that they may have right to the Tree of Life, and may enter in through the gates into the city. For without [are] dogs, and sorcerers, and whoremongers, and murderers, and idolaters, and whosoever loveth and maketh a lie."

I know it's hard for you to believe that someone like me can be inspired by the Holy Spirit, especially since you always considered me the weakest one. At times, it even overwhelms me, but I know what God has spoken to me.

I praise God that He has allowed me to see the truth. And it's only because I wanted to walk in His ways and have His wisdom that He allowed me to be released from the power of darkness. Please carefully read this next Scripture.

Galatians 6:7–8 "Be not deceived; God is not mocked: for whatsoever a man soweth, that shall he also reap. For he that soweth to his flesh shall of the flesh reap corruption; but he that soweth to the Spirit shall of the Spirit reap life everlasting."

Ira, I have not judged your heart motives in any of this, and I won't. That is only for God to do, but He has instructed that we look at each other and judge whether our actions are the fruit of His Spirit or the works of the flesh.

Exposed

Galatians 5:19–21 "Now the works of the flesh are manifest, which are [these]; adultery, fornication, uncleanness, lasciviousness, idolatry, witchcraft, hatred, variance, emulations, wrath, strife, seditions, heresies, envyings, murders, drunkenness, revellings, and such like: of the which I tell you before, as I have also told [you] in time past, that they which do such things shall not inherit the Kingdom of God."

If you will be completely honest, you know that you fit into almost every category that Paul has stated here. I don't bring this to your attention to condemn you but so that you might be saved.

God has so graciously allowed us to see that we were walking in lies and the deceptions of the Devil, but if you continue to reject the truth, you will surely die in your sin. I know in my heart that God desires for all men to be saved, but I realize that some people actually love death.

Proverbs 8:35–36 "For whoso findeth Me findeth life, and shall obtain favour of the LORD. But he that sinneth against Me wrongeth his own soul: all they that hate Me love death."

If you want God's wisdom, He is faithful to His Word, but you will have to turn from all the lies and earnestly plead for God's mercy, so that maybe He will grant you the great privilege of walking with Him in truth, instead of the shame and disgrace of walking with the enemy in deception.

Sincerely,
A servant of the Most High God,

C. Read

As signed by me in the presence of a witness on
the 14th Day of December in the year of our Lord,
One Thousand Nine Hundred and Ninety-Three.

{End of first letter to Ira}

*Riding high
above the Heavens!*
―――

chapter five

There is Still Time

"But of that day and [that] hour knoweth no man,
no, not the angels which are in Heaven,
neither the Son, but the Father.
Take ye heed, watch and pray:
for ye know not when the time is."
Mark 13:32–33

So many professing Christians today are conformed to the ways of the world, rather than the ways of God. As I have said many times before, sin is the doorway into the darkness, and if you walk in sin long enough, it will lead to a place you really don't want to be!

Remember, good and evil are rooted in the same tree, but godliness comes only from the Tree of Life. And unless men delight completely in the Word of God and are born again by His Spirit, they will never be able to put forth their hand "and take also of the Tree of Life, and eat, and live for ever" (Genesis 3:22).

False teachers, corrupt Bibles, and disorderly churches are abounding, just like God said it would be like in the final days. And only those who have eyes to see and ears to hear will truly understand the times we are living in.

God's people have wandered off the intended path because their faith is in the word of men, and *not* the Word of God. And I must say, woe, woe, woe be unto those who call themselves Christian, yet do not follow Christ!

There is still time to come to the Lord, and only those who are walking in the True Light, with their lamps brightly shining, will Jesus welcome into His Kingdom when He comes for His glorious Church. [Read Matthew 25:1–13 and Ephesians 5:27.]

This next letter is addressed to two remaining members of the Bible study group. As far as I know, they are still walking with the enemy, but they have been warned and told the truth. Apparently, they chose to dismiss it. I just hope they will repent before God pours out His wrath and indignation upon this wicked world and the children of disobedience.

Matthew 21:42–44 "Jesus saith unto them, Did ye never read in the Scriptures, The stone which the builders rejected, the same is become the head of the corner: this is the Lord's doing, and it is marvellous in our eyes?

Therefore say I unto you, The Kingdom of God shall be taken from you, and given to a nation bringing forth the fruits thereof.

And whosoever shall fall on this stone shall be broken: but on whomsoever it shall fall, it will grind him to powder."

29 December 1993

Dear Wendell and Candy,

The reason I am addressing both of you in the same letter is that my message to you is the same, and to anyone else who may also be walking in darkness and does not know where they are going. I realize you feel that I am the one who's walking with the enemy, but I contend that if you truly believe that, then you have been deluded into believing a lie because you loved not the truth.

I still have hope for you, though, and I would like to make one final attempt to try to persuade you to see the real truth. You may feel that I am being extremely presumptuous, but I want you to know that my primary purpose for writing you is because I am very concerned about you, and for all God's people for that matter.

Since God has directed that I bring these issues to your attention, what you do with them is of the utmost importance. All I ask is for you to read what I have written and take all that I've said into consideration as you allow God to speak to your heart.

Because you have remained with Ira and Bill's ministry, I can only assume that you still support them and their beliefs. I hope you realize that because you have stood by them even after the warnings, you have actually entrusted them with your very life—your eternal life!

There is still time to get out if you so desire, and in this letter, I will show why it is imperative that you must hurry, before the opportunity passes you by. I will also prove beyond a shadow of a doubt that they most definitely do not serve the Lord God Almighty in truth.

Candy, I know you have expressed doubts concerning Bill and his behavior, and even his teachings, but you always trusted Ira, just as I did up until 2 March 1993. I am going to include a transcript from a Bible study that Ira conducted right before the Lord intervened on 28 February 1993 to show that her teachings are also truth mixed with lies.

[I want the reader to know that both Ira and Bill are "enemies of the cross of Christ."[94] And even though the leaders of this Bible study group claimed allegiance to God and used all the right words to express their love for Him, it doesn't mean they actually served "the only true God, and Jesus Christ," Whom God sent to this world to give us eternal life (John 17:3).

And just because they spoke a lot about God and appeared to love and honor the Lord Jesus Christ and His great sacrifice, their actions proved otherwise. All of this is part of the deception!]

I have included the entire lesson so you will see that I have not taken her words out of context and also so you can get the full meaning of what she is saying. Please read this for informational purposes only. Do not hold onto this as being the truth.

TRANSCRIPT OF IRA'S BIBLE STUDY LESSON (VERBATIM)
4 FEBRUARY 1993, THURSDAY NIGHT[95]
[For italicized words the emphasis is mine. —C. Read]

Bill   Ira's going to share some things with you tonight.

Ira   Well, first of all, I'm going to tell you right off the bat that I'm going to do something that I swore I would never, ever do. And that I criticized other people tremendously for doing. And just in doing that, I want to say that the Lord has certainly dealt with my heart about some things. And He's shown me some things. And one thing more than any other thing, that I rejoice in the Lord in, is that His Word is true. And He very vividly promises us that anyone who diligently seeks Him, that He'll reveal Himself to them.

And if we continue to seek Him out and to search for His truth, that He will be faithful to accomplish the good work He started in us. And that's really not dependent on us. The only dependence on us is that we continue to seek Him. And as long as we do, no matter what, God is faithful to His Word. And He will go forth and accomplish that which He has said that He would.

And, um, as I was studying today, the Lord specifically impressed upon me the need to read this book that I got. And quite honestly, I had a different purpose in mind and intent in mind when I started reading this book today. And I thought the reason why the Lord wanted me to read it was for another reason. And it wasn't until I began to get into it that I realized that was not the reason at all.

And as we have continued to seek the Lord, and ask the Lord to reveal anything here that's not of Him, that *anything that's been twisted or distorted,* any teachings that might have gone forth that were not His heart, any areas that we may have been, um, out of order in—that He would reveal that to us.[96]

There Is Still Time

And today as I was studying again, when I get to the point where I finally think that I am beginning to get a handle on it, I'm finally beginning to see clearly, *it's like God jerks the rug right out from under me.* And I find out that all the ground that I've gained was not gained ground at all, and yet it was because I had to go through all that to see the truth.

The reason that, um, I'm going to share this with you tonight, rather than Bill sharing this—and he hasn't heard this yet, so this is going to be, um, for him, just like for you, the first time that he's heard it. But I prayed about it because there is a *spiritual authority,* and there is a manner God has ordained that we do things.

And the reason the Lord impressed upon me that I need to come and do this is because it has been through some of the things that I've taught, both publicly, you know, with the children's ministry, and privately in ministering to some of you all that *I have twisted God's Word in certain areas.* I've done so out of stupidity and, like Paul, out of total ignorance. But the Lord said I was to come and present this tonight so that, you know, no one that had received the things that I had said would be sitting here going, ah, that's not right. I'm—we've got this settled.

So as I bring this tonight, I want you all to know that I have humbled myself before the Lord, that I have asked God's forgiveness, and also ask you to forgive me. And anything that I said apart from God's Word was done in total ignorance. *Not in rebelliousness or disobedience to God.*

I'm going to read to—um, I'm going to read to you out of this book. And it's about four pages. But this is a very—this man is Watchman Nee. It's called *A Spiritual Man.* He wrote this in 1927 and 1928. He was a China-man. He was Chinese. This has been transferred from Chinese into—translated into English. He actually requested that his work was not to ever be translated, but they did. So people did translate, simply because the Lord instructed them to do so.

And I'm going to, rather than try to discuss in my own words, I'm going to read to you what God has shown me today, because these words are truly words of the Holy Spirit, and there is no way, even listening one hundred percent to the Holy Spirit, I feel, that I could even begin under the same anointing to state what this man has stated so beautifully. And I'm going to read slowly because there—almost every word is so compact, that you have to go through this slowly. And today I've read like seventy pages, and I'm a very fast reader, but you can't read this fast because *it's just like the Word of God*. Everything, every sentence means something very important that is so packed full of God's Word and His truth, that it's the same manner. This particular section is on salvation, and I'm going to start here.

Nee   If one believes in the death of the Lord Jesus as his substitute, he already has been united with the Lord Jesus in His death (Rom. 6:2). For me to believe in the substitutionary work of the Lord Jesus is to believe that I already have been punished in the Lord Jesus. The penalty of my sin is death, yet the Lord Jesus suffered death for me; therefore, I have died in Him.

Ira   Now, again, he's saying that to believe—if you believe that Jesus was a substitute for our sin, then Jesus has been punished in our place. He has taken our punishment. The penalty of my sin is death.

Nee   There can be no salvation otherwise.

Ira   And that's exactly what happened. Jesus suffered death. He suffered the penalty of death that was paid. The penalty of sin was death. And Jesus suffered that penalty. He paid that penalty on the cross. And because of that, if we believe and receive His substitution, Him being the substitution for our sins, then we have died in Him. That's the whole point of salvation. That's what the born again experience is all about.

Nee   To say that He died for me is to say that I already have been penalized and have died in Him. Everyone who believes in this fact shall experience its reality.

Ira   If you believe it, you have eternal life. It's that simple.

Nee   We may say then that the faith by which a sinner believes in the death of the Lord Jesus as substitute is "believing into" Christ and thus in union with Him.

Ira   Again, he's telling us that it's a matter of believing. When we believe that Jesus was the substitute, we are believing into Him, unto Him. We become in union with Him.

*T*HERE IS STILL TIME

Nee   Though a person may be concerned only with the penalty for sin and not with the power of sin, his being united with the Lord is nonetheless the common possession he shares with all who believe in Christ.

Ira   One of the things with me that has been such a deceptive force in my life, and in my walk with the Lord, has been over this one thing, because I've never been able to understand how you could separate someone who is concerned with the penalty for sin, yet not concerned with the effects of sin or the power of sin within the born again Christian.

And yet it doesn't matter whether that person is concerned merely with the penalty of sin or the power of sin. The whole point is that him being united with the Messiah is the common possession that he shares with all who are united with the body of Christ. The point is, if he is in union with the Messiah, he is—he is part of God's body, of Christ's body. Okay?

Nee   He who is not united with the Lord has not yet believed and therefore has no part in Him.

Ira   That's very self-explanatory. If you've not yet believed, this is not for you; don't worry about it.

Nee   In believing, one is united with the Lord. To be united with Him means to experience everything He has experienced.

Ira   And that's very true. If we are united with Him, we can't experience everything that He's experienced; we don't have to. But it's available to us to be able to. That again is a matter of choice. But nonetheless, whether you choose to appropriate the things of God or not, the fact remains that they've been poured out on you.

Nee   In John 3, our Lord informs us how we are united with Him. It is by our being united with Him in His crucifixion and death (vv. 14–15). Every believer at least *positionally* has been united with the Lord in His death, but obviously, if we have been united with Him in a death like His, we shall certainly be united with Him in a resurrection like His (Rom. 6:5). Hence, he who believes in the death of the Lord Jesus as his substitute is likewise *positionally* raised up with Christ. Though he may not yet fully experience the meaning of the death of the Lord Jesus, God nevertheless has made him alive together with Christ and he has obtained a new life in the resurrection power of the Lord Jesus. This is the new birth.

Ira Again, he says those who believe in the death of the Lord Jesus as their substitute are raised up with Christ. Just because he has not fully experienced the meaning of the death of the Lord Jesus, it does not change the fact of what God has said and what God has done, which is He has raised him up together to set the believer with Christ Jesus. And he has obtained new life in the resurrection power of the Lord Jesus. And this is the new birth. It comes through belief. It comes from what God has done. Not what we have done.

Nee We should beware lest we insist that a man is not born anew unless he has experienced death and resurrection with the Lord. The Scriptures deem anyone who believes in the Lord Jesus as already regenerated.

Ira There again, this is something I have always struggled with within my own life, and I know that all of us do because I've talked with each of you at length. It's very easy for us to look at other people and judge and think that because someone has not experienced certain things in their walk with Jesus, that they've not been made new.

But that's not true. We should beware lest we insist that a man is not already regenerated. When you believed, you were already regenerated. You're not going to be regenerated later. Even though it is a continuing process. You are regenerated at the time that you believed.

Nee All who received Him, who believed in His name were born of God (John 1:12–13). Let it be understood that to be raised together with the Lord is not an experience antecedent to the new birth. Our regeneration is our union with the Lord in His resurrection as well as in His death. His death has concluded our sinful walk, and His resurrection has given us a new life and initiated us into the life of a Christian.

The apostle assures us that "we have been born anew to a living hope through the resurrection of Jesus Christ from the dead" (1 Peter 1:3). He indicates that every born again Christian has been resurrected already with the Lord. However, the apostle

There Is Still Time

Paul in Philippians still urges us to experience "the power of His resurrection" (3:10).

Many Christians have been born anew and been thus raised with the Lord, even though they are lacking in the manifestation of resurrection power.

Ira Again, it's easy to look at someone, and if we don't see the regenerated, resurrected power of God working in someone's life, it's easy for us to say they're not born again, they're not walking with God. But the fact is, those that call upon the name of the Lord shall be saved.

Those who believe that Jesus was their substitution for sin have been raised again to sit in Christ Jesus in heavenly places. Regardless of whether they have experienced these things or not. Whether they've experienced anything in their Christian walk or not. God's Word is truth, and whether we like the way He does it or not, whether we like the way our brother or sister walks or not, His Word is truth. And us not liking it does not change the reality or the truth of His Word.

Nee Do not confuse, then, position with experience. At the time one believes in the Lord Jesus, he may be most weak and ignorant; he is nonetheless placed by God in the perfect position of being considered dead, raised, and ascended with the Lord.

Ira And most of us do. Except those of us who have been in churches all of our lives. Most of us come to the Lord Jesus very weak and ignorant. We don't know anything. And yet, simply by believing in the substitution that Jesus paid, confessing that before God, we immediately came to be considered by God dead, raised, and ascended with the Lord.

Nee He who is accepted in Christ is as acceptable as Christ Himself.

Ira And many times, we have stated here that, after we have been cleansed with the blood of Jesus—after Jesus paid the penalty for us—when God looks at us, He does not see us, He sees Christ, He sees Jesus. *That* stands in front of us.

And no matter where we've been or what has happened to us—*no matter what we're not able to get in control of our life*—the prerequisite is that we have received—we have believed and received what God has given in the form of His Son. And when we have, we've been accepted in Christ, and we are as acceptable to God as Christ.

Nee This is position. That's God's position. And His position is all that Christ has experienced is the believers. *And position causes him to experience new birth.* Because it hinges not on how deep he has known experimentally the death, resurrection, and ascension of the Lord Jesus, but on whether he has believed in Him.

Even if experimentally a believer is totally ignorant of the resurrection power of Christ (Phil. 3:10), he has been made alive together with Christ, raised up with Him, and seated with Him in the heavenly places (Eph. 2:5–6).

Still another matter should be carefully noticed with respect to regeneration; namely, that far more became ours than simply what we had in Adam before the fall. On that day, Adam possessed spirit, yet it was created by God.

It was not God's uncreated life typified by the tree of life. *No life relationship existed at all between Adam and God.* His being called "the Son of God" is similar to the angels being so called, for he was created directly by God. We who believe in the Lord Jesus, however, are "born of God" (John 1:12–13).

Ira And I want to stop there. He's commenting on a comment he made earlier in the book and, quite honestly, since I do not fully understand that, I'm going to let that go till the Lord gives me a more clearer understanding of it. And I don't even want to touch it. I don't know. Okay?

Nee Accordingly, there is a life relationship. A child born inherits his father's life. We are born of God; therefore, we have His life (2 Peter 1:4). Had Adam received the life which God offered in the tree of life, he immediately would have obtained the eternal uncreated life of God. His spirit came from God, and so it is everlasting. How this everlasting spirit shall live depends upon how one regards God's order and upon what choice he makes.

Ira Now we're talking about the person who has been born of God, who has been born again, and this is something that I want everybody to understand.

We are an everlasting spirit born again to God at this point if we're believers. How our born again, everlasting spirit will live depends upon how you and I regard God's order and upon what choice we make. It does not change the fact that we're born again, but it certainly will depend on how our lives will be lived and on the choices we make and how we view God and what God says.

Nee The life we Christians obtain in regeneration is the same which Adam could have had but never had: God's life. Regeneration not only retrieves out of chaotic darkness the order of man's spirit and soul; it additionally affords man the supernatural life of God. Man's darkened and fallen spirit is made alive through being strengthened by the Holy Spirit into accepting God's life. This is new birth.

Ira We certainly know that it is through the Holy Spirit that we are led into accepting the life that God offers.

Nee The basis upon which the Holy Spirit can regenerate man is the cross (John 3:14–15).

Ira And we know that the penalty that Jesus paid was on the cross. Therefore, the basis which the Holy Spirit can regenerate is through the cross. There is no other way except for the cross.

Nee The eternal life declared in John 3:16 is the life of God which the Holy Spirit plants in man's spirit. Since this life is God's and cannot die, it follows that everyone born anew into possessing this said life is said to have eternal life. As God's life is totally unfamiliar with death, *so the eternal life in man never dies.*

A life relationship is established with God in new birth. It resembles the old birth of the flesh in that it is once and for all. *Once a man is born of God, he can never be treated by God as not having been so born of Him.*

Ira It says the life relationship is established with God in new birth; it resembles the old birth of the flesh in that it is once and for all. When we're born in the flesh, we're only born once—that's it. If we die, we're not going to get born again in the flesh. What he's saying here is the new life, the new birth that we experience through the life of God, is the same way; once we are reborn, we cannot be reborn again.

That is it. That is the birth. It's forever. *Once a man is born of God, he can never be treated by God as not having been born of Him.*

Nee However endless eternity may be, *this relationship and this position cannot be annulled*. This is because what a believer receives at *new birth is not contingent upon a progressive, spiritual, and holy pursuit* after he believes but is the pure gift of God.

Ira God's Word plainly tells us that salvation is a gift from God, that no man may boast. No man may obtain it by works. And our new birth, our eternal life we receive from Him, *is not dependent upon a progressive walk with Him* or a spiritual and holy pursuit after what the believer believes God wants, even. It is given as a free gift. It is accepted as a free gift.

If there was any way we could obtain it, through holiness or purity or anything else, *God could have given us the standards by which to walk,* and we could therefore have walked by them.

It would have been absolutely pointless for Jesus to have died, because we could have done it. And having Jesus die on the cross, it is still beyond a shadow of a doubt *nonessential for us to do anything,* even after we are born again. If we can do anything that would save us, the gift would not be free; it would still be based on works.

[I had a question not picked up by the recorder, and this was Ira's response.]

Ira I'll cover that later, just don't be confused there.

Nee What God bestows is eternal life. *No possibility exists for this life and position to be abrogated*. Receiving God's life in new birth is the starting point of a Christian walk, the minimum for a believer.

Ira And I want to stop and share something here. I shared this earlier with C. today because, at the time, I did not realize that the Lord would have me share this tonight. And when I got to this point, C. goes, wait a minute, what about what God said in Revelation that, that—what was the question?

C. What if your name is blotted out of the Book of Life?

Ira Yeah, what about that verse that says, ya know, to be careful or your name will be blotted out of the Book of Life. Well, you know, I gave her some real lame excuse about we could make—

we could twist the Word of God and make it say anything we wanted to.

And, you know, it didn't satisfy either one of us. But both of us were willing at least to see God's point here, and we went on.

And I went on down, and after I read the next sentence—"Receiving God's new life in the new birth is the starting point of the Christian walk, the very minimum for a believer"—the Lord spoke to my heart and He explained that verse to me. And I want to explain because that is a question.

If we can never lose our salvation, why does God's Word say that we could possibly have our names blotted out? *And the Lord told me that everybody's name is written in the Book of Life.* It was never God's intention that anybody died.

His Word is very plain. He does not desire that any man perish, but all should come to know Him. It was not His desire that any man should be lost. He sent His Son so that all mankind might be saved.

All men were born alive to God; all mankind had their names written in the Book of Life. The only way your name can be blotted out of the Book of Life is if you receive—if you refuse to receive the sacrifice, the substitute of Jesus, then your name will be blotted out of the Book of Life.

Candy Is that great or wow!

Ira Correct? [Ira looked to Bill as she said that, and he just nodded in agreement.]

Candy Ah! So-o-o neat!

Ira And, C. and—I mean, that just blew me away. I just began to cry at that point because I just realized that the Lord loves us so much, and He wants us to know the truth so much, that even when we have questions, because He wants us to see the truth, *He gave us revelation knowledge of something I didn't even know* so that there couldn't be any ground for the enemy to come and say what about that? What about that? That's not true because if it was true, it would all be true.

So God immediately gave me revelation knowledge on exactly what that meant, so the enemy wouldn't have any ground, so the enemy wouldn't be able to come in and pick like the little foxes at the base of the vine.

And it blessed my heart so much that God immediately gave this revelation on that so we could know what He said here is true. That our salvation is—what?

[I made a comment that was not picked up by the recorder, and this was her response to me.] That's right. Hell was not made for man.

And it's God's heart that we all be saved. And it is God's heart that we do know the truth. And He will go to any length for those who truly want to know the truth. He will go to any length to reveal that.

Nee   Receiving God's life in new birth is the starting point of a Christian walk, the minimum for a believer. *Those who have not yet believed on the death of the Lord Jesus* and received supernatural life (which they cannot possess naturally) *are deemed in the sight of God to be dead,* no matter how religious, moral, learned, or zealous they may be.

Ira   No matter how religious, moral, learned, or zealous a person may be, if they have not yet believed on the death of the Lord Jesus and received supernatural life—this is not believing with your mind—I believe it. The devils believe. Believing with your spirit. Supernaturally allowing the Holy Spirit to recreate us and change us. It doesn't matter. *We're still dead if we haven't done that.* [I hope you are able to see the contradictions throughout this lesson by Ira. —C. Read]

Nee   Those who do not have God's life are dead. For those who are born anew, there is great potentiality for spiritual growth.

Ira   It's not a must, but there is great potential.

Nee   Regeneration is the obvious first step in spiritual development. Though the life received is perfect, it waits to be matured.

Ira   God has poured out on us at the time that we honestly believe in our heart and ask Him. He gives us everything completely. It is complete, and it is perfect. But that which He's given us remains inside of our human spirit until such time that the Holy Spirit begins to work in conjunction with our soul.

Because the soul is the mind, will, and emotions—that wait in perfection inside of us, in the inner man, until such time as the soul cooperates with the Holy Spirit, so that maturity can begin. The maturing process—Jesus grew in grace and wisdom. The same happens with us with the born again, renewed spirit.

Nee　At the moment of new birth, life cannot be full-grown.

Ira　At the beginning of the new birth, life is not full-grown. A baby doesn't come here fully grown. When we are born, we are not full-grown. Even though, as Bill has said numerous times, all the potential for a full-grown adult is there, everything they need is there, but it comes through maturity.

Nee　It is like a fruit newly formed: The life is perfect, but it is still unripe. There is therefore boundless possibility for growth. The Holy Spirit is able to bring the person into complete victory over body and soul.

Ira　I have just a couple more paragraphs here, and I'd like to mention that this is the thing that—this is the one thing that has caused me to stumble more and to begin to go back and doubt and disbelieve that you could lose your salvation. That you could really mess up and just blow it out the window. So I want everyone to pay really close attention to this because everyone in this room fits in one of these categories.

Nee　Two kinds of Christians: The apostle in 1 Corinthians 3:1 divides all Christians into two classifications. They are the spiritual and the carnal. A spiritual Christian is one in whom the Holy Spirit dwells in his spirit and controls his entire being.

Ira　His soul consisting of his mind, will, and emotions. And his body.

Nee　What is meant, then, by being carnal? The Bible employs the word "flesh" to describe the life and value of an unregenerated man. It comprises everything which issues from his sinful soul and body (Romans 7:19).

Ira　That's the flesh. It's made up of everything which issues from his sinful body and his soul.

Nee　Hence, a carnal Christian is one who has been born anew and has God's life, but *instead of overcoming his flesh, he is overcome by the flesh.*

Ira   Instead of allowing his soul, in conjunction with the Holy Spirit, to mature that which is already perfect within him and complete within him, he continues to allow his flesh to rule. He continues to be overcome by his flesh.

Nee   We know the spirit of a fallen man is dead, and he is dominated by his soul and body. A carnal Christian, therefore, is one whose spirit has been quickened, but who still follows his soul and body unto sin.

Ira   The carnal Christian is one whose spirit has been made alive, but who still follows his soul, which consist of the mind, will, and the emotions and body, into sin.

One of the things that he has pointed out before we got to this point is that the soul is in the middle. The soul is the one who is comprised of the mind, will, and the emotions. The soul makes all the calls.

The spirit doesn't override the soul. The soul makes the choice because God put within it the will. And God made us a free will. And for the spirit to override the soul, even a spirit that's alive to God, would be to remove from us the very thing that God gave us to make us people who have choices. So it's the soul who makes choices. But the soul is the one that makes the calls.

And after we're born again, it is the soul, not the body, but it's the soul that makes the choice on whether or not it will submit itself to the leadership and guidance of the Holy Spirit, or whether it will continue to operate in the flesh, or the soul of man.

Nee   If a Christian remains in a carnal condition long after experiencing new birth, he hinders God's salvation from realizing its full potential and manifestation.

Ira   It doesn't do away from the fact that he is born again. But if he continues to remain carnal, without allowing the soul to be under the influence of the Holy Spirit, and to take its suggestions from the spirit, rather than the soul—or the soul will either work in connection with the spirit who's born again to God, which works in connection with the Holy Spirit to produce God's life, to conform us and transform us. Or it will be dominated by its own desires, by the emotions, by the intellect of man, and his reasoning capabilities. Or either he will allow the body to begin

There Is Still Time

to do things outwardly. And when the body, the flesh, begins to do things outwardly, that almost immediately begins to control the soul.

Because *the soul will almost never be able to override what the flesh wants,* because *what the flesh wants is so strong.* It rises up within us. We want that piece of chocolate cake. We want it, we want it; *eventually, we're going to give in* and have it.

Certainly, we do, sometimes, exert that will power, but most of the time, *once we come under the power of the flesh, the soul usually gives in and goes with whatever the flesh wants because the flesh does exert so much power.* The flesh—then he will remain in that carnal position. And *this carnal position will actually hinder God;* it will hinder us from receiving what God has poured out on us. God has poured it out. They're there. They're available to us, but if we continue to walk in sin, if we continue to allow our flesh to rule, then we will not experience the full potential of our salvation.

We will not walk in all the things that God has promised. We will not receive from God all the things He has poured out. They are available to us if we would simply receive them. Even though they're there, even though they're inside of us, even though they're perfect in nature within us, as long as we remain carnal, and as long as we remain controlled by the soul and the spirit, we won't receive those things. Those things will not be matured inside of us.

Nee   Only when he is growing in grace, constantly governed by the spirit, can salvation be wholly wrought in him. God has provided full salvation in Calvary for the regeneration of sinners and complete victory over the believer's old creation.

Ira   One thing that Bill has said to me many times in the past, I guess, year or so, that's really hacked me off—where I just wanted to *rip his throat out*—is when he's told me that—um, probably my worst problem is that I try to make people conform to my standards of where I am.

And as I read this today, and as the Lord really bore witness in my heart by His Holy Spirit that this word is truth, *this has been the same truth that's been in my heart ever since I've known Him.*

A lot of things have swayed that. Actually, my soulish man with the intellect and reasoning abilities said one and one is two. And yet those principles don't work in the spiritual kingdom. They work here, but God has defied all logic. He has used things that absolutely do not make sense. *He's used the foolishness of the cross to save us.* And the wisdom of this world is foolishness to Him.

And while it is very, very true that many and most of the things that God has been showing me the last two years have been for a deeper walk with Him and a deeper commitment with Him—because those have stemmed out of a heart that truly desires to be committed to Him—it's also been very easy to say, well, if this is true for me, then it must mean that if everybody else is not doing it this way, that they're out of order with God, and God can't work with them. And God wants them to get their act straightened up, and God wants them to submit to Him.

And while all of those things are true, it is very true God does want us to submit to Him; He wants us to submit everything. But the whole point is, the only thing He asks you to do is to believe in His Son, to accept the sacrifice that He made for your sins. And if you do, He will meet you right there and will take the spirit inside of you that's dead to Him, and you will become born again and you will receive eternal life, which means exactly what it says, eternal life. And you will live forever with Him.

And that begins the process of your walk with Jesus. *It can be the beginning of the end.* You don't have to go any further. If you don't, then you have salvation forever and forever and ever. As long as eternity is, you will abide in the presence of God in His kingdom.

There is so much more that God desires for us to have. He has poured out everything in His kingdom. Not for later, but for now. He says we can have it now. If we will submit ourselves to Him and let Him do His work in our heart, He will change us from the inside out.

But it is not for the Christian who is submitted unto the Lord—*it is not their place to look and say, "But they're not doing that; they're out of order. You're not really walking—you're not really—"*

$\mathcal{T}$HERE IS STILL TIME

Only each individual person can make the decision of what they want and what they're really willing to receive from God.

And I can tell you that we're much more critical of one another than God is of us.

As we were singing tonight, God reminded me of that. I don't know if it was my own ears or God just wanting to—

{The tape ran out / end of transcript of Ira's Bible study lesson}

As I was writing this letter, I had initially included my thoughts within her lesson. But the Lord said He did not want His truth mixed with her lies, so I will take this time to refute some of Ira's statements, with the use of the Scriptures, to prove that her beliefs are quite contrary to the truth of God's Word.

Excerpt from Ira's Bible Study / 4 February 1993

Ira No matter how religious, moral, learned, or zealous a person may be, if they have not yet believed on the death of the Lord Jesus and received supernatural life—this is not believing with your mind—I believe it. The devils believe. Believing with your spirit. Supernaturally allowing the Holy Spirit to recreate us and change us. It doesn't matter. *We're still dead if we haven't done that.*

{End of excerpt from Ira's Bible study lesson}

Just because you believe in the death of Jesus is no great thing. Men die every day, but if you were to truly believe in His resurrection, now that would be something! Notice what God says about salvation.

Romans 10:9–13 "That if thou shalt confess with thy mouth the Lord Jesus, and shalt believe in thine heart that God hath raised Him from the dead, thou shalt be saved.

For with the heart man believeth unto righteousness; and with the mouth confession is made unto salvation. For the Scripture saith, Whosoever believeth on Him shall not be ashamed.

For there is no difference between the Jew and the Greek: for the same Lord over all is rich unto all that call upon Him. For whosoever shall call upon the name of the Lord shall be saved."

It's quite obvious, based on these Scriptures, that in order to be saved, you must believe with all your heart that God was able to raise Jesus from the dead and confess Him as Lord. If you can actually believe that God was able to bring His Son back to life, you will have no trouble believing all the other wonderful works of the Lord God Almighty.

If God is truly your Lord, you will most certainly want to please Him. And in order for you to know what the will of God is, you must allow your way of thinking to be changed by His thoughts and His ways. It is a continuing process of growing and learning of Him. The more you learn about God, the more you grow and the stronger your faith becomes, which will cause you to love God even more.

James 2:17–20 "Even so faith, if it hath not works, is dead, being alone. Yea, a man may say, Thou hast faith, and I have works: shew me thy faith without thy works, and I will shew thee my faith by my works.

Thou believest that there is one God; thou doest well: the devils also believe, and tremble. But wilt thou know, O vain man, that faith without works is dead?"

Romans 12:1–2 "I beseech you therefore, brethren, by the mercies of God, that ye present your bodies a living sacrifice, holy, acceptable unto God, [which is] your reasonable service.

And be not conformed to this world: but be ye transformed by the renewing of your mind, that ye may prove what [is] that good, and acceptable, and perfect, will of God."

It all starts with what you believe. If you are taught to submit to lies, you will believe lies and will have faith in lies. If you are taught to submit to truth, you will believe truth and will have

There Is Still Time

faith in truth. And it is so important to walk in truth, because only truth will be forever.

2 Corinthians 11:3 "But I fear, lest by any means, as the serpent beguiled Eve through his subtilty, so your minds should be corrupted from the simplicity that is in Christ."

Satan's whole purpose is to try to destroy what God has planned, and what better way to accomplish that goal than to convince people that they are born into the Kingdom of God when in reality, they are not?

The Lord brought the following Scriptures to my attention concerning the "new birth" as I was contemplating Ira's lesson on *The Spiritual Man* by Watchman Nee.

John 6:44 "No man can come to Me, except the Father which hath sent Me draw him: and I will raise him up at the last day."

John 1:12–13 "But as many as received Him, to them gave He power to become the sons of God, [even] to them that believe on His name: Which were born, not of blood, nor of the will of the flesh, nor of the will of man, but of God."

John 3:5–8 "Jesus answered, Verily, verily, I say unto thee, Except a man be born of water and [of] the Spirit, he cannot enter into the Kingdom of God. That which is born of the flesh is flesh; and that which is born of the Spirit is spirit.

Marvel not that I said unto thee, Ye must be born again. The wind bloweth where it listeth, and thou hearest the sound thereof, but canst not tell whence it cometh, and whither it goeth: so is every one that is born of the Spirit."

God is in complete control, and He's the One who decides who will be born into His Kingdom. Yes, He has given all men the opportunity to be a part of His Kingdom, but not all will be called the sons of God, and not all will rule and reign with Him.

The overriding tone of this lesson by Ira is that we are somehow in control of our own destiny, and that we're the ones who decide what we'll receive from God and what we won't. That we can pretty much do what we want and still be acceptable in the sight of God *as long as we believe in the death of Jesus as our substitute.* But I contend that these statements are all lies!

A person who is truly seeking the Lord, and desires a personal relationship with God, will most certainly allow His Word to take effect in his or her life. God offers His gift freely, and He will never force it on you, but you must come to God willingly. And a person who is truly born of God will strive to keep His Word and will pursue a life of holiness and purity with all sincerity.

Titus 3:8–11 "[This is] a faithful saying, and these things I will that thou affirm constantly, that they which have believed in God might be careful to maintain good works. These things are good and profitable unto men.

But avoid foolish questions, and genealogies, and contentions, and strivings about the law; for they are unprofitable and vain. A man that is an heretick after the first and second admonition reject; knowing that he that is such is subverted, and sinneth, being condemned of himself."

Those who claim to be born of God, yet refuse to obey God are liars and the truth is not in them. God will bring every work into judgment and hold all men accountable to what they do in their body whether it be good or evil!

1 John 5:2–4 "By this we know that we love the children of God, when we love God, and keep His commandments. For this is the love of God, that we keep His commandments: and His commandments are not grievous. For whatsoever is born of God overcometh the world: and this is the victory that overcometh the world, [even] our faith."

There Is Still Time

1 John 5:18–20 "We know that whosoever is born of God sinneth not; but he that is begotten of God keepeth himself, and that Wicked One toucheth him not. [And] we know that we are of God, and the whole world lieth in wickedness. And we know that the Son of God is come, and hath given us an understanding, that we may know Him that is true, and we are in Him that is true, [even] in His Son Jesus Christ. This is the true God, and eternal life."

Luke 8:17–18 "For nothing is secret, that shall not be made manifest; neither [anything] hid, that shall not be known and come abroad.

Take heed therefore how ye hear: for whosoever hath, to him shall be given; and whosoever hath not, from him shall be taken even that which he seemeth to have."

This next Scripture will prove that it is necessary to believe the testimony of Jesus Christ before God seals you with His Spirit. I realize there are many people under the false belief that they have been filled with the Holy Spirit, but just because you believe something doesn't make it true.

One very important factor to always keep in mind is that God is the One who's in control, and He is the One who decides with whom He will share His heavenly gifts.

As you read the following verses, keep in mind that the apostle Paul is speaking to a body of believers that has a strong abiding faith in the gospel of the Lord Jesus Christ.

Ephesians 1:12–14 "That we should be to the praise of His glory, who first trusted in Christ. In Whom ye also [trusted], after that ye heard the Word of truth, the gospel of your salvation: In Whom also after that ye believed, ye were sealed with that Holy Spirit of promise, which is the earnest of our inheritance until the redemption of the purchased possession, unto the praise of His glory."

Salvation is God's gift to give as *He pleases*. And when you become one with God the Father, a special union takes place that is not of this world. No amount of human effort can make it happen. It is totally *in the hands of God*.

And once God has granted you the great honor and privilege to become one of His sons or daughters, you become a new creation,[97] and you will see things from a completely different perspective. *This* is the new birth!

Then, as we learn to put to death our sinful flesh nature through the ability that only Christ can give us, as God's children, He will give us power over sin by His selfsame Spirit that raised Jesus from the dead.[98]

And as we become more knowledgeable of the tactics of the enemy, we will come to realize the many ways that the ministers of Satan have distorted, discarded, and disgraced God's Holy Word. And we can actually get to the point in our walk with God where we do not willfully sin against Him.[99] I know it could be hard to fathom, but according to God's Word, it is attainable.

1 Peter 4:1–2 "Forasmuch then as Christ hath suffered for us in the flesh, arm yourselves likewise with the same mind: for he that hath suffered in the flesh hath ceased from sin; that he no longer should live the rest of [his] time in the flesh to the lusts of men, but to the will of God."

I must proclaim, Christ is looking for a glorious church, one that is without spot or wrinkle or any such thing, one that is holy and set apart by Him and for Him in order to rule and reign with Him forever and ever! Amen!

1 John 3:2–6, 10 "Beloved, now are we the sons of God, and it doth not yet appear what we shall be: but we know that, when He shall appear, we shall be like Him; for we shall see Him as He is. And every man that hath this hope in Him purifieth himself, even as He is pure.

There is Still Time

Whosoever committeth sin transgresseth also the law: for sin is the transgression of the law. And ye know that He was manifested to take away our sins; and in Him is no sin.

Whosoever abideth in Him sinneth not: whosoever sinneth hath not seen Him, neither known Him.... In this the children of God are manifest, and the children of the Devil: whosoever doeth not righteousness is not of God, neither he that loveth not his brother."

I ask you, is it your desire to do the will of God? Or is it more important to satisfy your own will or the will of another?

1 Thessalonians 4:3–8 "For this is the will of God, [even] your sanctification, that ye should abstain from fornication: That every one of you should know how to possess his vessel in sanctification and honour; not in the lust of concupiscence, even as the Gentiles which know not God: That no [man] go beyond and defraud his brother in [any] matter: because that the Lord [is] the avenger of all such, as we also have forewarned you and testified.

For God hath not called us unto uncleanness, but unto holiness. He therefore that despiseth, despiseth not man, but God, who hath also given unto us His Holy Spirit."

I have taken great care to present the truth, but Ira shows little regard for the commands and laws of God. Her lesson was completely based on the thoughts and opinions of a man, but if those beliefs are not derived from the truth of the Word of God, they really aren't worth hearing or repeating.

Consider this passage Ira was referring to in the "revelation" that she received from her "god." You should be very familiar with this Scripture since it was the warning you received on the first day of the summer of 1993.

Revelation 3:1–6 "And unto the angel of the church in Sardis write; These things saith He that hath the seven Spirits of God, and the seven stars; I know thy works, that thou hast a name that thou livest, and art dead.

Be watchful, and strengthen the things which remain, that are ready to die: for I have not found thy works perfect before God.

Remember therefore how thou hast received and heard, and hold fast, and repent. If therefore thou shalt not watch, I will come on thee as a thief, and thou shalt not know what hour I will come upon thee.

Thou hast a few names even in Sardis which have not defiled their garments; and they shall walk with Me in white: for they are worthy.

He that overcometh, the same shall be clothed in white raiment; and I will not blot out his name out of the Book of Life, but I will confess his name before My Father, and before His angels. He that hath an ear, let him hear what the Spirit saith unto the churches."

That letter was written to the church, but obviously, most of the members had fallen away from the faith and were very deceived. This completely refutes Ira's claim about the Book of Life.

Excerpt from Ira's Bible Study / 4 February 1993

Ira All men were born alive to God; all mankind had their names written in the Book of Life. The only way your name can be blotted out of the Book of Life is if you receive[100]—if you refuse to receive the sacrifice, the substitute of Jesus, then your name will be blotted out of the Book of Life.

{End of excerpt from Ira's Bible study lesson}

Please seriously ponder these Scriptures in your heart regarding the death, burial, and resurrection of the Lord Jesus Christ.

2 Corinthians 5:14–15 "For the love of Christ constraineth us; because we thus judge, that if One died for all, then were all dead: And [that] He died for all, that they which live should not henceforth live unto themselves, but unto Him which died for them, and rose again."

Colossians 2:12–15 "Buried with Him in baptism, wherein also ye are risen with [Him] through the faith of the operation of God, who hath raised Him from the dead. And you, being dead in your sins

There is Still Time

and the uncircumcision of your flesh, hath He quickened together with Him, having forgiven you all trespasses; blotting out the handwriting of ordinances that was against us, which was contrary to us, and took it out of the way, nailing it to His cross; [and] having spoiled principalities and powers, He made a shew of them openly, triumphing over them in it."

Revelation 20:11–15 "And I saw a Great White Throne, and Him that sat on it, from whose face the earth and the Heaven fled away; and there was found no place for them.

And I saw the dead, small and great, stand before God; and the books were opened: and another book was opened, which is [the Book] of Life: and the dead were judged out of those things which were written in the books, according to their works.

And the sea gave up the dead which were in it; and death and Hell delivered up the dead which were in them: and they were judged every man according to their works.

And death and Hell were cast into the Lake of Fire. This is the second death. And whosoever was not found written in the Book of Life was cast into the Lake of Fire."

If you have an unsettling fear of dying, especially after you read this, I hope you will consider what is going on in your life. God wants you to know the truth and walk in it, but you must repent of the evils that you have become a partaker of and submit your whole heart, soul, and body to God above; and put all your faith, hope, and trust in the Lord Jesus Christ, and His Word.

There is still time, but this may be your last chance. Once the doors are closed, there will be no way to gain entry into the Kingdom of Heaven. And if you choose to reject God's Word, you'll wish you had listened when you stand before Him, but if you wait until then, time will have run out!

If you continue to trust in Bill and Ira, and anyone like them, you will no longer be able to justify yourself before the Lord God above by giving the excuse that you didn't know, because *you have most certainly been warned!*

Note this next excerpt, and carefully consider the Scriptures I use to refute Ira's statements. May you have ears to hear and eyes to see the truth.

Excerpt from Ira's Bible study / 4 February 1993

Ira One thing that Bill has said to me many times in the past, I guess, year or so, that's really hacked me off—where I just wanted to *rip his throat out*—is when he's told me that—um, probably my worst problem is that I try to make people conform to my standards of where I am.

And as I read this today, and as the Lord really bore witness in my heart by His Holy Spirit that this word is truth, *this has been the same truth that's been in my heart ever since I've known Him.* A lot of things have swayed that....

Actually, my soulish man with the intellect and reasoning abilities said one and one is two. And yet those principles don't work in the spiritual kingdom. They work here, but God has defied all logic. He has used things that absolutely do not make sense.

He's used the foolishness of the cross to save us. And the wisdom of this world is foolishness to Him.

{End of excerpt from Ira's Bible study lesson}

I would especially like to draw your attention to the Scripture regarding her false belief that *"He's used the foolishness of the cross to save us."*

1 Corinthians 1:18 "For the preaching of the cross is to them that perish foolishness; but unto us which are saved it is the power of God."[101]

Based on her own words and the conduct of her life, if this does not persuade you that you are walking with the enemy, nothing will! And you will just perish along with all the rest who continue to believe the lies and perversions of God's Word.

Romans 1:18–19 "For the wrath of God is revealed from Heaven against all ungodliness and unrighteousness of men, who hold the truth in unrighteousness; Because that which may be known of God is manifest in them; for God hath shewed [it] unto them."

God's wrath will come down upon all who pretend to be walking in the truth but are actually serving Satan and causing others to be entrapped by him. Ira and Bill's teachings are truth mixed with lies, but unless you are walking in the True Light, you will not be able to clearly discern truth from error.

The most important decision a man has to make is whether or not he will obey God and believe the testimony of Jesus, and the attitudes and actions of a person will determine what choice they have made.

If you decide that you are going to obey God and receive the truth of the gospel, you will have the opportunity and privilege of spending eternity with Him, but should you choose to disobey God and reject His Word, you will have the shame and disgrace of being rejected by Him forever.

I hope after reading this letter that you will no longer contend that I am walking with the enemy. If you do, it will only prove that your enemy is the Lord God Almighty, and your god is the god of this world, who is Satan.

Romans 6:16, 23 "Know ye not, that to whom ye yield yourselves servants to obey, his servants ye are to whom ye obey; whether of sin unto death, or of obedience unto righteousness?...

For the wages of sin [is] death; but the gift of God [is] eternal life through Jesus Christ our Lord."

If you are seeing the truth for the first time, it could be very disheartening, and I understand what you may be going through. It's so hard to accept when you find out you have been deceived by someone that you love and trust.

It's even harder to realize that you have been wrong all along, while claiming to be right, and have actually been an enemy to the cross of Christ. Please don't allow pride or humiliation to cause you to continue to reject the truth.

Just humble yourself before the Lord God and ask for His forgiveness, and if you truly mean it, He can be so merciful. He's such a great God to serve! Put your trust entirely in Him, and He will lift you up!

Here's a promise, among many others, that I can attest to being the truth. And should you decide that you're going to follow the Lord God Almighty in all truth and sincerity, it can be true for you too.

Isaiah 40:31 "But they that wait upon the LORD shall renew [their] strength; they shall mount up with wings as eagles; they shall run, and not be weary; [and] they shall walk, and not faint."

The next transcript is a prophecy Bill gave to Eve prior to her leaving the Bible study group.[102] I am just so thankful she got out of here when she did. Please keep in mind that this man claims to be a prophet sent by God to proclaim His truth.

Transcript of Prophecy / Poem as Spoken by Bill on 18 November 1992[103]

Okay, Eve, I want you to come sit right here. Right here on the floor before me. The Lord has instructed me to share some things with you. And I'm putting them on tape for you so you can take them home with you. Okay?

There Is Still Time

I want you to sit here. And I want you to receive these things. And the Lord wants you to receive these things from Him. So I want you to just shut everything else out. Close your eyes. Look down in your own spirit. Don't hang on to your hands. And turn your palms faceup to the Lord. Just like you're receiving something.

[There was a long delay before Bill spoke again, and these are the exact words recorded that night in my home.]

My daughter, I come to speak today,
and these are the words that I have to say.
The words that I speak are for your heart,
so that you might be strengthened
and established and whole and not apart.
For you've thought many things,
and you've seen many days
when you've even wanted to turn and run away.
And your mind told you that you really couldn't hear,
and it's even told you that I didn't even hold you very dear.
You've watched others seek me and say that they see,
and you've judged your own walk
by the things that you see.
You've let the things of the world be your guide,
but behind it all have been my holy eyes.
So I come to you now to bring some things out.
And darling, one day, you're going to give a shout!
For what I have for you, you've never imagined,
but it's all been my plan just for you in my heavens.
So listen to me, and listen well,
and heed what I say and that I tell.
You've thought in the past that yours was a hard lot,
and there's things inside that have just said, "Stop!"
You don't understand why you feel like you do,

Walking with the Enemy

and many times the ways you act,
or even what you want to.
The confusion abounds and runs rampant inside
and feels like a flood in a never-ending tide.
And your stomach's all torn up and tied up in knots,
and you think, "My God,
is this what I get for being Your child and Your tot?"
Listen, Eve, my dear daughter,
the apple of my eye, my joy and delight,
I tell you this, the things that have happened
were by my plan;
you didn't cause them to happen.
You think people don't like you because of how you look,
and I tell you I made you exactly like I wanted you to look.
You think you can't control some of the things that occur,
but if you could see in the spirit realm,
you'd know that I'm the one that stirs
and molds and shapes your steps as you walk
and gives you the words as you speak and you talk.
And you think that you are left alone because of you,
but I tell you, I had a hand in that too.
For if you knew the depths of my love,
you'd know how I protected you and kept you from harm.
You know that I've ordered your steps to this place,
and I've set you here so that you might taste
the goodness of my word
and the joy of my life.
For believe it or not, you are my wife!
And I've placed you in the body of the bride of my son
and made provisions upon provisions,
and darling, you've won.
Now I speak to your heart and tell you this,
if you really want to enjoy my bliss,

There Is Still Time

let go of the anger and rage inside,
and open your heart and get it real wide.
Cuz I've got a lot to give you and pour into you,
and darling, believe that I will give it too.
The rage and the anger are confusing enough,
and the road seems like it's gotten too tough.
But those feelings and emotions are not aimed at others;
you take the blame for the faults of others.
I don't ask you to hate 'em,
and I don't ask ya to reject them.
I simply ask ya to see the truth of what I've done.
Now listen, and listen, and listen well,
the faith walk is a life that spells out
every word that I've ever said
and opens the doors that seem closed instead.
I will guide you and lead every step,
but I want ya to trust me and depend on my help.
I don't ask great things that you do not know.
I simply tell you that I've made your way so.
If you will trust me and walk in my word,
I'll give to you everything that you've heard.
And as you take my word into your heart,
you'll find that you've got a brand new start.
Now receive my joy and my blessings as they abound,
and Eve, you no longer have to run around,
hoping and wishing that I'll answer your prayer,
for, my daughter, you've always been in my care.
Trust me, and receive from me, that which I've given,
and open your heart to receive what I've given.
Do not think you're less or the least
because, Eve, you sit at my heavenly feast.

{End of Bill's prophecy}

Do those words truly bear witness in your heart as being from a man who was actually inspired by the Holy Spirit of the Lord God Almighty? Would you trust this man with your eternal life? That's *exactly* what you are doing because of your decision to continue being a part of his ministry.

Candy, this next transcript is from a meeting that I arranged with your family right after we broke up. I realize you may be holding your former husband responsible for taking your daughter. But I want to dissuade you from blaming him, because as you read this, you will see that he was just responding as any loving and concerned parent would.

Excerpts from the Transcript of Meeting with the Families on 6 March 1993[104]

C. Just for the benefit of whatever reason this tape will be used for, my name is C. Read. I have been involved in a Bible study group for the last three years. Bill is the leader, so-called pastor of the Bible study group. Ira is like the co-pastor. My husband pretty much hasn't been involved in it. He was gone for a year and a half these last three years, so he was not a real part of it.

I want to state that my Lord and Savior is Jesus Christ. I serve the God of Heaven. All through this, that's who I served. When God and enemy were spoken in this Bible study group, we weren't talking about the same god. I was talking about the God in Heaven, and they were talking about the god, the prince of the power of the air, who is Satan. The *god of this world* is Satan. That's who they were talking about. Their enemy was my God. But at the time, of course, I didn't know this. And that is part of the deception.

I have no secrets. My heart is completely open to every person in this room, completely open to the Lord. I have nothing to hide, and they do.

And I would like for you to play this tape. This was a tape when we had a major confrontation last Tuesday night. It was like a showdown! It was beautiful! It was like light against darkness!

*T*HERE IS STILL TIME

And you could see it! It was so beautiful! I wish the world could see it. And it will. But go ahead and play this tape.

(2 March 1993 transcript is in Chapter 2, Heed the Call.)

C. You see the resistance against me speaking and having evidence against them. Not that that was my intent when we first had this meeting. God just laid it on my heart to have the tape player ready so that we could tape. I felt in my heart that we were not going to get to tape it, but since the Lord told me to still have the tape player ready, I had it ready. And what we got to hear was the resistance against the taping of anything.

They had to have the appearance of godliness around me because that was my whole purpose for even being in that group.

At that point in my life, I was crying out to the Lord. I had been studying His Word and really desiring a relationship with God. The One they talk about, how you can have the peace that passes understanding. And I read His Word, and I tried to do what His Word said, but the peace wasn't there. It just wasn't.

[My husband] wasn't seeking after the Lord. He was still after the world and doing his own thing. He didn't have the same goal as me. So I was almost at the point of leaving him. And then I met these people.

[Bill] lives with Ira and Tom. Bill and Ira sleep together. Tom has a room to himself. And how they did this, and why they did it, I have *no idea*, but I saw those two actually have sex together!

They live over there. He claims to be a pastor, a godly man, he's a Christian, but it's all lies. And to understand how I got sucked into it is through such deception and lying.

This is the Scripture I want to read pertaining to the pastor of [the Baptist church we were members of]. When I first got into this group, he came to me and [my husband] and tried to warn me.

He gave me this particular Scripture. And of course, when you are in the clutches of people who are working for Satan, they sneak in, and this Scripture will explain what they did. It is almost like you're in a hold by them, and it's a really weird thing.

They had a lot of different things that go on that they know about, but me being a very naive person, I didn't know about.

2 Timothy 3:1–5 "This know also, that in the last days perilous times shall come. For men shall be lovers of their own selves, covetous, boasters, proud, blasphemers, disobedient to parents, unthankful, unholy, without natural affection, trucebreakers, false accusers, incontinent, fierce, despisers of those that are good, traitors, heady, highminded, lovers of pleasures more than lovers of God; having a form of godliness, but denying the power thereof: from such turn away."

Everything that is written about these kinds of men—Bill is this man. He is this man! From those, turn away completely! You get away from them! They will taint you!

2 Timothy 3:6–7 "For of this sort are they which creep into houses, and lead captive silly women laden with sins, led away with divers lust, ever learning, and never able to come to the knowledge of the truth."

That was me at the point when I came to these people. I was learning. I was reading. I was trying to get the truth. But it was like I was never able to really come to the truth. And God wanted me to know the truth. And that's the thing about the whole deal, He wanted me to know the truth.

2 Timothy 3:8–9 "Now as Jannes and Jambres withstood Moses, so do these also resist the truth: men of corrupt minds, reprobate concerning the faith. But they shall proceed no further: for their folly shall be manifest unto all [men], as theirs also was."

Okay, that's what's going on right now. God has ordained and actually anointed me to go out and speak about these people because I was right there walking with them for three years. And this is something He has revealed to me recently. The thing I want you to realize, I was always serving the Lord God Jehovah! The whole way. The reason you can be so sucked in, because when they say God, you're assuming they're meaning your God. But they weren't.

Lynn Did you use the Holy Bible as your reference?
C. Yeah.
Lynn How could you use the Holy Bible?

C. Because they will state things in the Scriptures. See, if you do not really know the truth, you're at the mercy of man. If you really don't know the truth, if you put yourself in the position to receive from men—not that there aren't very good teachers out there. There are. But if you put your sole commitment to a man, that man can deceive you. That man can be deceived by the Deceiver. So you have to rely on what God's Word says to you and what He says to your heart.

Katie It was going around town that Bill was writing his own Bible. Is that true?

C. I don't know. Who knows? I wasn't privy to a lot of their stuff. They had secret meetings that I was not part of.

See, they had to appear godly in front of me because I was serving God. I was walking with God, but they did not want me to serve my God. God knew where I was, and Satan knew where I was.

And I'll read a prophecy that God gave me not long ago that will explain a lot of everything that's been going on. They did not want me to really catch ahold of the truth, because if I did, I'd find out who they were.

But because God was leading me, I found out who they were. He let me go through a lot of things to be able to know the manipulative, deceptive, lying, secretive tactics of the enemy, so I could come tell other people.

God does ordain certain people to do certain things. I am not any more important to God. You are just as important to God as I am, but I have been through an experience that God has shown me that the sole purpose of these two people is to drag as many people to Hell with them as possible through deception, through lies, through manipulation, and through very, very subtle tactics.

And if people can really learn what Satan's up to, they won't get hooked into it. And what I am here to do is first to expose these things, so that hopefully we can get Candy out of there. And get Rebecca and Kim.

They are not actually worshipping Satan. They're still under the guise or thought that they are serving God, Almighty God! And that's how the deception is. They're walking along thinking—and it's very hard to try to completely understand with your natural mind. That's why I want you to listen with your heart.

Your mind will say, "This is crazy. Forget it! No! Don't believe this woman. She's been walking with these people all this time. Why believe her now? She's probably one of them, and she's just trying to get into your heart."

If you accepted Jesus Christ in your heart, you got the Spirit of God; you got the same Spirit that raised Jesus Christ from the dead inside of you! Satan doesn't want you to know that. That's why he's leading silly women laden with sins away, so they won't know the power of God inside your heart. They don't want you to know about it.

(Break)

C. They alienated me from my [husband's] family. If you could understand the deception and subtlety that goes on, they don't want you to have contact with other people. And it's not something you consciously decide. It's part of the teaching and indoctrination that teaches you that everybody without doesn't want to serve God; they're just walking in their flesh, walking in the world. They don't really serve God. We are the only ones that truly want to have a real relationship with God.

(Break / phone call from Candy)

C. And I don't want to try to justify my behavior or what was going on, because I had the Holy Spirit inside of me, but God pointed out to me just recently that—

And I used to ask Ira about this particular Scripture, and she didn't ever want to let me know what she knew about it. It's like verses that I brought up to her she wouldn't tell me about them, because I was getting too close to the truth.

God was starting to open my eyes up to the truth, and certain Scriptures were coming up that she didn't want me to know about. She would always say, "Well, God hasn't given me revelation knowledge on that, and when it's time for you to know, you'll know." That was her excuse about Scripture that she couldn't explain to me.

There Is Still Time

Matthew 4:1 "Then was Jesus led up of the Spirit into the wilderness to be tempted of the Devil."

I don't know if you've ever read the temptations of Jesus, but there were three temptations: the lust of the flesh, the lust of the eyes, and the pride of life. Those are the three temptations that this pertains to.

And those are the three things that if a believer can actually get under control in their life, Satan will have nothing to tempt you with. Satan is the tempter. You are drawn off by your own lust, *your own lust!* And when that's conceived, it brings forth sin, and when sin is fully grown, it brings forth death!

So what I am saying to you is that God actually led me into this Bible study group. At the point that I came to this group, I didn't sin as far as obvious sin (at least from my perspective). I didn't commit adultery; I didn't lie or cheat; I didn't steal; I didn't do anything against the ten commandments. I didn't do anything against the laws of God. But there was still sin in me that I didn't know about.

It's not obvious sin in your body that you are committing. It is sin that through the knowledge of God you find out about. Through the *true knowledge* of walking with the Lord, you find out about it. And those are the sins Satan can come to you and tempt you with.

And one thing Bill used to tell me in our Bible study group, and he always said this: "God will meet you where you're at." His god will meet you where you're at. *Not my God!*

My God wants to bring you up and sit you in heavenly places in Christ Jesus! That's where my God wants you. And that's where you are if you follow Him. But the tempter comes out to tempt you away from where God has wanted to put you and puts these things in front of you to entice you through sins that you don't know. So Satan will meet you—if you are walking in your flesh, he will meet you right there. He does not even have to bother with you.

With me, and I am not trying to think highly of myself, but I was getting to a point where I really wanted to worship God in Spirit and truth. I knew there was more to God—I knew there was more to God than just the ten commandments.

And so Satan himself, a man led by Satan himself, had to come to me and tempt me. That's what God said happened in this situation. He led me there, and He knew that I would endure that temptation. And after I got out of it, He knew I would be strengthened and I would be able to come and tell people like you what happened.

So what I am saying to you—Satan's very real, very alive right now. He is wanting to—

Candy, she is very, very committed to God, the holy God. She thinks she's serving the holy God, but she is not! She has been captured alive by the enemy.

I do not want to take her daughter from her. I don't desire that for any mother, but if she is walking with Satan—If she continues, there is fear for Rebecca, for *any* little children in that group.

If Candy was to turn from this and get out of there, then there would be no need for taking her daughter. She'd be in a loving home. A home that would be very safe. But right now, she's not because she's walking with Satan, but she doesn't know it.

Lynn When you all are meeting, where are the kids?

C. For a time they had their own Bible study.

Lynn Did they use a Jewish Bible?

C. Most of the time, yes.

Lynn Who taught them?

C. For quite a long time, Ira did. Then Candy did. And Ira would go back to it. And recently, we have switched from the kids only having Bible study on one night.

See, we'd meet three nights a week: Wednesday, Thursday, and Sunday. And the kids lately have only been meeting one night, and the rest of the time, they've been down there with us.

This is done in my house. I don't know if I've stated that. First, it was done at Bill's house when he lived there, and finally, his wife got fed up with the junk. Most people don't stay long enough to get into it. It's like the Holy Spirit is warning them, "Get away! Get out! Don't come!"

THERE IS STILL TIME

But the kids were meeting with us most of the time. During prayer night, they'd go lay down, my kids would go to bed. We'd have a Bible study for the children; we'd have praise and worship where we sang and Bill would play the guitar and Ira played a keyboard. The kids would be involved in that, but then they'd go to bed.

Lynn Was it like they didn't want anyone to see what was going on?

C. No. There was nothing they could see that would be damaging to the children. It's the thoughts, and it's the teaching that would have been very damaging.

Lynn The reason I'm asking is because you said Rebecca's in danger. Because we love her, and if she's in danger, we want to protect her.

C. I'll tell you that the thing right now that's very serious is. I was going to read that Scripture to explain to you where Candy is and what we can do to get her out of that. And it's not what *we* can do, but what God can do.

> 2 Timothy 2:24–26 "And the servant of the Lord must not strive; but be gentle unto all [men], apt to teach, patient, in meekness instructing those that oppose themselves; *[Right now Candy is very much in opposition to me]* if God peradventure will give them repentance to the acknowledging of the truth; and [that] they may recover themselves out of the snare of the Devil, who are taken captive by him at his will."

That's where Candy is right now. She does not have the truth. God's the only one who can intervene right here. She has been taken captive by Satan. By people that work with Satan. That worship Satan. That bow their knee to Satan.

And I do not know any of their junk that they do in secret. And I couldn't even from experience tell you what they're doing, because I was never involved in any of that. And I am so thankful to God that I didn't get that deep into it. And that's the danger here.

(Break)

C. What finally broke me—

See, there were a lot of things that happened to me. Sexual advances, but it was alluring, deceptive ways of getting me to do that.

Lynn Was this during the services?

C. No. Not at all. See, during the services, they'd have to appear godly. This is when he had come over one time. Candy, Ira, and Bill had come over to watch a movie. This was after my husband left. And to understand how I could get to the point of doing something like that with a man, which is about the worst thing I could ever do against my husband. But Bill came to me. Just with these deceptive tactics. *Everything I did, I thought I was doing in the name of God. I actually thought this man was my husband!*

Lynn Was he that way with all the women?

C. Yes. He wants them to think that he is their husband. He lies. He brings Scripture to prove his point. If a woman won't get into the sexual thing with Bill, they'll try another avenue. That's where Satan is very, very sneaky.

Lynn He preys on, in other words, whatever your weakness is?

C. That's exactly right.

Lynn Does he do this to all of them?

C. Satan will meet you right where you're at. Wherever you're weak, he's going to come in and try to sneak in that door.

Lynn Do you know if Candy or Rebecca or Kim or any of them have ever been involved in any of this?

C. Okay, from personal experience and seeing things, Candy used to tell me that Bill tried it with her, but he didn't ever do it.

Katie Not with Candy. What I am saying is she's good about doing stuff and then turning around and telling somebody she didn't do it.

C. Oh, she is? She's good at lying?

Katie Yeah.

C. Okay, well, that's just part of this. And with the subtle tactics, the indoctrination, you have to understand how wicked it is when you're dealing with people that deal with Satan. They speak something, send a spirit to you, and put stuff in your mind.

And they'd come back to you and say, "Well, what'd God tell you?" And they knew exactly what spirit they sent to put stuff in your mind, and you're thinking God told you…and see, then you're confused about how to hear the Holy Spirit versus the junk.

There Is Still Time

Lynn Did he actually tell you that he was your husband?

C. Well, see, the first thing that he said to me when I started coming there was, "I want you to go pray and ask God who you are to me."

Lynn Who you are to him? To Bill?

C. Yeah. Or who he was to me. That was the question. And I said, "Okay." See, when you first come to this Bible study group, this man speaks some really profound truths.

Katie It's what you're looking for?

C. Yes. I was wanting the really deep truths of God. So he would say these things. Just like Eve in the garden, the serpent came to her and gave her some really profound truth, but mixed lies in it. The truth is what caught me. But I couldn't discern the lies because of the curses they were putting on me.

When I read the Bible, I couldn't truly interpret it because they were sending spirits to me; they were putting curses on me to keep me from really seeing the truth. That's what is so wicked and deceiving about this kind of stuff.

So when I went to God and asked Him, "Who is this man to me?" I went to *my God* and prayed. The main thing that was real clear was that I would learn a lot from this man. That's what I felt my God said, but also these other things came, that he was my husband. And my mind couldn't handle that. Since I was married, I couldn't accept husband. So I went back to him and told him what God said. I said, "God told me that I'd really learn a lot from you."

And he said, "Yes, I will be your teacher. What else did God say?" And I said, "Well," and I was very confused at that point. So I said, "He said you'd be like a father to me."

And I was very honest with these people, and you know, that is where Satan can get you. God wants you to be very wary and not to be deceived, but I was deceived. Very deceived!

And so he said, "No, that's not what God said."

I did hear something else, but I was very reluctant to repeat it. I eventually said, "I think He told me you would be like a husband to me." And he agreed that that's exactly what God said.

Lynn	*Bill actually said this to you?*
C.	Yes.
Lynn	He was to be your husband?
C.	Yes.
Lynn	And you're already married?
C.	Yes. The reason he could go with that, and the way he could substantiate that in my logical thinking—not in my heart. My heart had major question marks. But he would bring Scripture up to me and said, "But there is a spiritual mate. One man for every woman, and regardless of who you're married to in this lifetime, there's still one man for every woman." When you're hooked into this deception, they contradict themselves all the time, but you don't see the contradictions.
Katie	With Rebecca and Kim, is there a chance that Bill will tell them that he's their husband?
C.	Yeah. He tried that with Kim. I got to the point that I saw the wrong of it. Ira was trying to side with me, to act like she knows Bill is wrong, that he's just a little deceived in this area.
Lynn	With what?
C.	With trying to approach me.
Ron	Let me ask you a question. Is Candy, I mean Rebecca, in physical danger or spiritual danger?
C.	Both.
Ron	How is she? That's what we want to hear.
C.	Okay, we just have to establish that it's a very deceptive thing.
Lynn	And he feels like he's to be their husband? It's like the women that come in, he's to be their husband?
C.	He tries that with every woman who comes there.
Lynn	And so when Rebecca comes of age, it could be the same thing. Kim's already of age, so he's already approached her?
C.	Yes.
Katie	He's already had sex with her, if what we've heard is right.
C.	That was the accusation that was made to them Tuesday night and he—

There Is Still Time

Lynn He acknowledged it?

C. Yes. He did.

Lynn He acknowledged it? He acknowledged having sex with Kim?

C. Yes. And that's what got to me. I had these things happen to me, and I forgave Bill because Ira is right there to try to appease me, trying to tell me, "He's deceived in areas, but God's working with him. You have to hear the truth that he's preaching. He couldn't speak the truth like that except God be with him. He's 'God's anointed.'"

But the thing that got to me is Ira, through ignorance, or stupidity, or just wanting to crush me even more, told me about Kim. About how Bill went to Kim.

Katie Let me ask you this. Did Rebecca watch Bill have sex with Kim?

C. I don't know. No, no, because after she ran away—

Katie This is before she ran away.

C. Okay, well, I don't know anything about that.

Katie Well, we were told that she—that Bill had sex with Kim, and Rebecca walked in on them.

C. That's quite possible, but I don't know. I couldn't say.

Katie This happened at Candy's house before Kim ever ran away.

C. The thing about Kim—Ira told me about it over the phone, and I pretty much broke down. And I couldn't handle this man coming after a little baby Christian. And I said, "Ira, when are the lies going to stop? I can't handle this!" And she said, "You are just going to have to trust God."

Lynn What did she tell you?

C. When Kim had run away from her parents, she went to [a friend of Ira's]. She stayed there. And Bill went up there when she was there by herself and told her that she was his wife.

Lynn He told Kim she was his wife?

C. That's right.

Steve Did all ya'll know where Kim was when that court case took place?

C.	No. No. They would not—I had speculations, but they did not share this stuff with me. Purposely. Bill knew. Ira knew. And Candy knew. They knew.
Katie	And Rebecca knew? Rebecca did know.
C.	I don't know if Rebecca knew or not. Probably not. They wouldn't want a child to maybe slip. I am sure they didn't tell Rebecca.
Lynn	Okay, so he went up there to her?
C.	Yes.
Lynn	Had sex with her?
C.	That's what Ira told me. I did not experience it. I did not see it. That was the breaking point for me. And I went to my Father in Heaven and said, "Lord, I see what's going on. I am starting to see the truth. I am starting to see the lies. I am starting to see the deceptions. I can't handle untruth being spoken in my house. I can't handle this anymore. And I am giving it to You."
Steve	So what you're saying is that as long as they associate with Bill and Ira, as long as they're staying there, they're in danger, mentally and physically?
C.	Yes. That's right.
Lynn	And spiritually.
C.	Oh yes! Very much spiritually! That's my concern.
Lynn	Physically, what happened to Kim can happen to Rebecca?
C.	Sure. Very much. I saw Rebecca yesterday at the school. She's like she is in a little trance. And that's how they will keep her, because they don't want her to know. They don't want the truth to get to her. See, I gave this to the Lord, and He intervened Sunday. One night during prayer time—I could hardly pray around these people. And they intimidated me. They made me feel very inferior because I couldn't pray out loud in front of them. Near the end, I started being able to pray out loud as I got past the intimidation, but now I understand why I couldn't pray.
Lynn	So instead, you'd have these prayer meetings, and it was more of a condemnation?

C.	At the beginning it was—[Bill would say things like] we are just living in the world, we walk in our flesh, we don't go out and preach the gospel, condemnation like that.
	But see, near the end, those tactics didn't get to me because I knew I was walking with God. I knew I was starting to see the truth. I knew that I was actually seeing what God's Word was saying to my heart. God was strengthening me at the end.
Lynn	Did Candy see this?
C.	No. She doesn't. She's very, very blind to it. And let me tell you—
Bob	What he knew in making himself important was making everyone depend on him?
C.	That's right.
Bob	Is that right?
C.	That's *exactly* right!
Lynn	He makes them dependent on him?
C.	Yes. But all the while he's telling you that you have to depend on Jesus. But in his subtle tactics and his lies and his deceptions, it's really—you need to depend on him and Ira. Ira is the more powerful one in this thing. For Scripture's sake, he is the head, and she is the one who has to submit to him for appearance's sake.
Katie	I wondered about that.
C.	She is.
Lynn	In these Bible studies, does she—Ira and him both—what do they do?
C.	He's just out there preaching.
Lynn	He and she both?
C.	Sometimes. He for the most part. For a long time, she used to teach the children, and all the adults that wanted to be there were there. And I was usually there.
Lynn	Okay, she taught the kids? And she felt like she was his wife also, and she lives with him? And he lives in her house, and she sleeps with him?
C.	Yes.

Lynn You know that for a fact?

C. Yes, I do. I even saw them have a sexual, uh, this was really weird, and I don't know why they did it...but they did, and it's for their own demise, because they did it in front of me.

Lynn They had sex in front of you?

C. Yeah!

Steve What about the kids?

C. Now I don't know about any of that.

Steve You don't know if they were there?

C. They weren't there this particular time. It was after a Bible study meeting and everyone had left and I was just sitting there. They were wanting to talk to me about something, and then all of a sudden, they got up, started kissing and carrying on and taking off their clothes. And I'm sitting there saying [to myself], "*What are they doing?!*"

Bob The whole thing was intimidation?

C. Yes.

Lynn Where was her husband at this time?

C. Tom? He is, and I don't know the full story about him. I feel like—and this is certainly speculation. One time during a prayer meeting, Bill used to pray for people. Lay hands on them and—

Lynn He actually lays hands on you?

Katie That's a weird experience, because I saw them do it to Candy. When that happened, I liked to have freaked out. I went back to her bedroom and stayed back there in the corner.

Lynn When he lays hands on you, what happens?

C. I don't know. Just from my own of what God's revealed to me, he's passing stronger demons through you.

Lynn Does she prophesy, or what happens? Whenever he lays hands on you, what do they do?

C. They just kind of sit there and look into his eyes.

Lynn Like in a trance?

C. They, like, sit there in a little circle.

*T*here Is Still Time

Lynn Sort of like Rebecca...say for Brownies, right?

(Break)

C. Okay, where were we?

Lynn You were talking about Tom. Tom was there when they had sex?

C. No. No, he wasn't there. It was just me.

Lynn Oh, just you?

C. It was just me. And I just kind of freaked about it.

Lynn And they're saying this is part of the worship services? That this is spiritual?

C. No. No, it wasn't part of the worship. It was just part of the subtle tactics. That is what is so bad with pornography. See, when people look at books like that and see those bad movies, that is a deceptive tactic of Satan himself to get people. It's like it turns on the *enmity of God* that's inside each one of us. It's like it turns it on. Makes it alive. Turns on the lust there. And it is like you want to do it. You have to be around it. When you start looking at it, pretty soon, if you look at it long enough, you are going to start doing it yourself.

That's why we've got murderers and killers out there. But all this started with a little tiny seed that Satan planted. Then it's sin that goes unchecked, unconfessed, and then the sin gets a little worse, and then finally, you're getting into really bad sin. Finally, way down the line, you're raping, killing, cutting up people, and doing all kinds of wicked, evil stuff that Satan wants.

That is what's so evil about all of this. So if they stay in it a long time, if they keep in this without getting out, they will eventually—and this is something God has impressed upon my heart, why it is so important.

Right now, they are running scared, because I am speaking against them. They know something is going on. That's why they keep calling. They had Rebecca call first. Then Candy called. They know something's going on. They want to know where you all are. They're afraid I am talking to you right now. And by the spirit, they know I am.

The reason I am fearful for Candy is I am afraid she's in so deep that they're going to take her to one of their meetings and, through fear, force her to bow her knee to Satan. And if she does that, she'll be condemned to Hell. She will eternally live in Hell the rest of her life. I know that.

Lynn So this is sort of like a cult?[105]

C. Whatever a cult is, I really don't know.[106]

Katie How much contact does Bill have with Rebecca?

C. I don't know. Candy and Rebecca and Kim go over to their house a lot. I was never invited over there a lot. The only time I was ever invited was if they were trying another tactic.

Lynn Well, you know Candy and Rebecca lived with them for a long time?

C. Yes.

Lynn And Bill lived in that house? And Ira lived in that house?

C. I do not think Bill lived there during that time.

Steve He was there all the time.

C. He came a lot, but he didn't live there then. He did not move out until two years ago. If this all goes to a situation where you are going to try to get—

Steve We're *definitely* going to court.

Lynn Were Rebecca and Kim ever left with Bill?

C. I don't know.

Lynn Babysit? You know, a lot of times Rebecca—we would take her home maybe on Sunday evenings, and there would be some guy. I can't remember who it was. She would say his name. "He's going to take care of us." It was one of the guys—

Steve That was Wendell.

Lynn Okay. Wendell was to take care of them. Everyone else was going to be gone. Wendell was going to watch after them.

C. Now those were things I didn't know about.

Steve Wendell, I know Wendell. I've known Wendell since I was fourteen years old.

Katie Now Wendell, I don't really have a problem with.

There Is Still Time

C.   No, he's a helpless victim right now. He was invited to our confrontation last Tuesday night, and he just sat there in a little heap, wondering what's going on. "Here's this girl I really care about saying all these things against those people."

And here they're sitting there dumbfounded and not saying a word about the accusations I made.

I told you the reason I am fearful for Rebecca…because if Candy ever bows her knee to Satan, there's no hope for her. Once you do that—

Lynn   If Candy bows her knee and goes along with what Bill is saying, then she will allow him to have access to Rebecca? Whatever he wants to do?

C.   That's exactly right.

Lynn   That's what you're saying?

C.   That's what I am saying. If Candy actually, willingly…Scripture pertaining to that, Hebrews—

Lynn   In this thing that you're saying with this prophecy, is it something that they had?

C.   No. It's something that God—and when I read it in the church, I was so nervous, I could hardly even speak it.

Lynn   You read this in their church?

C.   At our church meeting.

Lynn   Will you read that so the tape could pick it up?

C.   Yes, very much. I sure will.

Lynn   Where did this come from?

C.   God gave it to me.

Lynn   When you're saying God—

C.   My God. *My God* gave it to me.

Lynn   And what was their reaction when you read this?

C.   Bill denied it. He said, "No, that's not from God."

Lynn   Okay. Would you read—

C.   Okay. This is the prophecy—this will give you the reason why there's still hope for all of them right now at this point. This is a prophecy God gave me. I was praying in the Spirit—

(End of first tape / beginning of second tape)

C.   This is a continuation from the first tape. The date, I don't think we stated the date. What's today's date?

Steve   Saturday, the sixth.

Lynn   Saturday, March 6, 1993.

C.   Okay…continuing in the seriousness of the ramifications of this situation. Tuesday night this week, I accused him—these are the accusations that I made to Ira and Bill. I stated to them that they are workers of Satan. I stated to them, through their prompting. It wasn't that I just came out with this.

At first, they tried to ask me if I believed they had the Holy Spirit inside of them. And I said, "I'm not going to make that judgment. That's not for me to judge. God's your judge."

They started saying something to the effect of—you know, they were pretty disgusted with me, because all I could speak was the truth to them, and they couldn't say anything, hardly. And that's how Satan is. If truth is spoken without doubt, Satan cannot stand that. So they were pretty silent that night.

But the reason they weren't vicious is because Wendell was sitting there. See, they couldn't let their true colors out, because there were two souls they were still fighting for. Souls they want to drag to Hell with them! That's the only reason why they were not as vicious.

I can't remember the sequence, and it would be wonderful to have it on tape, but we don't, so we'll have to just go by what me and [my husband] experienced.

Bill made a really snide remark like, "Which *god* do you serve?" And at that point, I said, "By the words of your own mouth, you are condemned yourself! If you can even ask me what *god* I serve, I know you don't serve the One I serve. You serve Satan! You walk with him! You work with him!"

And that's when I pointed to Wendell and started speaking very strongly to him that these people were out to get his soul and drag him to Hell with them. Their words actually condemned them, and it even says in the Scriptures that that's what'll happen.

And so I accused this man of being a false prophet. I accused him of being—and Ira stopped me and said, "What spirit is he?" And I looked her straight in the eyes and said, "The spirit of antichrist!"

And all these accusations were made, and they did not deny a single one of them. They could not deny them, because I was speaking them through the power of God. I was speaking the truth.

Lynn Did they ask you to leave at any time?

C. No, they were at my house.

Lynn They didn't get up and leave?

C. They didn't want to leave because they still wanted Wendell. See, he was sitting there, a little heap of a man. He had a lot of confidence in these people; he had a lot of confidence in me, and here I am accusing the man whose teachings he has been sitting under.

And I am accusing him of being antichrist! I am accusing him of being a false prophet. I am accusing him of lying, deceiving, and luring people in. I am accusing him of wanting to drag unstable souls to Hell with them. I am accusing these people of this, of being workers together for Satan. And Wendell is just sitting there. He couldn't say anything. I said, "So, Wendell, what do you have to say about this? What do you think?"

Lynn Well, what is Candy doing?

C. She's in a trance. She is in some kind of weird junk over there. She could not say anything. All she tried to do, and one thing—see, what happened Sunday night, the Spirit of God fell on me. His anger and wrath was being poured out of me. It was a wild, wild event! I have never, ever experienced anything like this in my life.

But see, the prayer I had to God at this point was: "I have given this over to You. I see the lies. I see the deception, but I don't know what to do." It was almost like I was powerless to do anything to get out of it. And I said to God, "You've got to intervene." And He did! He poured out His Spirit inside of me.

> [My husband] had just made a major commitment to the Lord to follow Him, and I felt like something was going to happen that night, but I thought it'd be through him.

Lynn Did he make a commitment with these people?

C. No, he made it to God. God, *alone*.

H. No, this was something separate.

Lynn You had gotten away from them?

C. [My husband] has been gone, so he hasn't been involved in it. Not like me.

H. And I was there. Did you tell them about—

C. And when he was there, they would put spells on him to make him sleep. He would sleep the whole time, and they would substantiate to me that he just was not interested. That the world was more important to him, that he didn't want to hear any of this. And in actuality, they had a spell on him so he couldn't hear it.

Lynn Well, see, most courts or judges or whatever, you know, I believe that, because I am a Christian, but most courts, they're just going to dismiss that.

H. Right.

C. That's why I am saying to you, this is in God's hands. God intervened. And don't try to rationalize this up here. God's intervening, and He's not going to allow this to happen. And let me read this to you, and you'll understand exactly why.

> Twenty-seven August nineteen ninety-two is when this prophecy came to me. I was praying by myself—not with these people—and God spoke to me and said, "Write these Words down."

> It's like this Scripture is coming true for my life. God said in the last days He's going to pour out His Spirit on mankind. People will prophesy. Men will dream dreams. And I actually—God allowed me to prophesy His Words.

(Break)

C. *The Words I speak to you are Spirit and Life. I Am calling My people, those whom the Father has given Me, unto Myself—*

> And I want you all to realize the way God had me write it down. It was like God was speaking through me. This wasn't C. Read

There Is Still Time

saying these things. This was God speaking through me to write these Words down. So I'll start over again...

{Break in Transcript}

I SENT THIS PROPHECY of 27 August 1992, and the following cover letter, to others as I was directed by the Lord. Considering the responses I have received, it would seem that what you are about to read is quite controversial. I sincerely hope and pray that you will have eyes to see what the Lord has revealed to me.

26 June 1993

My Dear Fellow Saints,

To those who truly love the Lord God Almighty with their whole heart, soul, and mind. To those who truly love the Lord Jesus Christ from a pure and sincere heart. To those who sincerely love their neighbor as they do themselves. To those who truly desire to worship God in Spirit and in truth. And to those who are willing to lose their life in this world so that they will gain more abundant life in the world to come.

My sincere prayer as you read these Words is that the Lord will truly prepare your hearts to receive only His truth. And may the eyes to your understanding be enlightened so that you can truly understand and experience the great love God has for us, and for all the world. And as you experience His great love, my prayer is that you will share that love with others.

I pray that God will continue to pour out His abundant mercy and grace on us individually and collectively as the body of Christ. God desires to have a very personal relationship with each one of us. He so wants to share all that He is with us, but sin stands in the way.

That's why I have found that it's so important to stay before the Lord God Almighty in His Word and by prayer, so that He can reveal to us the things that are keeping us from fellowship with Him.

He has so freely given of Himself, but the world and even some professing Christians just throw His love back in His face. There is such a sorrow in my heart because, as the Lord reveals Himself to me, I have started to truly understand who He is and what He really did for us at Calvary.

It so saddens me that I could have ever sinned against Him. He is everything that is wonderful and beautiful and precious. All He wants to do is love us and share His glorious Kingdom with us.

But now it's so hard for me, after having walked with Him for thirteen years, to understand why anybody would ever want to reject that. For some people, I realize it's because of their lack of knowledge of Him. And that is what this war is all about.

I have personally determined in my own heart that I want to serve Him no matter what that may entail. I so desire to be a vessel unto honor so that He can use me for any good work, if and when He desires.

My stand with Him is this: Not my will, but Yours be done, Lord. And my main objective is to keep on growing in a more intimate relationship with our Creator and try to be very sensitive to His Holy Spirit inside me.

I truly love and adore the Lord, not because of anything I have done, but because of Him and everything He has done.

I would like to share with you an experience I had with God that took place ten months ago from this date. At the time, I was a member of Bill's Bible study group. The meetings were

There Is Still Time

held in my home. I had been walking with them for approximately two and half years.

It was after a Thursday night Bible study. Everyone had already left, and it was just me and the Lord. I would also like to mention that we used to pray on Wednesday nights together as a group, but I had a very difficult time praying with them. It was very much of a struggle from within to pray in their presence. So I prayed many nights after everyone left.

This particular night, I was just sitting on my couch downstairs in the room where we met for services, just talking to the Lord.

As I was speaking, He interrupted and said, "Get up and get a piece of paper and write down what I speak to your heart." So I did.

And I testify this to be an accurate statement written by me, C. Read, as the Lord God Almighty spoke to me by His Holy Spirit.

C. Read

Signed and sealed in the presence of a witness
on the 27th Day of June in the year of our Lord,
One Thousand Nine Hundred and Ninety-Three.

Prophecy of 27 August 1992 [107]

THE WORDS I SPEAK TO YOU ARE SPIRIT AND LIFE. I AM CALLING MY PEOPLE, THOSE WHOM THE FATHER HAS GIVEN ME, UNTO MYSELF.

ALL MEN THROUGH ALL AGES HAVE HAD AN OPPORTUNITY TO COME UNTO ME, AND THEY WILL CONTINUE TO HAVE THAT OPPORTUNITY, BUT THIS AGE IS SOON TO COME TO AN END.

I HAVE A SPECIAL TASK FOR CERTAIN PEOPLE AT THIS TIME. I AM, AND HAVE BEEN PREPARING PEOPLE FOR A WORK THAT I HAVE CALLED THEM TO DO.

Walking with the Enemy

I HAVE IMPRESSED UPON THE HEARTS OF THOSE TO WHOM I HAVE CALLED, AND NONE OF THIS WILL COME AS A SURPRISE TO THEM. BUT THEY WILL STILL HAVE A CHOICE IN THE MATTER AS TO WHETHER THEY WILL ALLOW ME TO SHAPE AND MOLD THEM.

THERE ARE SOME VERY HARD STRUGGLES GOING ON WITH CERTAIN PEOPLE, AND THEY KNOW WHO THEY ARE. YOUR WORKS ARE BEING TRIED BY FIRE. THE ONLY ONES THAT I WILL PLACE THE SPECIAL ANOINTING ON ARE THE ONES WHO CAN PASS THROUGH THAT FIRE.

I AM TRAINING MANY PEOPLE ALL OVER THE WORLD FOR THIS TASK, AND THIS IS ONE PLACE WHERE THAT TRAINING PROCESS IS GOING ON. WHY DO YOU THINK THAT IT'S SUCH A STRONGHOLD FOR THE ENEMY?

SATAN DOES KNOW WHO YOU ARE. AND HE WILL TRY EVERY MEANS POSSIBLE TO DESTROY WHAT I HAVE PLANNED. THAT'S WHY IT IS SO IMPORTANT FOR YOU TO DEPEND ON ME AND MY WORD.

AS YOU NOTICED, MY ANOINTING DOES NOT COME AS YOU WILL IT, BUT AS I WILL IT. BUT THERE WILL COME A TIME WHEN EVERYTHING YOU SAY WILL BE MY WORDS. AND I WILL GIVE YOU THE BOLDNESS YOU WILL NEED TO SPEAK THOSE WORDS. AND YOU WILL HAVE MUCH OPPOSITION TO THE WORDS YOU SPEAK, JUST AS YOU ARE ENCOUNTERING NOW. LIKE I SAID, THIS IS A TRAINING PERIOD FOR YOU, AND ALL SOLDIERS MUST BE PREPARED FOR BATTLE.

IF YOU THOUGHT YOU WERE IN THE BATTLE ZONE BEFORE, YOU HAVE NOT EVEN GOTTEN INTO THE REAL WAR YET. YOU HAVE BEEN BEHIND THE LINES, BUT VERY SOON I AM GOING TO BE SENDING SOME OF YOU ACROSS THE LINES TO CLAIM THOSE THAT ARE MINE.

THEIR HEARTS AND MINDS HAVE BEEN BLINDED UP TO THIS POINT, BUT BECAUSE OF MY WORDS, THAT YOU WILL SPEAK, THE BLINDERS WILL BE REMOVED AND THEY WILL HAVE AN OPPORTUNITY TO RECEIVE LIFE OR DEATH. AND IF THEY CHOOSE DEATH, IT'S BECAUSE THEY ACTUALLY HATE ME IN THEIR HEARTS, SO DON'T HAVE SYMPATHY FOR THEM.

WHOEVER IS AGAINST ME IS NOT FOR ME. AND DON'T BE SURPRISED WHEN YOU FIND MORE AGAINST ME THAN YOU DO FOR ME. AS YOU

*T*HERE IS STILL TIME

NOTICED, MOST PEOPLE DON'T WANT TO LIVE BY EVERY WORD THAT PROCEEDS FROM THE MOUTH OF GOD.

A TRUE JEW IS NOT BY DESCENT, BUT BY CIRCUMCISION OF THE HEART. AND WHETHER YOU ARE ADOPTED IN MAKES NO DIFFERENCE TO ME, BECAUSE YOU WILL RULE AND REIGN WITH ME WHETHER OR NOT YOU ARE FROM THE BLOODLINE OF DAVID. THE SPIRIT GIVES LIFE; THE FLESH CONVEYS NO BENEFIT WHATEVER.

THERE'S BEEN TALK OF A LARGE CHURCH IN THE MAKING, BUT THAT IS NOT IN MY PLAN FOR YOU. AS THE TIME GETS CLOSER, I WILL REVEAL TO YOU MORE OF THE EVENTS OF THE FUTURE. BUT FOR NOW, ALL I ASK OF YOU IS TO CONTINUE TO LEARN OF ME, WORSHIP THE FATHER IN SPIRIT AND IN TRUTH, AND PRAY FOR MY PEOPLE.

AND REMEMBER, I WILL EQUIP YOU WITH THE AMOUNT OF FAITH YOU WILL NEED TO DO ANYTHING I CALL YOU TO DO. I AM YOUR STRENGTH. JUST KEEP ON LEARNING HOW TO DENY YOURSELF, TAKE UP YOUR CROSS, AND FOLLOW ME.

I AM THE WAY, AND I HAVE SOME PEOPLE I WOULD LIKE FOR YOU TO DIRECT THEIR WAY TO ME. YOU ARE MY SERVANTS BECAUSE YOU CHOSE TO BE. SO IF I ASK YOU TO DO SOME HARD THINGS, REALIZE I KNOW THE OUTCOME, AND TRUST ME COMPLETELY.

AFTER ALL, I AM THE LORD!

{End of Prophecy of 27 August 1992}

C.   This is the prophecy God gave me in August of last year. And I did not completely understand it. And I went before the church and—and I hate to call it the church. There were some people that were part of the church of Jesus Christ, but there were people that were part of the church of Satan. So when I got before that meeting, I tried to read this, and I could hardly read it. Bill was very opposed to it. He tried to make me think it was not from God, that it was not true.

When the Spirit fell on me Sunday, they tried to come to me and tell me that it just was not true—it was not of their god. *It was* of my God! The great Jehovah! The Almighty God is the One that gave me these Words. And He is the One that just poured His Spirit inside of me to anoint me to be able to come and to speak.

So what He says to me, which is very important right now, is to pray for them, to listen to Him, and do what He says in how to proceed with this whole thing.

And the thing that I perceive right now that we can do—and God will work it out. He will! He is wanting them out of there. He wants them. He knows their hearts' intent. He knows whether they want out. He knows whether they are serving Him, but in actuality being used by the enemy. And just in my heart, I feel—

I read this prophecy to Candy privately. First, I read it to Ira over the phone. She used to call me a lot, to make sure she knew what God was telling me, because she knew I was to the point that I was listening to God and talking to Him, and that He was talking to me. But I was not hearing Him as clearly as I could, because I had not learned how to really, actually, purge myself from all the different ways of sin that you just don't recognize as sin. And since God has taught me how to do that, He is talking to me very clearly.

And I did not completely understand this at the time, but when I read it to Candy, she just broke down crying, and she knew. I had no idea of the meaning of this prophecy when God gave it to me, but I understand it now. I did not realize that I would actually be, because of God leading me, able to help get people out from under Satan's control. And that is why I am talking to you here.

And the main thing I feel in my heart we can do for Candy is get her away from there and out from under their influence.

See, there are so many things that are said and done, that if my eyes had been completely open, I wouldn't have stood for. The indoctrination is that we are here for one another to point out sin to one another. So that person, if they are still sinning, God just has not been able to deal with them.

Bill would still have this spirit of lust on him because it is something he has not addressed with God; he hasn't confessed it. Ira would say, "But we still need to pray for our brother. We don't need to reject our brother." And since I am not spiritual, I didn't

	have the right to go to him. In Galatians, it talks about those that are spiritual, but since I wasn't spiritual in their eyes, I didn't have the right to go to my brother. But I still did at certain times.
H.	See, part of the indoctrination is also—in our case, and specifically in Candy's case, she lives two or three houses up from Ira and Bill, right across from Ira's mother's house. She knows who she is seeing. That is part of the manipulation and control, who you are in contact with. Explain all the times she'd call and want to pick your mind.
C.	Oh yeah, she would do that all the time.
H.	She does that. It is part of the psychological control of your thinking, and who you should be seeing. It's a control thing. It's a very subtle process. And once you are in, you don't really see that you are in it.
Katie	I think Ira and Bill put Candy up to trying to get me to come. She would come see me and want me to go somewhere, and then the whole time she was preaching all this stuff.
Lynn	We would like to hear how you were brought into it and what you saw that you think might have harmed Rebecca or Candy, since you were sort of an outsider and then came in. And how they got you in and everything.
H.	In my case—
C.	State your name.
H.	I am [H.], C. Read's husband. Well, basically, first C. had gone through her scenario in her search for the Lord. And we had gone through a discipleship program called MasterLife. I went through the program, but I was not really committed. Of course, C. was very committed, searching for the Lord and—
Lynn	This wasn't their church, right?
H.	No, this was the Baptist church. The program was over, and somehow or other, Bill had told us about the Bible study group. And C. was interested in going. I did not like it. For some reason, I did not like the idea of it. And she wanted to go, and I said no. And then she didn't go. And that went on for about three weeks.

And we were kind of at a very unstable point in our relationship. She became very insistent about going, and I had the idea in my head that if I didn't let her go, that she was going to be gone. And that's a fact!

So she started going. They met a couple times across the street, and then they started meeting at [Ira's] house. And I would stay with the kids, and C. would go. It was driving me nuts, her going over there. And it wasn't jealousy or anything like that. It was a concern.

Ron Curiosity?

H. No, not curiosity. I was not curious at all at that point. I was fearful for C.; for whatever reason, I was. I really didn't know why. Like I said, I really wasn't searching for the Lord at that time. A lot of things were going on inside that I didn't really understand. I could not stand it. I told C., "If you are going to go, I am going to go with you." Of course, that really upset Bill, the fact that I started going.

Lynn They didn't want you to come with her?

H. Oh, no.

Lynn Did they tell you that?

H. No.

Lynn Did they tell you?

C. No, of course not.

Lynn It was just their general—the way they acted?

C. [Yeah], and if you could really understand—

H. See, they want to work on one spouse—

C. They want to act godly, but see, since they're involved with satanic-type junk, which I am not really knowledgeable about, and just from my experience, I know it's true because of the different things God is showing me now that I am not with them anymore.

They say one thing with their mouth that would appear scriptural, but they would send spirits that would come and plant thoughts in your mind to make you think something else. And even act like they are prophesying to you as to what God told

	you. And it would make you even more convinced that these people were of God.
Lynn	Why would they not want him to come and be a part of that?
H.	Because, see, they want to separate you. That keeps you weaker to start with. What they want to do is, they want to split the relationship up. They want dissension. They prefer one spouse to be out of the picture. That way, they have control over half.
C.	Then they'll lure the other one in later. After one is caught, then they get the other one. And then you end up in a situation—because once you introduce sex into it, you don't sin just against God; you sin against your own body. You actually become one with that individual that you've joined yourself to.

So there's much more of a deeper tie that Satan has on you if you've actually indulged in a sexual relationship with either somebody of the same sex, or the opposite sex, or involving children.

Two weeks ago, Candy called me and said Rebecca finally got born again. That she finally accepted the Lord. I was so happy because I thought she meant Jesus. I was so excited that she actually was born again by God's Spirit. And I went over there that night. Rebecca was so accepting of me then. And she said, "Oh, I love you, Ms. C. I just always have." But she was so different. Before, it was a fight because she didn't want to be there. It was like she couldn't stand it. But after that point, she was accepting of me. And finally, she said she loved Ms. Ira, when she used to talk about her all the time.

Katie	She's never liked Ira.
C.	You'll find if you come across her now, she'll have a different attitude toward Ira. She won't have a different attitude toward me because I am out of the group now.
Katie	But she had a different attitude toward you the whole time anyway. She didn't talk about you like she talked about Ira.
	(Break)
H.	Basically, I went into the group with a lot of reservations. I was having a lot of personal checks inside, but once you are in there, you become numb to those checks. I'd have reservations about something, like a scriptural thing. They would interpret one

thing, say, interpret fornication and adultery. And Bill would come back and say the Bible says that, but let's go to the Greek translation and see what it says. The Greek translation says adultery and fornication are idolatry. So he discounts fornication and adultery in the Bible and says it really means idolatry. You are worshipping other idols. And that fornication and adultery are okay, basically.

Lynn He says that they're okay?

H. Right.

Lynn Did he come out and say this?

H. No. No, it's a real subtle thing in that area.

(Break)

H. As far as immoral? No, because for the most part, they did not want me to see anything like that. They did not want me to witness anything. The only things that I really saw, and it would not really do a lot of good, but the things are that Bill is a master at psychology. He is very well trained. Very well versed.

Bill is a very emotionally sick person, but you'd never know that up front. To me, he never revealed that.

C. I got a little tiny glimpse of it every now and then.

H. He's very unstable, like I said, but I never saw it. I am not really privy to his instability, but like C. said, she's seen it on a couple of occasions. He uses deception, manipulation, lies. He has all of that very well under control. He has the right answers for any question.

We were there as a Bible study group. And the really sad part, and the part that really does upset me, is the fact that my family gave them credibility. Here we've been going to the Baptist church, trying to serve the Lord and all this. And then comes Bill, who more or less enticed C. into the group.

C. I don't want to think more highly of myself, but I know, just looking back, that God led me through there. And with this prophecy, it substantiates some things.

Right now, the only thing we can do— I know you want to take this to court. The only thing I feel inside that you could do right now is—what's a temporary injunction?

There Is Still Time

Steve Temporary custody?

C. Do you happen to know a judge you could take that, so you could get temporary custody of her?

Steve Well, I'll have to go find a lawyer.

Lynn We don't even know that we have enough there. We need to get as much as we can on this tape.

H. Yeah. Let me just get back to Bill. He is very good at psychological control. And that is the part with the children that I know. Firsthand, as far as the children go, there is the psychological abuse that...the children are nothing. They are always subjugated, set apart. Not allowed to interact with the group itself. They're always pushed aside.

Steve If Rebecca's under a spell or whatever, how can we break it?

H. Get her out from their control.

C. No. Remember when I read this prophecy?

(Break)

C. Just by what I perceive in my heart, that whoever listens to this that is a Christian, they will understand and it will bear witness. That the sexual aspect is what holds people. Candy had told me that Bill never had sex with her. He tried—and even tried to say that she was his wife—but he could not get through that door.

See the thing with me—I couldn't handle it. I knew it was sin in my heart. I went to the Lord and asked for repentance, and He cleansed me of it. And I was okay for a while. And Ira would come right back and justify what had happened and try to take the blame off Bill and put all the condemnation on me, saying I was a stumbling block. I was the one who instigated it.

I said, "What do I do that's ungodly? I sure don't want to encourage this. What can I do to stop him from pursuing me? I don't want to be a stumbling block." I always took responsibility. But he'd come back after I was at a really weak moment.

Lynn Bill would come back to your house?

C. Yes. The first time was just like—I didn't even know it happened, hardly. I was so confused. It was just a weird thing. Then the second time was when I was just fed up with everything, and I just could not handle it. Why I couldn't handle it was the guilt, what I did to my husband, what I did to Ira. Because they were, at that time, apparently *married*. I mean, not married legally. They were *spiritually* married. And they *are* spiritually married!

Lynn Bill and—

C. And Ira. But it's in *Satan's* kingdom! Satan has joined them together. *Not* God!

Lynn Do you think any of the women might be abusing the kids?

C. Not that I know of. I know that I did not. And I do not think that Candy did.

One thing I want you to know right here, as far as Candy getting out, if she truly loves God with her whole heart, soul, and mind, when I speak—I don't know what I am going to say to her. Just like when I came to you, I did not know exactly what I was going to say.

I just know that my heart's been open, and I am very honest and willing to state to you anything that has taken place. And that has been my statement to people.

Then, when God has me speak to Candy, she will have the opportunity—when God anoints me to speak to her, she will have the opportunity to receive life or death. If she chooses death, it's because she hates God in her heart, so don't have sympathy for her.

And realize that God is still going to take care of your little daughter. You pray for her. And every Christian in this room, pray for her. That is what God said to do. He will rescue that little girl out.

If Candy, and she decides, if she hears the truth and it breaks her free of it, she will come out of it. She will drag her daughter with her. She will not let anything happen to her daughter. She will be as turned on to the Lord as I am. She will be released from the chains that are binding her. She will be free! The truth will set her free!

And when those people left my house Tuesday night, they took their junk with them. You will never know the freedom I felt inside my heart! I felt like I had my house back. I felt like I was truly married to [my husband] and had him back. He had

	me. It was almost like I could feel that the chains were gone. Everything that was binding me up was gone.
Katie	Well, do you think it would help any if we just go to Candy's and get all of her stuff and take it back down to the country?
C.	No. You can't do anything. God can do everything. You can't do a single thing. I can't do anything. *It's only through the power of God.*
Lynn	The only way that any of them is ever going to change is to get away from Bill and Ira's influence. In other words, are you saying that their influence is making them do things and see things that happen?
C.	And act like they're okay. Act like they're okay with God. It's part of the deception.
Lynn	Like the sexual encounters that are happening?
C.	And it is not a lot of sexual encounters. That's the thing. See, it happened to me the second time, but I was so guilt ridden and broken that I couldn't handle it anymore.
Lynn	But he's supposed to be your pastor? Right?
C.	Yes.
Lynn	And he is saying he is your husband and doing this? And he is her pastor also?
C.	When I presented Scripture to him—
H.	Yes.
Lynn	This is her pastor. And she is saying that what he says and what he does is right? This is what I am going to follow? This is what I believe?
C.	No. No, see, when I got Scripture to back up why the adultery was wrong, they had to go through another angle and say, "Okay, it was wrong. Bill repented of it. He is not going to do that anymore. God's dealt with him in that area, so you don't have to worry about that anymore. God's dealt with him. So you forgive your brother. Do what God's Word says. If you can't forgive your brother, God can't forgive you." See, they use all kinds of Scripture.
Lynn	Did Candy ever know any of this went on between you and him?

C.   Yes. I went to [them] with it. Bill and Ira, the first time—I just could not handle it. I had to confront them with this. Bill was freaked that I really admitted it.

Lynn   Was Candy—what did you do?

C.   Candy was not there. Okay, after the second time, this is something I was very ashamed of. This is not something I was really willing to talk about. It was a real struggle to even go to these people, to confront these people with this. I did not even want to discuss it with Candy. I did not want to discuss it with *anyone*. If you committed adultery with a man, you wouldn't go telling people about it. It's shameful.

Steve   But did you tell her?

Lynn   She was aware?

C.   She confronted me. Well, no, let me tell you what happened. And I'll tell you why God even let me go by Scripture to—do you know where it talks about if your brother has something against you?

    (Break)

Lynn   Bill was used by God?

C.   They would say Bill was used by God in such a way to point out people's failures, their sins, the things that they were weak in. So that he would actually be used by God to show people their faults. See, he was led by God to do these things, but I was weak in this area, and it was just showing how I fell into adultery. That was my weakness.

    So because of the experience I went through, Ira's comment would be, "Look at all the things God was able to show you." And that is true. Scripture is true where it says God can use all things for the good of those who love God and are called according to His purposes. That was a true Scripture, but they perverted it. He was saying the truth when he was saying "god" used him to show people their weaknesses. *Satan* used him to show people their weaknesses, and he tried to pull people in *because of their weaknesses!*

    The thing with me, and with Candy, I feel her heart is to follow the Lord. She is deceived into thinking that these people are following the same God as her. And so when these sexual encounters happened with me, I went to them first, based on this Scripture:

Matthew 18:15–16 "Moreover if thy brother shall trespass against thee, go and tell him his fault between thee and him alone: if he shall hear thee, thou hast gained thy brother. But if he will not hear [thee, then] take with thee one or two more, that in the mouth of two or three witnesses every word may be established."

And that's what I did. After it happened the second time, and that was right before I was planning to get out of that group...I was so beaten down. I couldn't handle it anymore, and he came to my house that night. I remember that night very clearly, how upset I was. It was like my heart was ripped out of me, but thank God, He is a healer. He does heal those kinds of things. But we had an encounter that night that hooked me back in.

Lynn This is when the two or three witnesses came in?

C. No, when we had the encounter, nobody was there.

Lynn No, I mean afterwards.

C. Okay, then finally, I got to the point where I saw Bill was not going to wake up. He was definitely having problems...and Ira all along is appearing to be on my side with all this. She is my friend. She is my confidante. She speaks about Bill and says how wrong he is, but we'll pray for him.

Lynn Okay, you said Ira and Candy, you took them with you?

C. I took them and made the accusations to Bill.

Lynn Was it just Ira and Candy?

C. Yes.

Steve Was Wendell aware?

C. Wendell didn't find out about all this until Tuesday night.

Lynn He found out about the encounters, Wendell did?

C. Yes, Tuesday night he did. (On 2 March 1993), I went through everything that had happened.

Lynn Tuesday night you brought all this stuff up?

C. Yes.

Lynn And what caused all the ruckus?

C.   Yes. Well, Sunday was the beginning of God intervening—

Lynn   Well, what did Candy say about this, when you went forward?

C.   She didn't agree with the sexual encounters, she just agreed that there was sin that people needed to repent of, and that's why she was willing to go with me that night.

Lynn   And *forgive* him?

C.   Yes. To forgive him. But if you only knew, he has already committed the *unforgivable* sin! He has *blasphemed* the Holy Spirit! He has turned the grace of our Lord God into lasciviousness and *despicable acts!* He is *not* going to be forgiven! He is going to *Hell!*

He does not have a chance to repent! He has gone through his chances of repentance! He will go to Hell! And he wants to take anybody that will be willing to go with him! Through deception! Through lies! Through any means! That is what is going on here. And that is why only God can stop this.

I know you are very concerned—

Lynn   Candy does not see this?

C.   No, she doesn't! She does not see this yet. She is going to have a chance to hear the words God wants her to hear. The blinders will be removed at that point. God, like His Word has said, [His] disciples will have the authority to bind and loose things—things that are bound in Heaven, and things that are loosed in Heaven. They have that authority.

The thing about God's Word, if you doubt it, it's not going to help you. I am at the point where I have been through so many things that I don't doubt God's Word. He has strengthened me in this, because I went through all these temptations.

It's not to say that I am anybody more important, but God will anoint me to speak to her, and the blinders will be removed for her to see the truth. It will be able to go into her heart, and she will hear the truth, and she will either accept it or reject it. And if she rejects it, she's going to go to Hell with them!

Lynn   The thing right now that we're so concerned with—right now we have got to get to the point—

C.   Yes, so you take this tape.

There Is Still Time

Lynn Just in case it didn't copy earlier for some reason, just say again why you feel they are in danger.

C. The reason why I feel, and I sense in my heart—and [some of] these are things that I have not ever experienced, so this is pretty much just things that I feel that God has told me.

Lynn And things that have happened to you.

C. Well, just the sexual encounters are things that have happened to me, the sexual encounters I have seen other people in. Those are the only things that I can actually say that I have seen. Now I know, just because of the spell that they had on me, because of the ways that they were able to take something right out of my mind when I was talking, I know that they can cast spells on you. I know that, because it happened to me. I know they can put thoughts in your head. So people who do that kind of junk... when you are really heavy into worshipping Satan, you start doing all these things.

Lynn So you are saying if Rebecca really stays in this, that they are being exposed to this?

C. They are in danger of—see, right now, I have not been in contact with these people since Tuesday night, since I kicked them out of my house. And I did!

Lynn You asked them to leave?

C. I told them they will not— [My husband and I were both talking.]

Lynn And what did they say when you told them this?

C. They were trying to—

H. They wanted to know what they could do to convince her, convince us, that they had changed.

C. They were empty words.

H. Yeah. What they could do to get back in our graces. He started out—she went through the whole thing, all the accusations. Bill denied everything that she was accusing him of. I forget the question exactly.

C. Oh, yeah. I think I asked him if he denied any of this.

H. Right. That's it. He was sitting down. He got up. He was nervous. He was pacing around. And then he sat down. And he's,

	like, he's fixing to say no. And he said, "Yes. You know, yes. Everything you said is true."
Lynn	He admitted everything was true? That you accused him of?
H.	Yeah, right.
C.	The sexual things, *even with Kim*.
H.	Right.
Lynn	And he admitted to the sexual things with Kim?
H.	Yes. And then he looks at [my wife] and goes, "C., I'm sorry for all the things I've done to you." Then he looks at me and says, "I'm sorry for—" What did he say?
C.	I think defraud you.
H.	And [he] says, "Candy, I'm sorry for all the things I've done to you and your family."
C.	Then she jumps up and says, "I forgive you." I didn't say *a word*.
Lynn	So she forgave him for all that he's done?
C.	And she brought up the Scripture to me. She said, "C., if you cannot forgive your brother, God cannot forgive you."
	That's perverting the Scriptures!
H.	Bill turned to Ira and asked forgiveness of her, and of course, she says, "You haven't defrauded me."
C.	That wasn't the story *yesterday!* She always used to say how disgusted she was with Bill.
H.	Right. So Bill admitted to everything C. accused him of.
Lynn	But you did not actually get this on tape?
H.	No. What you heard is all that we had on tape.
C.	And Ira, in the beginning, said that we are going to use this for the world. And I am not using it for the world. I am using it for God's people. I want them to know the truth. I want them to hear it, so that they can be aware.
Lynn	Well, see, we are not aware that these things really are going on. We know that they go on, but you don't think that it is going to affect your family or your loved ones.
H.	No. Not at all.

THERE IS STILL TIME

C.   It can, though. That's what is so serious about it. And it has happened with you.

Lynn   I guess what concerns me is he up and says it's okay, and then he denies it. And now he turns back and acknowledges it, like when he thinks he's lost you.

H.   Once confronted, it seems like, from what she had told me, when she would go to him…he denied everything, but Ira came back to her at a later date and admitted that Bill had admitted to her that it had happened. Of course, he would never admit to C. that it happened. It was always that it didn't happen when he was confronted.[108]

Even there Tuesday night, he was denying it until he realized that after C. said, "We are not like-minded in this. I do not agree. We are not in agreement. You people are going to have to go. Take your stuff and no more." And that's when he came across and said, "What can I…." And went into the thing about admitting to everything.

Lynn   When you say admitted, will you say what he admitted to?

C.   All he admitted to were the sexual encounters with me. Sexual encounters with Kim. He just said, "Whatever I've done to you, Candy, I'm sorry. Ira, the way I've defrauded you." And Ira was so adamant and said, "You haven't defrauded me."

Lynn   He said Candy and family. Right?

H.   Right.

Lynn   Whatever he's done, he's done to the family, also?

H.   Right.

C.   Yeah.

Lynn   Well, is there any way we could find out what he's done to Rebecca?

(Everybody was talking at once)

C.   If you could get her away—

H.   I don't know if there is anything there, but I do know that she had a change a couple of weeks ago.

C.   It's possible that if you get her away, I could talk to her.

Lynn   But you did see an actual change in her life after Candy let—

Ron	Do you think it was sexual or spiritual?
H.	I would love to think it was spiritual—
Lynn	The change in Rebecca, do you think it was sexual or spiritual?
C.	Probably both. But the spiritual is what truly matters here.
Ron	I think the best thing to do is get Rebecca and let Katie get her off—
Lynn	We cannot talk to anybody right now.
C.	No, you can't. They don't need to know that I have come to you today. They don't need to know that you know as much as you do.
Lynn	She's a child. She's having to live in this house.
C.	There is nothing that's going to break that. Like I said, if you go the way God has said to go, you will get that little girl out of there.
	This has been a very painful situation for everyone concerned, but if you can be a little patient and longsuffering. Just rest and relax and know that God is in charge.
	You know, even through all this, looking back, here I am walking with this man. And you know, this is when I am looking back, sitting in my living room, imagining him sitting there on my fireplace hearth, thinking I have actually had a man that was serving Satan sitting in my house. And then I think about—

(The tape ran out)

{End of letter to Wendell and Candy}

BY DIRECTION OF THE LORD, I have not yet sent this letter to Wendell and Candy. Most likely the only way they will be able to read this is if they obtain a copy when it's a matter of public record. Regardless of how God chooses to get His message out, I have learned that if I wait on the Lord and trust Him completely, He most certainly will work out all of the details in order for His will to be accomplished in His perfect timing—which is truly all that matters.

There Is Still Time

You can see, from my experience of walking with the enemy, what can happen when your trust is in something other than God. You will never truly understand the things of God *and* the tactics of the Devil unless your complete trust and faith is in the Lord God above and His Word.

If you depend on your own knowledge or the knowledge of others, you are extremely limited in your ability to discern truth from error. And it is so important to be found standing on the side of truth at the return of the Lord Jesus Christ.

No matter how convinced you are that you're walking in the truth, just because you believe it, doesn't make it truth. Just because you have it all figured out, doesn't make it truth. And only the Holy Spirit of the Lord God Almighty can lead and guide you into the truth that will prevail.

If the Holy Spirit has revealed to you that you are not walking in the truth, or if God has convinced you that you need to be born again, please heed the call! I hope you won't allow pride or humiliation to cause you not to submit yourself to the Lord God Almighty. There is still time, but please hurry before They close the door. This may be your last chance!

I have to say, if you dismiss God's voice and disregard the prophecies within this "little book," you will deeply regret that decision on the Great and Dreadful Day of the LORD.

Malachi 4:5–6 "Behold, I will send you Elijah the prophet before the coming of the Great and Dreadful Day of the LORD: And He shall turn the heart of the fathers to the children, and the heart of the children to their fathers, lest I come and smite the earth with a curse."

Your Name shall be praised in the mighty gates of Zion!

chapter six

Shining Light on the Darkness

> "Then Jesus said unto them,
> Yet a little while is the light with you.
> Walk while ye have the light, lest darkness
> come upon you: for he that walketh in darkness
> knoweth not whither he goeth."
> John 12:35

God had me deliver the following letter to Candy's workplace so that I could be certain she received it. I had hoped that the remaining members of the Bible study group would finally wake up and see the truth, but as far as I know, they are still walking with the enemy in darkness.

21 February 1994

Dear Ira and Candy,

It's been almost a year since the night we broke up, and I feel the Lord is leading me to write one final letter to you. I have written separate letters to both of you that you have not received as of yet, but I'll have them delivered to you when and if the Lord directs me.

After Bill's letter, I am sure you're not really eager to receive another one from me, especially since it was so long. And because I consider the time I spent with Bill's ministry as a type of wilderness experience, it was very significant for me that the original letter ended up being forty pages long.

I don't know if you realized it, but the Lord arranged for Bill to receive that letter on 24 September 1993, which was the eve of Yom Kippur. Since you both claim to be Jewish, you must realize the importance of this Jewish holiday. Not until after the fact did I realize that this Day of Atonement is the holiest of all Biblical holy days, which gives men the final opportunity to repent and seek forgiveness for their sins.

Because the purpose of my letter was to persuade Bill, and whoever else might read it, to see the error of his ways and to repent before it was too late, it was very fitting that he would receive it on this particular day. And I attribute it completely to the Lord God. Praise His blessed Holy Name!

Every letter I have written to you was under the inspiration and direction of the Lord God Almighty. And I don't make that statement lightly. It's quite a responsibility, plus a tremendous honor to be entrusted with His Word.

Because the Lord has given me more of an understanding concerning how Satan works, I know you may not even realize that you are the one that's walking with the enemy. And if you love your sin, and do not have a sincere love for the truth, God will send you a strong delusion to believe the lies.

This Scripture will help establish what I am saying.

2 Thessalonians 2:8–12 "And then shall that Wicked be revealed, whom the Lord shall consume with the spirit of His mouth, and shall destroy with the brightness of His coming: [Even Him], whose coming is after the working of Satan with all power and signs and

Shining Light on the Darkness

lying wonders, and with all deceivableness of unrighteousness in them that perish; because they received not the love of the truth, that they [might] be saved.

And for this cause God shall send them strong delusion, that they should believe a lie: That they all [might] be damned who believed not the truth, but had pleasure in unrighteousness."[109]

I hope this makes you realize just how important it is to walk in truth. The Lord God is certainly no respecter of persons, and regardless of who you are and what your profession is, you will be held accountable as to what you do with His truth.

As you should well know, the only way to the truth is through Jesus Christ, who is the Anointed One that God sent to reveal that truth. And because He was obedient to the will of God, all men will be without excuse when they stand before Him on that Day.

In regard to Jesus being the only way to the truth, I would like to reference this passage of Scripture where Peter had just healed a man in the name of Jesus Christ of Nazareth, and because of this sermon, many believed.

Acts 3:13–26 "The God of Abraham, and of Isaac, and of Jacob, the God of our fathers, hath glorified His Son Jesus; Whom ye delivered up, and denied Him in the presence of Pilate, when he was determined to let [Him] go.

But ye denied the Holy One and the Just, and desired a murderer to be granted unto you; and killed the Prince of life, Whom God hath raised from the dead; whereof we are witnesses.

And His name through faith in His name hath made this man strong, whom ye see and know: yea, the faith which is by Him hath given him this perfect soundness in the presence of you all.

And now, brethren, I wot (or know) that through ignorance ye did [it], as [did] also your rulers. But those things, which God before had shewed by the mouth of all His prophets, that Christ should suffer, He hath so fulfilled.

Repent ye therefore, and be converted, that your sins may be blotted out, when the times of refreshing shall come from the presence of the Lord; and He shall send Jesus Christ, which before was preached unto you: Whom the Heaven must receive until the times of restitution of all things, which God hath spoken by the mouth of all His holy prophets since the world began.

For Moses truly said unto the fathers, A prophet shall the Lord your God raise up unto you of your brethren, like unto me; Him shall ye hear in all things whatsoever He shall say unto you.

And it shall come to pass, [that] every soul, which will not hear that prophet, shall be destroyed from among the people. Yea, and all the prophets from Samuel and those that follow after, as many as have spoken, have likewise foretold of these days.

Ye are the children of the prophets, and of the covenant which God made with our fathers, saying unto Abraham, And in thy seed shall all the kindreds of the earth be blessed. Unto you first God, having raised up His Son Jesus, sent Him to bless you, in turning away every one of you from his iniquities."

I hope you realize that the purpose behind my correspondences is to persuade those of you that are headed for destruction to repent of your own sin and believe the truth, so that you may be saved from eternal death.

I don't know what is going on in your personal lives, but it would seem that you are no longer recognized as a viable church by the editor of the local newspaper, since they no longer allow your "church" listing.

And it seems that many who were with you while I was a member are no longer standing with you in support of your ministry. I would think all of this would cause you to look at

Shining Light on the Darkness

your life and question your beliefs, especially in light of what was spoken to all of us on the night of 28 February 1993.

I still have hope, though. And I realize it's possible that God could have allowed our blindness to continue for a time, so as to have His will accomplished, especially since that's exactly what He did with the nation of Israel in regard to the Lord Jesus Christ being the Messiah.[110]

This nation is under God's judgment, due to the acceptance of other gods! And He is in the process of revealing the darkness so as to give His people an opportunity to stand apart from the lies and deceptions of the Devil.

As you read the following Scriptures, notice what God did when they tried to put other gods before Him, and know that it wasn't God's people that did it, but they were completely responsible for what happened. Due to their attempts to manipulate God and His power, many were destroyed. I encourage you to go back and read the entire story of how this came to be.

1 Samuel 5:1–6 "And the Philistines took the ark of God, and brought it from Eben-ezer unto Ashdod. When the Philistines took the ark of God, they brought it into the house of Dagon, and set it by Dagon.

And when they of Ashdod arose early on the morrow, behold, Dagon [was] fallen upon his face to the earth before the ark of the LORD. And they took Dagon, and set him in his place again.

And when they arose early on the morrow morning, behold, Dagon [was] fallen upon his face to the ground before the ark of the LORD; and the head of Dagon and both the palms of his hands [were] cut off upon the threshold; only [the stump of] Dagon was left to him.

Therefore neither the priests of Dagon, nor any that come into Dagon's house, tread on the threshold of Dagon in Ashdod unto this day.

But the hand of the LORD was heavy upon them of Ashdod, and He destroyed them, and smote them with emerods (or tumors), [even] Ashdod and the coast thereof."

It's obvious that the Lord God is all-powerful, and other gods cannot stand in His presence. One day, God will destroy all other gods / idols, but until then, it's so important to be found standing on the side of the Most High God.

The following will show how far America has gotten off the intended path, by compromising the truth and acknowledging the worship of other gods, despite the fact that this nation claims to be "one nation under God."

EXCERPT FROM *THE HORNBLOWER* / NOVEMBER 1993 [111]

The National Council of Girl Scouts of the USA, in the meeting assembled in Minneapolis, Minnesota, 22–25 October 1993, took the following action:

Proposal #3: Flexibility in wording for spiritual beliefs in the Girl Scout Promise.

Motion: That, since the Girl Scout organization makes no attempt to interpret or define the word "God" but encourages members to establish for themselves the nature of their spiritual beliefs, it be the policy of GSUSA that individuals when making the Girl Scout Promise may substitute wording appropriate to their own spiritual beliefs for the word "God."

Action: Proposal #3 adopted.

{End of excerpt from The Hornblower*}*

It was very hard for me to believe that the Girl Scouts of the United States of America would actually endorse the acceptance of other gods, but it has become even more apparent

Shining Light on the Darkness

to me, especially since I've left Bill's ministry, that the subtle tactics of the enemy are at work in every facet of our society.

For the Girl Scouts of America to pledge they will serve "God and country" while acknowledging and accepting the worship of other gods is a contradiction in terms and completely against the very precepts that this nation was founded upon. These United States will not stand if this practice is allowed to continue.

The question before us all: Are we going to serve the Lord God above with our whole heart, soul, and mind, or will we allow other gods to be a part of our life? And based on our personal decisions, it will determine what kind of relationship we will have with God and where we will spend eternity.

My hope in sharing this with you is that you will understand how turning away from the One, True, and Living God can enable this sort of evil to become very prevalent in our society and way of thinking.

[I would like to note, that because of the Girl Scouts decision to acknowledge other "gods" as an acceptable practice, my husband and I decided not to allow our daughter to continue to be a member of this organization. And I praise God that she was in complete agreement with our decision.]

One thing I can say with certainty, with which I think you will agree: One day, every man will bow their knee to the Lord God Jehovah and acknowledge that Jesus Christ is Lord, all to the glory of God!

God *will* deliver His people, who truly love Him, from all that is evil one day, and then truth, justice, and mercy will prevail.

Ever since the Lord exposed Bill's ministry, He has been showing me where He's been exposing the lies and deceptions in other places—even at the highest level!

I would like to share an excerpt from the radio interview whereby I became aware of this particular matter. The date is very significant because it was the exact date a year ago that the Lord God gave me that enlightening prophecy.

The topic they spoke of was very fascinating in light of all that the Lord has been revealing. This issue has enabled congressmen to be very secretive about what they truly support, but in public stand for something different.[112]

Guest Speaker: Congressman Inhofe from Oklahoma
27 August 1993

Host   C. Read joins us. Thanks for calling.

C.   Well, thank you. I'm kind of nervous.

Host   That's all right. Don't be nervous. It's just the four of us.

C.   Well, I just want to make a comment, and then a question. When I heard you talking about this, this morning, such an excitement came over me because it's so important to walk in truth, and that's one thing I've come to realize.

And I really see the Lord starting to open things where darkness is no longer able to operate without being exposed. And I see this bill as doing that.

Host   Shining light on the darkness. You're exactly right!

C.   And I just want to encourage you to not back off, because this is something that is so important. And it'll hold people accountable for the decisions they make in their lives that affect us and our country.

I'd like to ask you, Congressman, what is it that voters can actually do that will really make an impact on their representatives?

Guest   That's the whole reason for being on these talk shows. I mentioned, C., that this is my forty-fifth one in two weeks. What you can do is the list that [was] read…those individuals that signed discharge petition number two, they all know which one it is, you don't have to identify it to thank them for having the courage to stand up against the elitist leadership of Congress. It took courage to do it.

Specifically, what you can do, C., and all the rest of the listeners, is call the people that are not on this discharge petition and encourage them to get on.

Host I think you believe in prayer, don't you, Congressman?

Guest I think your listeners might be happy to know that there are two strong Christian groups in Congress. One is the House Prayer Breakfast, which is a very large group. We have a prayer breakfast every Thursday morning, and I am the president-elect of that group.

Host Good!

Guest The other group is the Christian Embassy, which is an off-shoot of Bill Bright's operation. And we have a Bible study at one o'clock in the chapel in the Rotunda of the Capitol every Thursday. So there is, uh, Christ is in Washington, despite what some people might think.

Co-host There are probably some things happening that the Lord is doing that we will someday know about.

{End of excerpt from the interview}

I took Congressman Inhofe's advice, and I wrote a letter to the congressmen from my state. I received a response from most of them, but many times what they wrote to me did not match up with their final vote.

I have learned that it is not only important to pay attention to what men say, but their actions as well. And only through the Spirit of God can we truly discern whether we are listening to the spirit of truth or the spirit of error.

If you wonder why I have shared all of this with you, suffice it to say that if you are truly on God's side, you should be very concerned with how our government operates. And if you're not, it's time to consider whose side you are on. Please notice what God's Word says about it.

Walking with the Enemy

Zechariah 3:7 "Thus saith the LORD of hosts; If thou wilt walk in My ways, and if thou wilt keep My charge, then thou shalt also judge My house, and shalt also keep My courts, and I will give thee places to walk among these that stand by."

1 Corinthians 6:2–3 "Do ye not know that the saints shall judge the world? And if the world shall be judged by you, are ye unworthy to judge the smallest matters? Know ye not that we shall judge angels? How much more things that pertain to this life?"

Jesus Christ won the victory! And it's time for the body of Christ to stand up in the power and might of the Holy Spirit and denounce the hidden things of darkness. Truth will prevail! And it is so important to be found standing on the side of the Most High God and the Lord Jesus Christ on that Day!

I take no pleasure in the thought of you or any other man burning in Hell for eternity, and I believe the hardest thing for me to accept is how you could choose death over life. It still saddens me that things have turned out the way they have between us, because I really felt like we would be friends forever.

If God ever reveals to me that you have come to Him with a sincere and repentant heart, and have turned from all the wickedness that you have become a part of and have decided to follow Him with your whole heart, soul, and mind, you will always have a friend in me if you ever need one.

Sincerely,
A servant of the Most High God,

C. Read

As signed by me in the presence of a witness on
the 28th Day of February in the year of our Lord,
One Thousand Nine Hundred and Ninety-Four.

chapter seven

Then It Will Be Too Late

"And death and Hell were cast into the Lake of Fire. This is the second death. And whosoever was not found written in the Book of Life was cast into the Lake of Fire."

Revelation 20:14–15

THE FOLLOWING LETTER WILL FURTHER PROVE that the Lord God Almighty will use whatever the Devil intends for evil and turn it around for the good of those who love God and are the called according to His purpose.

8 March 1994

Dear Ira,

I was a little presumptuous about that being my final letter to you, and after receiving the article entitled "The Holy Spirit Versus Demon Spirit Guides" in the mail, I feel led to respond. Since you didn't include your own comments (but highlighted certain sections), I can only assume you are still contending that I am the one who's being controlled by demonic spirits.[113]

I must say that, in a way, I am delighted that you would think that of me, especially since they also used to wrongfully accuse my Lord and Master of the same thing. But I am equally disappointed because it shows me that you are still walking with the enemy and completely under his control.

Ira, you have to know it would be so much easier if I'd just put all of you out of my mind and not be concerned about anything in connection with you or Bill's ministry, but the Lord has not allowed me to do that.[114]

My ultimate desire in all of this is for the truth to be made known in regard to the tactics of the enemy, so as to free God's people from the bondage of sin and Satan. And then, we the people of God can truly serve and worship Him in the manner in which He so deserves.

You probably will never openly admit that Bill's Bible study group is a cult, but I am very certain of it, especially since I was personally involved with all of you for three years. I just praise God that He didn't allow me to gain knowledge of the very depths of Satan, but just enough to know and understand many of his deceptive ways.

Even though you were secretive about many things, I was always very open and honest with you about everything. Of course, you tried to lead me to believe that I was your trusted friend so as to obtain information from me, but now it's quite apparent that you had ulterior motives.

After I joined the group, I was led to the following passage of Scripture. But Satan was always one step ahead of me in order to dissuade me from seeing the truth of the Word of God. I praise God that His truth has prevailed in my life!

2 Corinthians 11:3–4 "But I fear, lest by any means, as the serpent beguiled Eve through his subtilty, so your minds should be corrupted from the simplicity that is in Christ.

𝒯HEN IT WILL BE TOO LATE

For if he that cometh preacheth another Jesus, whom we have not preached, or [if] ye receive another spirit, which ye have not received, or another gospel, which ye have not accepted, ye might well bear with [him]."

Because of my misunderstanding and lack of knowledge, I didn't realize that just because a man claims that Jesus Christ is his Lord and Savior, and he would lay down his life for Him, doesn't mean he's referring to the only begotten Son of the Most High God.

Because of my misunderstanding and lack of knowledge, I didn't realize or even understand what it meant to receive another spirit. But due to my affiliation with Bill's ministry, I was exposed to many other spirits that were quite contrary to the Spirit of the Most High God.

Because of my misunderstanding and lack of knowledge, I didn't realize that a man could claim to be anointed by God, sent to preach and proclaim the truth, yet preach another gospel while using the Holy Bible to distort and pervert the Word of the Most High God.

Since we did not serve the same Jesus, our relationship could not remain the same after the truth was revealed during our meeting on 2 March 1993. Had I stayed with the Bible study group after that, I would have forfeited my relationship with the One, True, and Living God.

The shroud of secrecy and deception has been removed, and I now understand why many things occurred as they did. Since I've been away from Bill's ministry, the Lord has been revealing to me the many ways that Satan has control of people without them even being aware of it.

The Lord has brought to my attention the various ways that Satan is able to introduce his demonic spirits through the medium of television and motion pictures. Some seemingly innocent and wholesome programs are tainted with evil so as to acquaint children and adults alike with demonic spirits.

Just to give you an example: This past weekend, I watched a movie with my children called *Free Willy*. By all outward appearances, it was a nice little movie about a whale called Willy, certainly nothing to be alarmed about, *or so I thought*. But I should have known something was wrong due to the unusual fascination my children had for this movie, but I just dismissed it.

When I found out that one of my girls was willing to lie so as to encourage me to buy the movie in the first place, I really should have known something was wrong, but I dismissed that too.

When I discovered that a music video with (ungodly music) was at the beginning of the movie, I assumed that's why I had a problem with it, so I just had them fast-forward that part. But not until I watched the entire movie did I finally understand why I had the nagging doubts.

The scene that I was most concerned about is where the little orphan boy has learned how to repeat an incantation that he hopes will give Willy the power to jump over the wall to freedom. Of course, it worked, and Willy was free! And everybody was happy!

But the movie didn't explain, or even lead you to believe, that this occult practice of chanting can teach unsuspecting viewers how to conjure up evil spirits and prepares them to be very accepting of these demon spirit guides.

Most people don't even recognize this as something to be concerned about because their minds have been so conditioned to be accepting of this kind of evil; thus, they unwisely regard it as harmless.

But because the Lord has been giving me insight into this sort of thing, I know this subtle tactic of the enemy will enable Satan to control people's thoughts and actions by the use of these demonic spirits. Which is why this is very important to understand and to be extremely cautious of.

Because this practice is so prevalent in every aspect of our society, we have been reaping the effects of this sin in our land. It's very evident that something is terribly wrong, and it can no longer be ignored! If it is not acknowledged, the people of this nation, and the world, will continue to be distressed by this evil and wickedness.

When you hear of someone, whether a child or an adult, committing a despicable act of violence, you can be certain demonic spirits were involved. And part of the problem is that the perpetrator may have no recollection of it, nor understand how they could have committed such a terrible thing. And in many cases, the demonic spirits that they are controlled by will lead them to take their own lives after they have carried out the horrible deeds of the Devil.

[I published this in the first edition of my book in March 1995, and many of the concerns that I addressed then are even more prevalent today.]

God's people need to wake up before it's too late! The Scripture that says, "My people are destroyed for lack of knowledge" is so true, but the wonderful thing about it is that God is exposing the many evils of Satan in order to give His people the opportunity to stand apart from the wickedness of sin. (Hosea 4:6)

In fact, the main purpose behind this letter or any other letter that I've written since the Lord God Almighty delivered me from the power of darkness is to share the truth of what God has revealed to me concerning my walk with the enemy, so as to warn others.

But since you still seem to be trying to convince me that I am wrong and hopefully sway me to your way of thinking, I will take this opportunity, with the guidance of the Holy Spirit, to show you why I perceive the article that you sent me to be Satan's attempt to distract me from the truth.

I know that it would give the Devil such great pleasure if he could cause me to doubt what God has said to me, but I am finally standing on the Rock. And it's only because of the Lord Jesus Christ that I will continue to stand.

Excerpt from "Holy Spirit Versus Demon Spirit Guides"

"The Holy Spirit wants us to be in control and responsible for our own actions.... Demons want total control. They will frequently knock the person unconscious and then use them in any way they want. The Holy Spirit is gentle. When He comes into a person, He is so gentle that when you look inside yourself, you can't tell what is the Holy Spirit and what is you."

{End of excerpt from Ira's article}

The main thing that comes to my heart and mind as I read some of these statements is that of my conversion experience. I know when I finally gave my life to the Lord Jesus Christ over fourteen years ago (in November 1979), there was most definitely a change in me.

When the Holy Spirit was given to me, I knew it! There was no doubt that the Spirit of the Most High God was with me. There was an obvious change in my thoughts and actions, and since then He has been continually changing my old personality to be more like the nature of His dear Son, Jesus Christ.

I agree the Holy Spirit is very gentle, but because I have asked my Father to purify my heart, it has been an extremely painful and difficult process of realizing the sin I have walked in.

And when my old selfish nature rises up, the Holy Spirit is right there to lovingly remind me. Of course, it's my choice as to whether I am going to submit to the Lord Jesus Christ and His Word, or am I going to allow myself to give in to the desires of my old nature.

Moreover, He has never knocked me out so He could work through me. I have always been aware of what God has been doing inside my heart, although it was mixed with fear and confusion while I was with you and Bill.

The night of 28 February 1993 was a different matter altogether. It was very evident that we were in the presence of the Holy Spirit, and I could have repeated what the Lord was speaking to my heart, or I could have allowed fear and intimidation to stop me, but obviously, that was not to be.

On that night, there was such a supernatural strength about me that was completely unlike my normal personality. And like you said, with which I will agree, *there was no stopping me!* You have to admit, that was definitely a very extraordinary experience for everyone involved.

This article that you sent me is exactly what God warned us about that night in February. It is also truth mixed with lies! I'll continue with the other things you noted so that you can see why I believe this attempt to persuade me that I am wrong to be a form of subterfuge on the part of my enemy.

Excerpt from "Holy Spirit Versus Demon Spirit Guides"

"One of the most common deceptions of demon spirit guides is to give the person many false 'words of knowledge,' which is really simple divination. Demons also give many individual 'prophecies,' which is really fortune-telling. Prophecy in the Scripture is usually for the whole body of Christ, *rarely for individuals, and certainly not on a frequent basis.*"

{End of excerpt from Ira's article}

Ira, I don't even want to imply that I know everything there is to know about God and how He works, but I know He is in complete control! And He is working to have His perfect will carried out no matter what Satan or his ministers may do. Praise the Lord God Almighty!

Consider the following Scripture.

Proverbs 5:22 "His own iniquities shall take the wicked himself, and he shall be holden with the cords of his sins."

I realize if you are not able to discredit me, you will be forced to admit you have been wrong all along and have wronged many others in the process. If you ever come to this realization and are truly repentant, it could be an extremely hard thing to bear, but consider the alternative should you stand before Almighty God condemned.

You obviously do not know *my* Jesus, and the reason I can say with confidence that you don't is because if you had been able to grasp what the Son of God did for mankind, you would fall on your face and worship Him.

My Lord is the only begotten Son of the Most High God, who was sent to this earth to reveal the truth to a lost and dying world. And due to the great love that Jesus had for His Father, He obeyed Him in all things, even unto death.

And to prove that God the Father is all-powerful, He raised His Son from the grave, and death was forced to release its control over Him. And now this same Jesus sits at the right hand of the power on high in all glory and honor! Praise His blessed, Holy Name!

And because I have committed my heart, soul, mind, and body to the Lord, He has washed away my sins with His own blood. And I will forever be with my Lord and Savior Jesus Christ, the eternal King!

He is, and has always been, the true love of my life, and I will never give Him up for anything this world has to offer. And if you knew Him, you would feel the same. Unless, of course, you love the darkness more than you do the light.

2 Corinthians 13:5 "Examine yourselves, whether ye be in the faith; prove your own selves. Know ye not your own selves, how that Jesus Christ is in you, except ye be reprobates?"[115]

My humanness cannot stand the thought of you, or any other man, burning in Hell for eternity, but if you find yourself in the Lake of Fire, you'll wish you had listened to that servant my Lord Jesus put in your path while you walked this earth. But *then* it will be too late!

A servant of the Most High God,

C. Read

As signed by me in the presence of a witness on the 17th Day of March in the year of our Lord, One Thousand Nine Hundred and Ninety-Four.

*Your Kingdom
shall reign forever!
And ever!*

chapter eight

WHOSE SIDE YOU ARE ON

> "And if it seem evil unto you to serve the LORD,
> choose you this day whom ye will serve...
> But as for me and my house,
> we will serve the LORD."
> Joshua 24:15a, c

THIS TESTIMONY SOLIDIFIES ALL THE ALLEGATIONS that I made against Bill and Ira. How you respond to this compelling evidence presented here, between an attorney and former group member, will reveal who you truly believe, which in turn will determine whose side *you* are on.

THE INTERVIEW OF FORMER GROUP MEMBER
TRANSCRIPT OF 17 MAY 1993[116]

Q. Eve?

A. Yes, sir.

Q. Again, my name is [Arthur].[117] And today is May the 17th, 1993, and it's pretty close to 3:30 in the afternoon. And the purpose of my call is to take a recorded statement from you relative to your knowledge of a situation that exists, and particularly as it may affect Rebecca. Do I have your permission to take a recorded statement at this time?

A. Yes, you do.

Q. When did you last live [there]?

A. I moved permanently—I think it was the middle of February of this year.

Q. Of '93?

A. Yes, sir.

Q. That's when you left?

A. Yes.

Q. Why did you leave?

A. Oh, the problems I was having with my husband…we were going to get a divorce and—

Q. You don't need to go into details now.

A. Well, it was a personal thing with our family. And I decided to move somewhere with my son, and that's where I chose to go.

Q. Okay. Did you and your husband get a divorce?

A. No, sir.

Q. Okay. Now, what I want you to do is just tell me about your knowledge and involvement with this group that's led by Bill. Just talk to me a little bit about it.

A. Okay, um, I guess I was probably first introduced to everybody—everybody being [C.'s family], and Bill and Ira, and Tom. And the fall or winter of '89, I drove out a few times to the meetings. We moved in January '92, and maybe a couple of months before we moved out here, I started coming again. And then I would say I was a full-time—I attended Wednesday, Thursday, and Sunday.

Q. All right, now. When did you become a full-time member?

A. I would say it would have been January '92.

Q. And you left in February '93?

A. Yes, sir.

Q. Okay, so over a year, then?

A. Yeah.

Whose Side You Are On

Q. All right. During that time, did you get to know Candy and Rebecca?

A. Yes, I did.

Q. Tell me what you know about the group, and the activities of the group, and what occurred while you were a member.

A. Well, on the surface, it appeared to be just a fellowship of people with a common faith in God and who loved the Lord. And we all just wanted to hear more and get closer and know Jesus better. And it was nice having the camaraderie, the likeness of people with the same faith. And we were encouraged not to have unbelieving friends.

Q. Is an unbeliever a non-Christian or just a non-member of the group? In other words, I am a member of the Methodist church. Would I, based on what you're talking about, would I be considered a nonbeliever, or an unbeliever?

A. Well, they would probably ask me if you believe in Jesus, and if you said yes, then they would probably just ask what kinds of things would we talk about and what kind of things would we do. And they would just warn us to be careful of who we associated with outside the group.

Q. Okay. Basically, they would want you to spend all your time with group members?

A. They would prefer that. Yes.

Q. What were some of the activities that you participated in as a group member?

A. The worship services that were here at [C.'s] house. I did attend a couple of the ones that were at [Ira's] house.

Q. Can you describe to me what went on at those meetings, in general terms?

A. In general terms, uh, we would gather, and there would be iced tea and refreshments. And we would have small talk, and then a Bible study session, and then small talk afterwards.

And we would sing for about twenty to thirty minutes before we had Bible study. And then, when it came to C.'s house, they also started having dinner, at least on Wednesday and Thursday.

Q. Did you also socialize together at times other than the meetings?

A. I spent quite a bit of—you mean on the days of the meeting, or at other times?

Q. At other times.

A. Well, during this last year, I spent an awful lot of time with Candy because I wasn't working. She was out of work with her knee—

Q. Were you and Candy friends?

A. Yes.

Q. Are you still friends?

A. Well, I've spoken to her since I've moved. But when, after the incident that initiated the breakup of C. from the group, um, it just came to me to call C., and I did. And so the next day after it happened—

Q. All right, what incident are you talking about that caused C. to leave the group?

A. Um, I don't know what the date was, but when—

Q. But what was it?

A. At a prayer meeting, at a Bible study meeting, uh, the Holy Spirit had some words for Bill, which she spoke, and um—

Q. Was that the confrontation meeting?

A. The confrontation was a couple days later, I believe.

Q. Okay, yes, I know. So in other words, basically in my language, ah, when C. got on to him about what he was doing was when they pretty much forced her from the group?

A. Right.

Q. Okay. And so then you contacted—

A. I called C. the Wednesday after the confrontation, and I said, "I don't know why I'm calling you, but I—" Because generally, I don't like to call C. because she likes to talk a long time. And it cost too much money. [She started laughing.]

Q. And I understand.

A. She's a talker, now.

Q. I know, C. and I have engaged in several conversations.

Whose Side You Are On

A. But I said, "No, I have to talk to C." So I called her, and she said, "Why did you call, Eve?" And I said, "Well, something just urged me to call." She proceeded to tell me everything that had happened. And then, after that time, I did call Candy once. And I called her for the purpose of getting back a vacuum cleaner that I had loaned her.

Q. Okay.

A. And I told her that I loved her, but I really didn't want to talk about anything that had happened in the group because I knew that she would try to tell me that C. is crazy.

Q. Okay.

A. And I—C. is driven, but she's *not* crazy.

Q. All right. Now let me ask you a couple of things about what you brought up so far.

A. Okay.

Q. Do you have any personal knowledge of any of the sexual activity that went on in the group while you were a member?

A. I did not know about C.

Q. All right, tell me what you do know about.

A. The only thing that I do know about is an obvious, uh, relationship between Ira and Bill.

Q. Now how do you know about that?

A. Just the way they act toward one another. I've never seen any sex…but they treat one another as husband and wife.

Q. Well, now explain to me what you mean by that.

A. They embrace. They kiss. They—

Q. When they kiss, is it a kiss on the lips?

A. Oh yes, sir.

Q. In other words, what's a better word—

A. Intimate.

Q. A real sexual-type kiss?

A. Well, something that is reserved only for a husband and wife.

Q. I know, but—

A. Well, I don't believe I've ever seen any passionate kissing.

Q. Okay. All right.

A. But I would still describe it as a husband and wife type of an embrace.

Q. Have you seen, and I apologize for being so explicit, but any fondling of any kind between the two of them?

A. No.

Q. I guess what I'm saying…in a lot of religious groups, the friendship hug is something that is very traditional.

A. Yes, sir.

Q. And even a kiss on the cheek is a Christian greeting.

A. Yes, sir.

Q. Are you saying that what you have seen on more than one occasion, between these two people, is more than that sort of hugging and kissing?

A. Yes, sir.

Q. Okay. And have they done this in the presence of the children, *specifically* Rebecca?

A. I don't know. For a time, they didn't seem to show that much emotion for each other, but toward the last six, seven, eight months, they didn't seem like they were trying to hide anything at all. But in the beginning, they wouldn't do even much around me.

Q. Did they do this in front of Tom?

A. Oh, *yes*.

Q. Do you have knowledge that they sleep together, ah, in Tom's house?

A. Um, you mean by admission of either of the two parties?

Q. That's sufficient.

A. Well, um, the only conversation and admission of any kind was maybe after Ira and Bill had gone to—they went on a vacation together.

Q. Just the two of them?

A. Yes. When she came back, she was very upset because she thought she was pregnant.

Q. And she told you that?

Whose Side You Are On

A. Yeah. She went out and bought a pregnancy test.

Q. And she told you that? And told you she had—that she was afraid Bill was the father?

A. She didn't mention his name, but that was the person that she was with.

Q. Okay.

A. She wouldn't come out and admit it to me. She never did.

Q. All right, have you witnessed any French kissing with Bill and any of the male members?

A. No, sir.

Q. Okay. Have you witnessed any inappropriate physical contact by Bill, or any of the other members of the group, and any of the children?

A. No, I can't say that I've ever seen him, uh—

Q. And one of the children in particular that I'm talking about, who I consider a child, is Kim.

A. Um, well, I, you know, she was drawn to him when she first came. She wanted to spend time and be close to him. And I have seen him, you know, with his arms around her.

Q. Are you aware that they had sexual relations?

A. Only by hearsay.

Q. By hearsay, would it have been from Kim or Candy? Either one of them ever tell you?

A. No.

Q. Only from C.? [There was a delay in her response.] *Or from anybody else?*

A. *Well*, I have a stepdaughter. And she lived with us for a period of time. She is Kim's age. She went to high school, and she palled around with Kim. As a matter of fact, she is the reason that Kim was introduced to the group.

Q. Okay.

A. She told her friends that he tried—he put his hands down her pants and kissed her.

Q. Kim?

A. Yes.

Q. Okay.

A. But she never told me that. She was telling her friends, her peers, this. Something Kim had told her, and it got back to me.

Q. Okay, now do you know when this—

A. It had to have happened within the first month to two months after she joined the group.

Q. All right, was this while she was being hidden out? Or was this—

A. Prior.

Q. Do you know where it occurred? This was while she was living with Candy, correct?

A. I don't know where it was supposed to have taken place. I would assume it would have taken place either at Candy's or at Bill's, but I believe it was before she came to live at Candy's.

Q. When she was still kind of babysitting?

A. Yeah, I believe so.

Q. Okay.

A. Because they really didn't have all that much to do with one another after Kim went to live in [another city].

Q. Okay.

A. Or wherever she went to live. I was never told where she went.

Q. So the only—is that the only knowledge you have of any sexual activity by Bill, with Ira and Kim? Are there any others? I know about C., but are there any others?

A. He was inappropriately—uh, he would try things with me, but I really wouldn't have anything to do with it.

Q. All right, can you explain? And I apologize again.

A. That's all right. That's all right.

Q. But what would he try with you?

A. Sometimes, he would share something with you that got you really emotionally going, and you would cry, and then he would put his arms around you and comfort you. And it was like—it wasn't like *he* was comforting you. You really felt that the Lord was comforting you. But then he would take advantage of the situation and try to kiss you on the mouth and stuff like that, but I would always turn my head because that didn't seem appropriate to me. And I just said, "Well, he's just, he's just a sensual person, and he gets carried away, but I'm not going to participate in that."

Q. Would he also attempt to touch you in inappropriate places?

A. No.

Q. So really it was just the kissing part?

A. Yep.

Q. All right. Ah, now—so you never had any type of a relationship with him?

A. No.

Q. Again, I apologize. Did you have any other relationship with any other member of the group?

A. No, sir.

Q. Okay. The cause of your possible divorce with your husband had nothing to do with your involvement with the group?

A. Oh, I believe it had everything to do with the group.

Q. All right. Well, explain that to me so I can understand.

A. Well, when we moved out [there], um, I spent more and more time with the group. And my husband spent more and more time—he's a hunter and a fisherman. And possibly, we had problems, but they were just completely made worse by the situation.

Bill and Ira, non-directly, they never did anything directly, but they would put, you know, they would suggest things. That I didn't need the man, and he was no good for me, and he was a terrible influence on my son, and that I would be much better off to raise my son by myself, with their help, with the help of the church. And God really had a plan for my life. And didn't I feel better here anyway? And they would take care of me. And hadn't they pulled through for me before?

Q. Is that the emotional type of experiences that you would be going through when he would attempt to kiss you on the mouth? Is that the type of thing that he'd be doing?

A. No.

Q. Okay. All right. Did anybody else witness him attempting to kiss you?
A. Possibly.
Q. Such as?
A. Probably C.
Q. Okay. Any children?
A. No, generally, something like that would probably have happened after we prayed or at the culmination of Bible study, and by then, the children would have been in bed.
Q. As you know, this is a rough type of thing to be involved in, as far as a child custody battle. Because all we're interested in is Rebecca being in an environment where she can grow up and learn to love the Lord in her own way, without being influenced in anything happening to her, such as happened to Kim or anything like that.
A. Right.
Q. While it is on my mind, did he ever make any advances toward your stepdaughter? Bill? Or any other member of the group?
A. I don't know what he did with her. I know he kissed her. To what extent, she never told me.
Q. Do you think she would be willing to talk about this if she had to, or is this too emotional for her?
A. Oh, I'm sure she'd probably be willing to talk about it.
Q. Now talk to me a little about your relationship with Candy, because what I need to know—any testimony that, you know, that would lend itself to show that she was not caring for Rebecca as she should. Such as any type of sexual activity she may have had that would be improper. Improper or maybe like neglect of Rebecca by leaving her alone or unattended, unsupervised, those type of things. Tell me what you know about that.
A. I think Candy really thought she was doing the best for Rebecca. I knew of no, uh—from the time I met Candy, she wasn't, she didn't have an involvement with any man that I knew of. So as far as Rebecca witnessing something like that, I have no idea.

As far as neglect, the only type of neglect would have been what Ira used to do, always be on the telephone with her. Candy was always on the telephone either to C. or to Ira. And it wasn't so much that she wasn't there, but they monopolized a lot of her time that she could have spent with her child.

Q. Are you not aware of any boyfriends, or men friends, that Candy had spend the night at the home?

A. No.

Q. You're not aware of any of the physical or sexual encounters that Candy had with Bill?

A. No.

Q. You're not aware that she was disrobed on at least one occasion?

A. She never discussed it with me.

Q. Okay. All the time that you were friends, she never discussed that with you?

A. Never.

Q. Is there anything that you can tell me?

A. We did discuss at one point that—because I'd constantly ask C. and Candy, I said, "How could...?" You know, I would always question the household that lived together. How could they be believable if they lived that way? And they would always say, "Well, you just have to trust God."

And we did talk about the time, about the way Bill, the way he kissed. It was more sensual than just brotherly. And she said, "Well, yeah, he does that, but that's just Bill." As far as her offering any information, it never went any further than that.

Q. What do you think? I mean as far as Rebecca. Is she being taken care of in a suitable manner by Candy?

A. I think Candy means well. I don't believe Candy fully understands what influence that group has on her. I don't think she's intentionally neglectful or anything.

Q. What influence is that group having on Rebecca?

A. Well, I would say in some respects it has a good influence because she did make a commitment to the Lord. I haven't seen her since her mother called to tell me that. It was after I moved. She was all excited. She said her daughter made a commitment to the Lord and it was great, because she was kind of a rebellious girl—spoiled.

No more spoiled than my son, who is five. Of course, now Ira and I had a lot of discussions about that. She didn't agree with the way I was raising my son. We butted heads a lot about that.

Q. Do you see any bad influences of this group on Rebecca? Do you feel like Rebecca is in any danger and needs to be removed from this group?

(The tape ran out)

{End of 17 May 1993 transcript}

I DID NOT GET THE END OF THIS CONVERSATION, nor do I remember her response to that question, but apparently, the Lord wanted her removed from that group, since the judge granted full custody of this little child to her father.[118]

Unfortunately, Eve did not seem to understand the demonic nature of the "spirit" that Bill and Ira belong to. And I just pray that God will open her eyes to truly see whose side *they* are on!

chapter nine

Christ or Antichrist

> "Now the Spirit speaketh expressly, that
> in the latter times some shall depart from the faith,
> giving heed to seducing spirits, and doctrines of devils."
>
> 1 Timothy 4:1

THIS IS MY LAST CONVERSATION with Bill, and he actually validates everything that I said against him. It still saddens me that we do not serve the same God, and because I am very certain that he is of the spirit of antichrist, I will never walk with him again!

EXCERPTS OF CONVERSATION BETWEEN C. READ AND BILL
SUNDAY / 2 MARCH 1997

C. The last time I called you, my husband was home, and that's why I let him listen in on the phone, because he needs to be aware of whenever I talk to you all. He's asked me not to have contact with you unless he knows about it. And I am recording our conversation so he can listen later, if that's okay with you? If you'd rather I didn't—

Bill It's fine with me.

C. I am concerned about some of the things that [Ira] wrote in the letter [she had sent me last week]. Mainly, I guess, about you. She was saying that you had said that you're finally getting through this and recognizing that the things that you did were sins against God? Is that right?

Bill *C., my whole life is a sin against God!* That's the way I look at it. I don't see any good that I've done. I don't see any blessing that I brought to anybody. And I don't see any good thing that I've done at all. I wrote somebody a letter a couple years ago, and I told him, "All I was, was death." And you can record that. I don't care. Because that's about the way I feel.[119]

C. Do you not believe that it was the Devil leading you, though?

Bill No, it wasn't the Devil leading me. There's a big difference in being deceived into doing something that you think is right—

C. I mean, if you're in a deception, you know, he could be the one doing it.

Bill You got the Word right there before you. What the Word says is very plain. It's very clear. God doesn't hide it. He makes it very, very plain for us to see it. Very, very plain for us to follow it. Doesn't make it easy to do it. But it's there.

C. Well, how come you don't think it was the Devil? I mean, he's the Deceiver!

Bill If you think for one minute that I'm going to put responsibility for my sins off on anybody else, or even a devil, the Devil, Satan, Lucifer, or the angels of deception, or anything like that, then I'm not going to stand before God and say, "Oh God, it was, you know, the Devil made me do it." That's not what this is all about. What this is all about is being accountable for your own actions.

C. That's true.

Bill And what my actions were, I'm accountable for them. It doesn't have anything to do with deception or—

C. So you weren't deceived, then? Is that what you are saying?

Bill No, I wasn't deceived.

C. Oh, so you just knew full outright what you were doing? And it wasn't a deception?

Bill Well—

C. I mean, that's what I am trying to understand.

Bill Well, what I am saying to you, I didn't follow the Word, okay? As misguided as I may have been, and misled—

C. Well, you used the Word to justify everything.

Bill You can use the Word to justify anything, C. You can pull Scripture apart and dissect it. Take this verse and that verse, and you can make it all add up to doing what you want it to do.

C. Yeah, I know. A lot of people are doing that these days.

I had asked Ira if you all knew anything about that Pensacola thing. You hadn't heard about any of that going on down there?[120]

Bill I hadn't heard a word about it.

C. I mean, the only way I knew anything was from the radio. They had a program on it. But I see that as a major deception.

You know, I don't judge your heart. And I will never do that. But what's in your heart does come out of your mouth. Even now, you don't admit that any of that was the Devil working? I mean he—

Bill Look—

C. I considered—when I look back, your Bible study group was a cult. I mean, it was! The Devil, he was the leader of that group. He was the head *man* that people looked to. I mean, not me. If I felt like the Devil was involved with anything I did, I would not have done it. I think you believe that. But the things that were done there, that was not God, the Almighty. It was—I believe it was the "god of this world." Are you saying you don't believe that?

Bill Don't you see anything that people have to do with this, C.? I mean, this isn't just a battle between God and Satan here.[121]

C. Well, it's when you submit to sin, which will lead you to walking with the Devil.

Bill C., if you do not follow the Word of God, if you do not listen to it, and do not heed it—

C. You fall into a trap.

Bill No, if you don't do it, it's called sin.

C. Well, yeah—

Bill   And sin separates you from God. You know, for whatever purpose, for whatever reasons that people do it, you know, do their own thing.

There are certainly evil influences out here. There are certainly satanic forces at work out here that disrupt God's people, to disrupt the work of the Lord, to destroy people's lives.

C.   But you know what? In our last conversation, you even said that if I think I can't be deceived by the Devil, then I already am. Do you remember that?

Bill   Yeah.

C.   I mean, that thought has just come to me, that you said, "If you don't think that you can be deceived by the Devil, then you already are."

Bill   Very much so. I mean, I'm not going to sit here and say that Satan didn't have any influence. And Satan didn't have any, you know, guide, guidance, or something like that involved in the things that took place at the Bible study, or anything else. I'm not saying that. I'm just telling you that I'm not going to put the responsibility off on somebody else, because I had a choice.

C.   Well, that's true.

Bill   I had the choice to respond godly by the Word of God and follow His teachings, or I had a choice not to. There were many times that I chose to, and there were times that I chose not to.

C.   Yeah, well, you—

Bill   Well, we could call it, well, you were deceived. You could say, "Well, yeah, Lord, I didn't understand all that. And I was misled and all that." But that doesn't relieve me for the accountability before the Lord for it.

C.   Well, I understand that, actually.

Bill   You know, I'm just not going to run around here and call everything satanic and deception and say it wasn't my responsibility and it wasn't my fault. Those things *were* my fault. Those things *were* my responsibility. And I didn't honor that responsibility very well. And because I didn't honor that responsibility, things happened. Sin got planted and it grew a crop. And when that crop came to fruition, it wasn't very pleasant.

C.   *No, the Devil's work never is.*

Bill   But we all have a choice of whether we are going to listen to the Word of God and do what He says, or whether we're going to allow ourselves to be tempted into sin, or fall away from the Lord, or seek the things that the flesh desires or whatever. You know, we all have that choice.

C.   Yeah?

Bill   But the bottom line is, the Word has something to say—a truth to say about our conduct, about our thoughts, about our intentions, about our actions, and about the way we live.

C.   Oh, yeah.

Bill   And we can live according to the Word of God if we so choose to. If we choose not to, things happen. Things happen both ways, but that's just how it is.

C.   You know, this is a four-year anniversary of a date that's really important to me. I don't know; do you realize that?

Bill   No.

C.   Oh.

Bill   I don't keep up with days.

C.   Oh. Well, I do, actually. You know, the twenty-eighth of February is the day that the Lord revealed the truth to me about [you and your ministry]. And you know, that's kind of become a bittersweet day for me. I have to tell you that I'm not pleased about the way things have ended up between some people that I really loved. You were among those people, but, um, I still would—

Bill   C., I am not worthy of anybody's respect or anybody's love.

You are doing yourself an injustice by not—if you have the truth, then you are doing yourself an injustice by not associating with Ira. Because she is a very godly woman. She sees the truth. She knows the truth. You know, Candy listens to Ira, and she knows the truth.

I am not about to begin to have relationships with anybody. You know, I'm not having leadership, ministry, discussions, or anything with anybody. I've done this on the phone, but this is the first time in about four years, because I'm not doing that. That's not who I am.

C. I guess you quit—

Bill But you are doing yourself a great disservice. You know, you really ought to be before the Lord about whether you need to go ahead and begin to make some contact with her. I told you this two years ago.

You know, I didn't call you to try to reconcile yourself to me. Because that ain't going to ever happen. But I called you to tell you that, you know, you ought to at least open yourself up to the possibilities of being able to stand upon the truth that the Lord's given you—

C. Oh, I believe I already do that.

Bill And carry that truth to Ira and discuss it. You know, because if you're wrong, if you've missed it in some areas or something, you know, let the Lord open your eyes to that. If she's missed it in some areas, you might be the instrument God uses to open her eyes in some areas.

C. Well, can you tell me, do you still have the same opinion of the twenty-eighth of February 1993 as you did when I talked to you last?

Bill What was my opinion then? I don't remember.

C. Oh, you don't remember?

Bill No.

C. Well, basically, you didn't believe it was of the Lord. It was just C. leading, you know, standing up and saying some things. At first, I know Ira had, through a letter, told me that she thought it was of the Devil, and then she changed her mind and said it was just me. You know, what I was doing. Do you still believe that?

Bill Well—

C. That event really is kind of like a turning point in my life. It's kind of an instrument I use to gauge where people are at with the Lord. Because I know that that was not C. Read. That was not, certainly not the Devil. *It was Jesus Christ coming into that room. And you were a witness to it.*

And it amazes me, when I think about it, that God would actually show up in such a way. And He did! And it seems like I am the only one that believes that it was. My family does. They know that it was the Lord. There has never been any question there. But you and Ira, and even Candy—I haven't talked to Wendell about what he really thinks—but you all don't feel like that was God, and I would like to understand why not. Why is there a major division there?

And that is one of the main reasons why there hasn't been a reconciliation between me and you, or her, and any of you. That is, I think, *the defining moment in all of it.* Because, you know, everything that happened between me and you, and between me and Ira, and any of you all could be set aside, I believe. But it's the way that the Lord was treated, is my concern.

And it's the same—I mentioned in a letter to her that I am not attending a fellowship right now. And it wasn't meant to imply that she knew my business. It was meant to say that she would understand. I didn't realize or think that you all had knowledge of what I am doing.

But I would think that you would understand that the Lord is not well received among many churches. *And He is with me.* I know He is! But He is rejected. Him inside of me is rejected. And when it's just C., she is very welcome. When it's Him, though, He is not welcome. And I guess I would like to understand why you don't think it was Him.

Bill   Well— [He was extremely reluctant to answer this question.]

C.   And why do people reject Him so much? I had really hoped in that letter that I wrote to you—I know it was a long letter, and I was trying to work out, even in my own heart and mind, why the things happened between us. And I was hoping that you were so deceived and deluded and overcome by the Devil that you came to the point that you realized that, and came out of it, and asked God to forgive you. I mean, you take credit for what happened, but it's almost like—I don't really understand there.

Bill   What do you want people to do? I mean, how do you want—how do you want me to respond to my sin? Do you want me to excuse it away by saying, "Well, gee Lord, Satan deceived me here?" And, you know, because I was so deceived, I'm not really responsible for my actions?

C. Oh no, you're responsible and held accountable. Even me, I have been greatly affected by what I did. I have never said that, but I know if I had gone in full well realizing that the Devil was influencing my thoughts and my actions, I wouldn't have done much of what took place.

Bill Well, I'm not going to sit here and tell you, yeah, I sat there and said, "Well, gee, I'm just deceiving these people. And you know, the Devil's in charge of my life." That's not what happened at all. I don't think anybody—well, I don't know, maybe there are. Maybe you believe it. I don't know. I can tell you that that's not the way it was. You know, I went in there with the best of intentions of serving God and—

C. Well, I believe people start out that way—I believe a lot of people start out with great intentions, and they go down the wrong road, and then they end up doing things that they don't understand the ramifications to, or what influence has taken them over. And it's through sin that they get into that condition. Their own personal sin. But then it's like you get to a certain point, and then it's definitely the Devil taking control. Do you not believe that?

Bill At times, that happens. You know, there's a whole spectrum out there. You can't lump everyone into one category. You know, some things happen in people's lives. And some people are doing it through the very good heart intentions and yet are either, by their own lusts, or cares and concerns for other things, you know, get misled and get off track.

Some people may even have an evil heart. And they do have a heart of evil. And they masquerade as wolves, masquerade as sheep wearing all the clothing and the right words, and with all the looks and the right stuff, but inwardly they are ravenous wolves. Jesus talked about those.

So you're asking me to define me. Well, that's what I've tried to do. I'm not trying to classify everybody into one particular group of people or make everything fit a formula for sin occurring in their lives. The whole formula is this, if you want a formula, you know, the formula is this. You know, without Jesus Christ and His blood shed on the cross, there's no forgiveness of the sins. And if a person refuses to accept Jesus and accept that blood sacrifice for an atonement for their sins, then they will die in their sins.

C. *Well, are you refusing to accept the fact that He showed up in our living room that night? Do you not believe that?*

Bill What night?

C. The twenty-eighth of February. The last night you preached in my home. *You don't remember that night?* It should have been an eventful night for all concerned. It was for me!

Bill C., the events—to be honest with you—

C. I hope you will be.

Bill I'm not really thinking about what's, you know, what all that has—I do not remember the specifics, okay?

C. Well, that night, I mean it was the last night you preached. You have to remember that very well. I mean, I started praying in the Spirit. That was definitely not my normal character.

Bill I remember the night. I remember what happened. You want me to give you my assessment of that? That I—

C. Yes, I would love to know that.

Bill Okay, my assessment was this: You were right on with the fact that there was sin in the camp. That there was sin in my life. That there was sin leading and misleading and permeating every aspect of what we were doing. It's not so much that night that I disagree with. It's what happened after that night.

C. On the second of March?

Bill No.

C. That night you all came over to talk?

Bill No, it's what happened with you in beginning to be—in taking on the role, or whatever it was, I don't know. You know, all I know is—

C. Taking on what role?

Bill That you somehow decided that you were going to make everything that had ever transpired, you know, in all of our lives, a matter of public record. And you know, the attacks, and the, you know, the degrading of individual people.

C. What do you mean by that?

Bill Well, I mean, you went to other people. You talked. You wrote letters. You shared. You know, well, I don't really know. I mean, the only thing I got is what you wrote to me. Okay. I'm not going by—

C. Well, go by what you know. Not necessarily—

Bill By hearsay here. But I'm just going on what you've written to me.

C. Yeah?

Bill Ah, you know—

C. Is anything in that untrue?

Bill What the Word has to say about that is, you know, if you find your brother in sin, you go to him.

C. I went to you, don't you remember?

Bill And I got no problem with you rejecting me. And I got no problem with you blasting me and calling sin, sin. I don't have any problem with that, C. *What I have a problem with is you doing it outside the realm of God's love.* Now that may be my personal preference. And that may be my personal choice. But for me, it's almost like the woman caught in adultery, or any sinner that Jesus came to. He reached down to them and said, you know, "Thy sin be forgiven thee, go and sin no more."

C. Yeah?

Bill And to, you know, to almost treat somebody like, "Well, I know that you are not going to repent, and I know you are not going to stop sinning, and I know that you're not going to, you know, acknowledge anything here. Then I'll just become your enemy, and I'll just blast you up one side and down the other." And—

C. And that's what you've taken, as what I've done?

Bill *Well, you asked me!*

C. Well, that's okay. I'd like to understand.

Bill I just tried to tell you real honestly that I think you were right on with what you said concerning sin. I think you were right on with, you know, your personal assessment of the situation.

C. Yeah?

Bill But when it came to reaching out in love—

C.   It's what I've done afterward? That's what your problem is?

Bill   And not responding—and, you know, a godly response to a sinful person. I mean, it just doesn't add up in the Word of God. That's not what the Word says to do. The Word says, yeah, if they don't stop sinning—it says to separate yourself from them. It doesn't say one word about taking them into the judicial courts of the world.

C.   I haven't ever done that. That was someone else having me come.

Bill   You didn't feed Steve all that information? You didn't, you didn't, you know—

C.   Yes, well—

Bill   Here you took all the things—

C.   Well, I—if you really want to know what happened. I don't know if you do or not.

Bill   Yeah, I'd like to know.

C.   You know, after 28 February 1993, that *very significant date,* and then on 2 March, it was really obvious that we were against one another in our views, if you want to put it *mildly.*

That was the Lord working in me. And it wasn't C. Read saying, "Okay, I'm going to get at you." Because there has never been revenge in my heart toward you. I don't know if you realize that or not, but there has never been.

But I know that, based on everything that took place, I felt very inclined for people to know about what had happened to me and that I had been involved in a cult group for three years. That I was definitely being influenced by an evil influence. Not by God!

Because I professed to be a Christian all that time. I professed to be serving the Lord. And there was just something in me that I wanted people to know what I had been involved with. And the only desire in having people know what I went through—because I was very willing to go into the adulterous relationship I had with you. You know, people that are trying to hide something, they would not have talked about that, but I told everybody what I had done. I wanted them to know that I was in a deception. I was!

And you know, Candy's family, it was very important for them to know. And [my husband's] family, I told all of them. You know, it was on the sixth of March that I got together with Candy's family. And it was only—the only purpose in mind there was to warn them of these dangers. And that's why any of that took place.

(The tape ran out. End of first tape / beginning of second.)

C. Well, I was just mentioning to you what I think about what happened. After I got out of your Bible study group, there was a real desire in me to let people know what I had been involved with.

And there wasn't—and there still is not—a desire to hurt any of you. It seems that you see otherwise. And you seem to think I am not very loving, but I know that the more I see how God is, a lot of what looks to not be loving actually is.

He knew where I was when I went to your Bible study group. He knew what would happen to me, and He let me go through that place. Actually, that was very loving of Him. Because of the things that happened, I—kind of what you all said at the beginning, I was very self-righteous. And you remember—I don't know if you remember some of the things. Like you would cuss in front of me.

And that time when you and Ira had sex right in front of me. You said it was to break me of my self-righteousness, to be accepting of some of the things that go on and not be so shocked. Do you remember that?

Bill C., I remember that a lot of things that took place were ungodly. You want me to focus on the things that were godly. It's very difficult for me to come and see very many things that were right or very many things that were godly here.

C. Well, Ira stated in her letter that you admitted that your relationship with her was wrong from the very beginning.

Bill It was. I was married, and I should have honored that commitment.

C. Well—

Bill My question back to you is what we were talking about. You know, it's not me here anymore. Because I'm not leading anybody. And I'm not trying to lead anybody. I'm not out here trying to—

C. Have you not led anybody, or had a group since the—

Bill Right after—a few months after all that happened—you know, this one just passed into oblivion, and that's been it.

CHRIST OR ANTICHRIST

C.   Yeah? So actually the prophecy did come to pass?

Bill   *What prophecy?!*

C.   The twenty-eighth of February. You seem to think that that's *so insignificant.* Actually, everything that was said that night by the Lord is coming to pass.

Bill   Well, whatever. I don't care! I mean, I really don't! You know, good, bad, or indifferent, it doesn't make any difference to me!

C.   But you still don't think it was the Lord? Is that right?

Bill   *I never said that, C.!* I told you that I thought you were right on—

C.   Well, now, now. I know C. can be right on if she is with the Lord. But do you still not believe that that was His Spirit coming into my room?

Bill   There was the Spirit of the Lord there, but there was something else there also.

C.   What?

Bill   There was a spirit of condemnation. And that's not from God. There was a spirit of hatred that was there. And that wasn't from the Lord. You know, if your brother is in sin, or your sister's in sin, and you really have the heart of the Lord to bring them out of that sin—

C.   You talk to them first, of course.

Bill   Well, now there's an overriding love that Jesus had in His heart for people that overrode everything. The whole point here was—I can understand your vengeance against me. I can understand that. I can understand—

C.   I don't have a vengeance against you, actually.

Bill   Look, I can understand your words against me. I can understand you wanting to go out in the society, in the world, and to the church, and Christians, or families or anywhere else, and saying, "Look, this man is not from the Lord. This man has done this, this, this, and this. I was an eyewitness to these things." I got no problem with that.

C.   You don't?

Bill   No. The point is here, you drug other people into it. But you carried it beyond that. You carried it to the innocents.

C.   To the what now?

Bill *The innocents!* Those who were innocent.

C.   What do you mean?

Bill Other people got caught up into it who were innocent.

C.   Like who?

Bill Ira is innocent.

C.   How is *she* innocent?

Bill She didn't buy into this. And because of it, Ira today is branded as a witch in this world!

C.   *Really?*

Bill Candy didn't see it. Candy didn't go along with it. Candy was listening to the truth and trying to follow that. It didn't have anything to do with them siding with me or siding with you. It had everything to do with them siding with Jesus. With the truth.

And you know beyond—you did go out. And March the sixth, as you just said, you went. And you talked to an ungodly family. Who took Candy to court. And took her daughter away from her. And now that daughter is in worse shape than you could ever imagine.

C.   How's that?

Bill How's that? She sold herself to the world, because she has no godly influence in her life.

C.   Well, they go to church don't they?

Bill C., you've been around out there in the church world enough to know that people that go to church are not necessarily godly, spiritual people.

C.   Well, I am quite aware of that, yes.

Bill Well, these aren't godly, spiritual people. But yet, because of your desire to share everything, and tell everything, you went beyond where you needed to go. That wasn't from the Lord. That wasn't from God.

C.   Well, do you remember that conversation when I first came there? You had asked me who you were to me.

Bill And that was as ungodly as all get out!

C.   But you know what? I did hear those things that—

CHRIST OR ANTICHRIST

Bill   I'm sure you probably did hear those things.

C.   —you had suggested that I heard. Of course, the first thing was that you would be my teacher. I mean, not actually teacher. That "I would learn a lot from you" was more accurate. And so we deduced from what I heard that you would be my teacher. But also the fact that you would be my husband. And that was the seed planted that kind of helped lead the other stuff on.

But I heard those things. Those were real voices. And do you not admit that you can pray and cause people to hear voices? You know, because how would you know that I would hear the same thing?

Bill   I'm not going to pray—I don't have that kind of influence in people's lives! I can't pray and ask God to reveal *some voice* in somebody's head; that's ungodly! You got a Scripture sitting right there that says be the husband of one wife. I mean, that is what the Scripture has to say. It doesn't say go out here and attract unto yourselves women and men who call you their husband. That's not what the Scriptures say. We have the Word. The Word is the guide.

C.   You used to bring David into it. Remember him and all his wives? That He would give him all those things?

Bill   Absolutely. You can take the Word of God and justify anything you want to do with it. But that doesn't necessarily make it true. Doesn't make it godly. And it doesn't make it right on with the Lord. And what I'm just saying to you is, that, you know, the things—

I didn't have any problem with you standing up and saying—I mean, well, my flesh did, but looking back on it four years later, I'm saying, "No, this woman was right on when she said, 'Yes, there's sin in the camp. Yes, there's things that need to be taken care of.'"

But instead of allowing the Lord to take care of it, *you took the sword up in your own hand*. And you somehow heard and—you know, you ought to—need to remember, if you heard a voice that told you something that was ungodly, such as, "He's your husband," that you could also hear a voice that—that there's also another possibility, that you could hear a voice that says, "You need to go out here and reveal this truth to everybody."

Because what happened in the long run of revealing the truth was you not only isolated yourself and alienated yourself from people who could probably benefit from a loving, kind, gracious, humble spirit, teaching them how to avoid sin in their life. But in the process, a lot of other people were affected by it. A lot of other people became victims of that sword.

Ira never did anything to you except encourage you, love you, care for you, talk with you, plead with you, pray with you, and beg you to listen to the Word of God, and flee from sin. And yet, *she's branded as a witch in this entire community* because of some of the things that have been written and said about her.

C.   Because of me?

Bill   Yes. I mean no one—C., when you offer a testimony to people in a letter that says "the spirit of antichrist," what do you think ungodly people are going to do with that?

C.   Well, they are going to have to take it before the Lord and let—

Bill   They're ungodly! How are they going to take it before the Lord?

C.   And know if it's true or not.

Well, that night, the second of March, which is exactly this date four years ago. Do you remember when I accused you of being of the antichrist? And you would not deny it? You didn't deny it! You didn't deny it that night, and are you denying it tonight or today? Do you deny that the spirit of antichrist led you in the activities that took place when I was with you for those three years?

Bill   What do you want me to do, C.? Which gate do you want me to go out so everybody can *stone me*? So you can prove the point that I'm of the antichrist! Which one? I'd be glad to! My life doesn't mean squat to me!

C.   Well, do you remember what you used to tell me? That your life would be one of suffering and pain and that you would die for your faith? Do you still believe that? Remember? That's what you used to tell me. And I—

Bill   Yep.

C.   I used to be so concerned about that. And I used to even hate the way people would treat you.

Bill   That was nothing more than a fleshy ploy to get people to be sympathetic with me, and to get me what I perceived that I needed, and convince them that that's exactly what they ought to do. Not *knowingly* doing that. I mean, I'm not going to sit here and tell you that, boy, I had this wonderful plan. Cause that wasn't the plan.

But instead of committing—

C. But you know what? You know what would make all of this more credible? Is if you did admit that it was of the Devil. I mean, good grief!

Bill C., what it—I mean, I—

C. I mean, it was! It had to be!

Bill That everything that I did was opposed to God? That everything that I taught, preached, lived—

C. Well, no, it was truth mixed with lies.

Bill —was totally outside of the Word of God? And you want me to confess, make some kind of confession that the Devil made me do it? And I'm not going to do that to you! I told you that *I'm not going to give Satan credit.*

I know that Satan had an influence here. And I know that he corrupted me. And he corrupted a lot of things that I did. And he, you know, in his influences, and his demonic spirit world, and all the spiritual ramifications of evil took hold here. I know that. But if you think for one minute that I'm going around confessing before the world *that I'm some kind of antichrist—*

C. Well, what's antichrist? It means against—

Bill C., the spirit of antichrist is denying Jesus Christ as Lord! Denying that He is the Son of God! That He died on the cross for man's sins! It is trying to get people to acknowledge that there is another god out there, other than Jesus Christ. I have not done that! And I never even did that! I never preached that! I never said, "Deny Jesus!"

C. Something that I am reminded of—it was a dream I had about you, that I was telling Ira about. Do you remember that dream?

Bill No.

C. It was a very strange dream. And it was like you were fixing to bow your knee to the Devil. And she freaked out when I said that. I brought that up in that letter. I know it was kind of long. I don't know if you got back to the—did you read the whole letter?

Bill Yes.

C. It was brought up in that.

Bill It's been a while.

C. But, you know, I actually dreamed that you were going to do that. And I know that there's people that do that. And I—

Bill But I *don't!* And I *haven't!* Not knowingly, willingly, with all the faculties, and senses, and intelligence, or lack of, that I have, or don't have, have never gone out to worship Satan. I have never bowed my knee to the Devil!

C. Yeah?

Bill But the ramifications of the things that I've done are exemplified by evil, which means that I was not listening to God. That I was not following the Word. No matter how pretty it sounded. No matter how great it might have come across. Now if that isn't enough for you—for a man to admit that he's sinned before God, that he's sinned against God, that he's sinned against humanity— then, you know, I don't know anything I can call it beyond that. It's a spirit of revenge, or anger, or bitterness, or resentment, or something.

Because that's all God asks us to do. That's all that Jesus said for us to do, is repent of your sins, confess your sins before God, and He's faithful to forgive you of those sins. Well, let me tell you, I've spent a lot of time before the Lord confessing my sin, and I still have to spend a lot of time before the Lord. And I have to live with what I have done. My sin, like David, is ever before me. I live with it every day. Day in and day out.

C. Have you not been forgiven?

Bill *Yes, I have been forgiven!*

But that doesn't mean that I can ever attain to the positions, or fulfillment of the plan, that God had for my life, because of the kind of sin of standing up proclaiming myself to be some kind of spiritual leader and teacher to other people, have them to follow me, only to find that we're all in the same pit together.

The blessed thing about it is that if it—

If there's anybody in a pit, I'm the only one in it. Everybody else has seemed to get out of it, which is a blessing.

C.   For them or you? It's not a blessing to you?

Bill   Yeah, it's a blessing to me. I'm glad people aren't wrapped up in me. I'm glad people aren't sitting there going, "Ewe, ah, come on, ya know, whoop de do." I'm glad they're not there. I rejoiced that people could find Jesus.

But I also will not stand behind something that says I'm being godly when the things I've done out here caused nothing but destruction.

And what I'm saying to you is perhaps there are things that have taken place because of the things even you have done with a godly intention, and yet have backfired out here. And virtually caused misery, grief, pain, anguish, suffering, and untruth to be placed in the lives of other people.

C.   Now I don't believe untruth. Anything that I have spoken or written has not been untruth.

Bill   Well, I'm not going to argue with you on that one, because for the most part, I can't even remember what you've written. And I mean, the letters are here, but I don't go back and read them. And I, you know, I read them when they came, and that's it.

C.   Well, I—that is something that I do not ever want to believe, is a lie. And I know I did when I was with you all. *I believed a lot of lies.* And something that I will always stand for is the truth. And if I should speak a lie, I would not mind it being brought to my attention. In fact, I would welcome that. If I speak lies, I would have no problem with someone addressing that with me.

You seem to think that, just by what you are saying, that I have vengeance and hatred. And actually my hatred is more toward the Devil, because he—

Bill   Well, I tell you what, C. If you don't have hatred and vengeance in your heart, then you go to the godly people. The people who really seek after the Lord. Who are really earnestly seeking after—

C.   I would like to find them, actually.

Bill   Well, there's one of them right here! There's two of them right here! Ira and Candy. If you really want to know the truth, then prove it!

I've proved it! I've proved that—that I will not preach lies, and deceit, and ungodliness, and untruth out here. By backing off, by not accepting any kind of speaking engagements, by not trying to organize any kind of ministry. In fact, I don't have one.

C. So you don't have your ministry anymore?

Bill I don't have *anything!*

C. You quit doing anything to do with—

Bill That's what I'm telling you. I'm not doing anything! That was it. But what I'm saying to you, if you really, honestly want me to believe, or want anyone else to believe it, that you really are after the truth and that you do have the truth, then you go to the people who are seeking that same truth. And be reconciled to your brothers and your sisters. And find, you know, a common ground to stand on here. And go to them. And share with them. And listen to them. And learn.

C. Well, I have read her letters. And I have read some of the stuff she sent me. And I know if I get into that self-righteous mode again, I will certainly fall. And I hope that I don't.

But everything that I do, I feel led by the Lord. In fact, I felt led to call you. I was very nervous at the thought of speaking with any of you all, because I believe that much of what took place was the working of Satan.[122] And even though I despise him, I respect him.

And my hope is that people can learn from my mistakes, because I have made many in my walk with the Lord. But ever since the twenty-eighth of February, I have been walking in a completely different light than I ever have in my life. And I was hoping that maybe your view of that day, *that very important day to me,* was different. But I see that it is not.

And I do not have a vengeance for you. God will be the One that exacts His vengeance upon those who do not love Him and those that have evil motives. And He is the One that will determine everything. I don't. And I want you to know that what I do is because I truly feel He is leading me.

It is not because I am out to hurt you, or hurt Ira, or hurt Candy. I have no desire for that. Actually, my desire right now would be to

ℭHRIST OR ANTICHRIST

        move away and never come back. That is really what I would like to do right now. And if the Lord desires for that to happen, it will.

Bill Maybe the Lord desires for you to reconcile with your sisters, who never did anything to you in the first place.

C. Well, I don't know— I know Candy. I don't feel like she ever had evil motives toward me. I don't really know. But you know, I am just basing things off of the results of what has happened, and what has taken place.

Bill What are you basing it on? And what has taken place?

C. Well, do you remember the night when you all came over on the second? The night that, you know—the twenty-eighth wasn't really a day that I feel like we broke up. There was some revealing of things that night, but the second of March is when we got together. And privately I—it was still very private on the second. It didn't become public until the continued refusal of wrongdoing. But on the second, she was very mean toward me that night. Very, very hostile. And quite agitated at me, because I wanted to bring up to Wendell and to Candy and to my husband that what had taken place between me and you was absolutely wrong.

        But you tried to deny everything that night. Even with Kim and everything, when Ira and Candy had already admitted to it having taken place. And you were still denying it until you saw that it was completely over. And that night, she was even, ya know, wanting to deny it. And I guess it's—

(The tape ran out)

{End of 2 March 1997 transcript}

IF YOU NOTICED, BILL COULD NEVER CONFESS that it was the Spirit of Christ who appeared in my home on that February evening. The spirit of antichrist that is inside of him would not let him, and it is because he *does not belong to God*.[123]

1 John 4:1–3 "Beloved, believe not every spirit, but try the spirits whether they are of God: because many false prophets are gone out into the world.

Hereby know ye the Spirit of God: Every spirit that confesseth that Jesus Christ is come in the flesh is of God; and every spirit that confesseth not that Jesus Christ is come in the flesh is not of God: And this is that [spirit] of antichrist, whereof ye have heard that it should come; and even now already is it in the world."

May this testimony dissuade people from trusting in a man, a movement, or even their own selves and persuade them to call upon the name of the Lord from a sincere and repentant heart. He is true and faithful always! And that is *the definitive truth* you can trust and believe![124]

C. Read

2 John 1:9–11 "Whosoever transgresseth, and abideth not in the doctrine of Christ, hath not God. He that abideth in the doctrine of Christ, he hath both the Father and the Son.

If there come any unto you, and bring not this doctrine, receive him not into [your] house, neither bid him God speed: For he that biddeth him God speed is partaker of his evil deeds."

Final Note

I just could not conclude this book without saying that I am so thankful to the many members of the body of Christ that God has put in my life, especially during this time of healing that I have been going through.

That's not to say I am completely over my experience, but I have come to terms with how and why I came to be in that situation. Even now, I can say that I am a much stronger person because of everything I went through. Not because of Satan's attempts to lead me astray, but because of what I saw God do in spite of what Satan and his workers of iniquity intended.

All praise, honor, glory, and thanksgiving to Almighty God for His love, mercy, and amazing grace!

You may not be aware of the ways that you help those in need, but if you are led by God's Spirit, whether it is through word or song, you are impacting this evil world and making a difference in the lives of those you touch.

God's people are scattered about, but it won't always be. We may stand alone, but we are not alone because the author and finisher of our faith is with us. I can attest to the fact that He is true and faithful, always![125]

When God's Word is spoken in truth, as we are led by His Spirit, it can affect the hearts of men; and depending on the condition of our hearts, His Word can either give us strength because it establishes the truth more fully, or it can cause our heart to grow faint because it convicts us of our sin. And it is so important to acknowledge and repent of our sin while there is still time.

For those who have not yet trusted Christ for your life, I pray that you will. The shame and disgrace you experience now cannot even be compared with what you will face should you stand before Almighty God condemned.

My last word to all those who have given their lives for the cross of Christ, no matter your situation, please don't give up! The Lord knows exactly what you are going through for His name's sake, and He will reward you accordingly. Jesus will be your strength in time of trouble! And you must know that evil will not always be with us.[126] Keep contending for the faith!

And know, if God is for you, it doesn't matter who is against you. His truth will prevail! Praise the Holy Name of Yeshua HaMashiach, Jesus the Christ!

Luke 4:17–21 "And there was delivered unto Him the book of the prophet Esaias (Isaiah 61). And when He had opened the book, He found the place where it was written, The Spirit of the Lord [is] upon Me, because He hath anointed Me to preach the gospel to the poor;

He hath sent Me to heal the brokenhearted, to preach deliverance to the captives, and recovering of sight to the blind, to set at liberty them that are bruised, to preach the acceptable year of the Lord.

And He closed the book, and He gave [it] again to the minister, and sat down. And the eyes of all them that were in the synagogue were fastened on Him. And He (Jesus) began to say unto them, This day is this Scripture fulfilled in your ears."

Hear, O Israel: The Lord our God is one Lord! And may YHWH, the Holy One of Israel, truly bless those who love Him with all their heart, with all their soul, and with all their might. Amen!

Sincerely,
A servant of the Most High God,

C. Read

As signed by me in the presence of a witness
on the 12th Day of May in the year of our Lord,
One Thousand Nine Hundred and Ninety-Four.

Final Note

IN CONCLUSION…

I would like to address those who have rejected the Lord God Almighty for whatever reason. Whether it is based on a misunderstanding because of your own perception or the misguided views of another, either way, the end result is the same: *You need the Lord!*

Or you could possibly be someone that was also purposely misled into believing lies in place of the truth; either way, the end result is the same: *You need the Lord!*

Or maybe you are one that has rejected the church altogether because of an encounter with an improper representative of the Lord Jesus Christ; either way, the end result is the same: *You need the Lord!*

Regardless of your individual circumstances, if you have never experienced the amazing grace of God and incredible forgiveness of the Lord, either way, the end result is the same: *You need the Lord God Almighty in your life!* And I pray that you have come to that same conclusion.

As you can see from my story, I have made many mistakes during my walk with God, and even now, I still have times I feel so unworthy to be called a servant of the Most High God, but that just reminds me of how much *I need the Lord!*

Let me tell you, if and when you ever truly meet up with the One, True, and Living God, while on this earth, He can, and He will, fill the void in your life if you sincerely call upon Him. He will replace despair with hope, emptiness with purpose and meaning, hatred and bitterness with love and joy, discontentment with satisfaction, along with an abiding peace that nothing or nobody in this world could ever give you, *only Him!*

All of us have an inner desire to love and to be loved, and only true love that lasts forever comes from God. He purposefully meant it to be that way, so that if we ever left Him out of our lives, we would realize that something was missing, and hopefully, we would go searching for Him. But I am so sorry to say that most people are looking for the love and joy that only God can give in all the wrong places.

In order to give all men the opportunity to receive His genuine love, God sent His Son, Jesus Christ, to this earth to reveal the truth about Him, His Kingdom, and eternity. But so many people refuse to allow Him to become a part of their daily lives so that He can reveal that truth.

John 3:16-17 "For God so loved the world, that He gave His only begotten Son, that whosoever believeth in Him should not perish, but have everlasting life. For God sent not His Son into the world to condemn the world; but that the world through Him might be saved."

As God has allowed me to understand more fully what took place as He watched Jesus live out His time here on this earth, the hardest thing for me to deal with is the pain and anguish that I am sure my Heavenly Father went through as He stood by and watched as they made a mockery of His dear Son.

Can you imagine what it must have been like? Who would even consider giving up their only son with the knowledge that he was going to be ridiculed and laughed at by the entire world, beaten almost to the point of death, and nailed to a cross as a criminal, even though He was perfectly innocent?

But God knew it all! In fact, He planned it all! He knew that Jesus's sacrifice was the only way to win the ultimate victory over sin, death, and Satan. That's what His love is all about. To love someone so much that you are willing to give up everything that you are, everything that you own, and even your very life, so as to prove your love. What an *awesome* God He is!

And you must know: That has to be the most heartbreaking of experiences, for a Father to stand by and watch the misuse, the abuse, and the murder of His only begotten Son, unless, of course, the same was to have happened to His wife. And I am here to tell you, He has experienced that sorrow as well.

Final Note

But just as the death of His dear Son was not in vain because Almighty God was able to raise Him up again, so too shall He bring back to eternal life His glorious bride that shall rule and reign with Him, forever and ever, world without end. Amen!

My Lord and my God has most certainly endured great pain, suffering, and sorrow for all of mankind, even to this very day, and if you have not yet begun to understand what He has done, then you don't know Him very well.

However, the most important thing that you need to seriously consider right now is whether or not you will be allowed entry into His heavenly Kingdom. And it all hinges on what you do while it is called Today.

Hebrews 3:7–13 "Wherefore (as the Holy Ghost saith, To day if ye will hear His voice, harden not your hearts, as in the provocation, in the day of temptation in the wilderness: When your fathers tempted Me, proved Me, and saw My works forty years.

Wherefore I was grieved with that generation, and said, They do alway err in [their] heart; and they have not known My ways. So I sware in My wrath, They shall not enter into My rest.)

Take heed, brethren, lest there be in any of you an evil heart of unbelief, in departing from the living God.

But exhort one another daily, while it is called To day; lest any of you be hardened through the deceitfulness of sin."

I ask you, who are you going to follow? There are only two choices. There is no middle ground in this battle for your soul. Satan would love for you to continue in his kingdom, but my dear Father would rather that you joined Him in His.

And God proved it by giving you a way to be reunited back to Him through Christ Jesus, His Son. And you *must* come through that door! There is no other way to God the Father and His Holy City.

God will forgive you for any rejection of Him because of your ignorance of the truth, but if you purposefully reject the voice of

God, and blaspheme His Holy Spirit, you will never be forgiven in this world, or in the world to come.

One of the greatest pleasures I could ever receive is if the Lord will use my experience to show the world that they need to be saved from eternal death and Hell. And for those who are lost, I hope they will be persuaded to embrace the truth and turn from their sin and come to the Lord Jesus Christ by faith in Him and His Word. After all, it is God's Son who holds the keys of Hell and of death!

As I have always told my children, the greatest gift I could ever receive from them is if they would truly love, honor, and obey the Lord God Almighty with all their heart, soul, mind, and strength and genuinely love their neighbors as themselves—that would please me immensely.

The same holds true for you: If you were to humbly come and give your allegiance to God the Father and sincerely worship Him in Spirit and in truth, due to the testimony of Jesus Christ in my life, that would bring such a tremendous joy to my heart, and not to my heart only, but more importantly, *to the heart of God!*

"I Am Alpha and Omega,
the beginning and the end,
the first and the last."
Revelation 22:13

Something to Think About

IF YOU HAVE READ my entire testimony of *Walking With the Enemy*, you know that 27 August 1992, along with other commemorative dates, are very important to me.

Several years ago I sent some letters to different folks with the hope that it would wake up the "Sleeping Giant." Based on the condition of so many in the churches today, men are still asleep!

In the previous edition, I just touched on the essence of those letters, but the actual letters are much more powerful. I pray that these words will cause men to really think about why the Devil has been able to deceive so many people to the degree that he has. And may this testimony encourage faithful men, who are led by God's Holy Spirit, to stand against the evil schemes of the Wicked One.

27 August 2014

To Friends, Family, and Acquaintances:

So many people in this nation, even Christians, are conformed to this world and not the Word. Sin is the doorway into the darkness, and if you walk in it long enough, it will lead to a place you really don't want to be.

Remember, good and evil are from the same tree, but godliness only comes from the Tree of Life. And God is looking for a people that is holy and set apart by Him and for Him, and only through Christ can we get there.

Christians have gotten off the intended path because their faith is in the word of men, rather than the Word of God. And I must say: Woe, woe, woe be unto those who call themselves Christian, yet do not follow Christ!

Walking with the Enemy

False teachers, corrupt Bibles, and apostate churches led by those who have fallen away from the truth are abounding, just as God said it would be like in the final days, and only those who have eyes to see and ears to hear will understand what I Am saying.

As long as God's people continue to turn a blind eye to sin or willingly participate in it, they are subject to error and deception, and they will never be the holy people that God greatly desires, and requires, for His Church to be.

I came across the following letter that I would like to share with you, and even though I wrote it over twenty years ago, it is still just as relevant today, and even more so considering the state of the churches.

I truly love God and His people, and I will continue to keep you and your loved ones in my prayers to Him!

Sincerely,

C. Read

John 12:35 "Then Jesus said unto them, Yet a little while is the Light with you. Walk while ye have the Light, lest Darkness come upon you: For he that walketh in Darkness knoweth not whither he goeth."

May 19, 1994

To the Editor of The *Clarion-Ledger*,

I just couldn't stop thinking about the man who had lost his three children because he had fallen asleep. I can almost imagine the horror he must have experienced when he found their lifeless little bodies in that old refrigerator. It must have been his darkest hour!

My heart goes out to him and his family, and I just pray that they will turn all this over to the Lord, if they haven't already. The unbearable shame, guilt, anger, and resentment will just destroy their lives completely if it's allowed to continue.

Something to Think About

It may be extremely hard to understand how God could even possibly use this tragic situation and turn it around for his good and the good of others, but He can and He will if we would only look at it from His perspective.

As I read the front-page article on May 18, 1994 describing what happened, the Lord brought to my attention that the condition of most fathers in this country is that they are spiritually asleep, thus they are unable to see the imminent danger their children are in.

If they don't wake up while there is still time, they will ultimately be responsible for the eternal death of their families; and if they find themselves and their children in outer Darkness separated from God forever, there will be no turning back them.

My hope and prayer is that the pain and sorrow of this family can be eased if they know their situation has sounded an alarm to all of us for the need to humbly submit our whole heart, soul, and body to Almighty God and His Word before it's too late.

It's so important for the men and fathers of this country to stand up and be the spiritual leaders that God has ordained that they must be! Should they refuse, they will be held accountable for that decision! And in so doing they will ultimately help contribute to the demise of the United States of America as a nation that stands for truth, justice, and freedom for all.

Sincerely,
A servant of the Most High God,
C. Read

THIS IS A VERY SPECIAL POEM that I would like to share, and here's a little background to show why I was inspired to write it.

My parents divorced when I was ten years old, and I never really knew my real father. My mother always painted a terrible picture of him, and I never saw him while growing up. After I was married and had children of my own, to my pleasant surprise, he contacted me.

I found out that he had retired from the US Navy after over twenty years of service. He seemed to be a very lonely, brokenhearted man who was mourning the loss of his second wife who had passed away. He talked of great plans of us getting together, but sadly, that never took place.

Even though I was not able to have a relationship with my father after my parents separated, God, in His wonderful way, made up for his absence. As I reflected on the final conversation that I had with my father before he died, I wrote the following poem. I have come to realize that God always has a much higher purpose in mind, and I am so thankful for the way He turns my disappointments and heartaches into blessings!

My Real Father

I have truly enjoyed the conversations we've had of late,
and I am so thankful You are nothing like I assumed was Your fate.
Those assumptions were based on dissimulation.
I know the truth now and have accurate information.
That is truly all that really matters, You see,
because You are just like the real Father I'd want You to be.

I have always had fond memories of You in my heart,
and I've longed for a relationship when we are together and not apart.
I am so very thankful and I must confess,
that I have truly been so wonderfully blessed,

*S*OMETHING TO THINK ABOUT

with others to stand in and take Your place,
until the great day that we meet again face to face!

I am so sorry for the pain that You have been through,
and the sense of loss that I am sure has been there too.
It's hard to think that, due to death, we are finally going to meet,
but I can even be thankful in the face of seeming defeat.

I truly trust and believe all that has taken place
was in Your mighty plan that You hoped we'd embrace.
And due to the great knowledge and my genuine faith,
death is the beginning if we believe what the Prophet sayeth:
Repent and believe for the day is at hand,
and it's time for God's people to make a stand!

God truly desires to give and to share,
His glorious Kingdom with those He holds dear.
I hope you will be spared from the wrath that is to come,
and there is only one way, through Jesus Christ, His Son!

For unto us a child was born.
And They have called His name Emmanuel.
The Mighty Counselor! The Prince of Peace! The Almighty God!
Who is Jesus my Lord, my Savior, my Redeemer, and my Friend.
And He's given Himself for all those that call upon Him.

Blessing, and honor, and glory, and power, and might
be unto Him that sitteth upon the Throne,
and unto the Lamb, for ever and ever! Amen.

C. Read

{2 January 1994}

This was not in previous editions, but I am compelled to include this thought provoking message in my testimony. The Lord led me to write this poem many years ago, but the words are timeless. God has such a wonderful way of using bittersweet situations to show me deeper Spiritual truths. God's gift is freely given to those He has chosen, but you will have to lose your life in this world to obtain eternal life in the world to come. As you read this, I pray that you are one who truly appreciates the Gift that God has given because of the life, death, and resurrection of His beloved Son, the LORD Jesus Christ!

The Gift

When I gave you the Gift, due to the birth of the King,
I truly felt that It would bring you great joy and delight.

I also imagined that you would display It in a place for all to see,
But obviously that was not to be Its plight.

And when you kept It hid away and out of plain sight,
I was greatly disappointed
that It was not as important to you, as It was to Me.

Maybe It wasn't for you what you thought It would be?

The things of the world will indeed fade away and be diminished,
And only what God has given will matter when all is finished.

So it's best to keep in mind
that only the things of Heaven will last and be forever,
And what you do for the LORD Jesus Christ
will be applied to that treasure.

Something to Think About

God most certainly takes into account
all that we do in this present life,
And depending on what we do with His Word
will either bring us joy or brings us strife.

And as the LORD reveals the true condition of our hearts,
we must totally submit to Almighty God if we are smart.

So that He can cleanse, and purify, and remove all that is evil,
But should we refuse, we will be guilty of serving the Devil!

Never forget that what The Father has given
is much more important to procure,
And could be taken away from those who do not keep It secure.

The Gift of God's Spirit
should be protected with our very own life,
and cherished, and honored, and adored,
As a man should be toward his wife.

And if we ever willfully ignore God's Voice and speak evil of Him,
We will most certainly be in danger of blasphemy the sin,
That could cause us to be eternally separated from Them,
Who have prepared the Way for all men
to be a part of God's Family.

C. Read

{24 January 1995}

Timeline Index

4 November 1979: I called out to God. (Pages 382)

18 June 1989: Father's Day letter to my husband. (Page 93)

Fall of 1989: First letter I gave Bill. (Page 84)

29 March 1990: First Bible study meeting with Bill and Ira. (Page 96)

19 April 1990: Bill "laid hands" on me and prayed. (Pages 100, 117, 154)

14 May 1990: God gave me the gift of praying in the Spirit. (Page 103)

4 January 1991: My husband left for military training. (Page 122)

18 June 1992: My husband returned from active duty. (Page 122)

27 August 1992: My first prophecy from the Lord. (Pages 265–267)

18 November 1992: Bill's prophecy. (Pages 238–241)

4 February 1993: Ira's last Bible study lesson. (Pages 212–227)

16 February 1993: My journal entry: "Can I trust them?" (Page 73)

28 February 1993: The appearance of the Lord! (Pages 31–39)

2 March 1993: The True Light pierced the darkness—again! (Pages 77–79)

6 March 1993: Meeting with the families. (Pages 242–282)

21 March 1993: Letter to Bill and Ira after I left the group. (Pages 150–152)

25 March 1993: My sworn statement. (Pages 183–188)

14 April 1993: First and last page of warning letter. (Pages 154–157)

19 April 1993: Mount Carmel destroyed by fire. (Pages 21, 361–362)

20 April 1993: My testimony broadcast over the airwaves. (Pages 22–23)

7 May 1993: Recollection of Prophecy of 28 February 1993. (Page 35)

8 May 1993: My proclamation of faith to God. (Pages 178–180)

12 May 1993: Commissioned by the Lord. (Pages 176–178)

17 May 1993: My courtroom appearance. (Page 188)

17 May 1993: Eve's recorded statement. (Pages 305–316)

5 June 1993: Letter to the churches. (Pages 26–39)

26 June 1993: Cover letter for Prophecy of 27 August 1992. (Pages 263–265)

𝒯IMELINE INDEX

29 June 1993: My husband's encouraging letter. (Pages 58–59)

2 July 1993: Transcript of taped recording to Candy. (Pages 45–49)

24 August 1993: Final letter to Bill. (Pages 89–157)

27 August 1993: Shining Light on the Darkness transcript. (Pages 292–293)

2 January 1994: My Real Father. (Pages 350–351)

18 September 1994: My first taped conversation with Bill. (Pages 158–167)

2 March 1997: My last taped conversation with Bill. (Pages 317–337)

27 August 2014: Something to Think About. (Pages 347–353)

14–15 May 2015 / 25–26 Iyar 5775 / 40th & 41st Day of the Omer: I have finished this edition of my testimony! (Except a little polishing.) And what an amazing journey it has been! I am certain that everything is in God's timing, and it is so providential that I would conclude this work on this very important day in the history of God's chosen people and nation.

"On May 14, 1948, on the day in which the British Mandate over a Palestine expired, the Jewish People's Council gathered at the Tel Aviv Museum, and approved the following proclamation, declaring the establishment of the State of Israel. The new state was recognized that night by the United States and three days later by the USSR."

These are the first and last paragraphs of that amazing declaration, as posted at the Ministry of Foreign Affairs at Gov.il, Israel's government website.

THE DECLARATION OF THE ESTABLISHMENT OF THE STATE OF ISRAEL

"ERETZ-ISRAEL [(Hebrew) - the Land of Israel, Palestine] was the birthplace of the Jewish people. Here their spiritual, religious and political identity was shaped. Here they first attained to statehood, created cultural values of national and universal significance and gave to the world the eternal Book of Books.

PLACING OUR TRUST IN THE 'ROCK OF ISRAEL,' WE AFFIX OUR SIGNATURES TO THIS PROCLAMATION AT THIS SESSION OF THE PROVISIONAL COUNCIL OF STATE, ON THE SOIL OF THE HOMELAND, IN THE CITY OF TEL-AVIV, ON THIS SABBATH EVE, THE 5TH DAY OF IYAR, 5708 (14TH MAY, 1948)."

Holy Scripture Index

Colossians 1:12–14 18	2 Corinthians 5:10–11 199
1 Corinthians 1:18 236	2 Corinthians 5:14–15 234
1 Corinthians 10:9–12 133	2 Corinthians 6:14–18, 7:1 201
1 Corinthians 13:1–13 73	2 John 1:9–11 338
1 Corinthians 14:27–28 103	2 Peter 1:10–12 137
1 Corinthians 14:33 129	2 Peter 1:21 175
1 Corinthians 15:1–4 174	2 Peter 2:20–21 116
1 Corinthians 2:14 172	2 Peter 3:17 116
1 Corinthians 2:4–5 197	2 Peter 3:2 175
1 Corinthians 3:18–20 197	2 Peter 3:9 107
1 Corinthians 5:1–13 202	2 Thessalonians 2:8–12 286
1 Corinthians 6:18 146	2 Timothy 1:7 73
1 Corinthians 6:2–3 294	2 Timothy 2:15, 3:16–17 196
1 John 1:9 107	2 Timothy 2:16–18 199
1 John 2:15–21 86	2 Timothy 2:19–26 205
1 John 2:18–19 .... 131, 198	2 Timothy 2:24–26 249
1 John 2:26–28 57	2 Timothy 3:1–5 244
1 John 2:26–29 .... 109, 173	2 Timothy 3:6–7 244
1 John 3:2–6, 10 232	2 Timothy 3:8–9 244
1 John 4:1–3 337	2 Timothy 4:10a,14–15................. 200
1 John 4:1–6 190	3 John 1:9–11 200
1 John 4:6 198	Acts 13:6–11 189
1 John 5:18–20 231	Acts 3:13–26 287
1 John 5:2–4 230	Colossians 1:12–14 18
1 Peter 3:1–2 60	Colossians 2:12–15 234
1 Peter 4:1–2 232	Colossians 2:4, 8 118
1 Peter 4:18 111	Deuteronomy 13:1–11 141
1 Samuel 5:1–6 289	Ecclesiastes 3:14–15 11
1 Thessalonians 4:3–8 233	Ecclesiastes 12:13–14 .... 69, 157
1 Timothy 1:19–20 200	Ephesians 1:12–14 231
1 Timothy 4:1 317	Ephesians 2:8 63
1 Timothy 5:22 98	Ephesians 5:14–16 120
2 Chronicles 7:14 69	Ephesians 5:24–27 105
2 Corinthians 10:4–6 81	Ephesians 6:10–20 74
2 Corinthians 11:13–15 173	Ezekiel 18:20–32 132
2 Corinthians 11:3 229	Ezekiel 2:1–9 52
2 Corinthians 11:3–4 296	Ezekiel 3:1–27 53
2 Corinthians 13:5 303	Galatians 1:9b 152

Holy Scripture Index

Reference	Page
Galatians 3:27–28	114
Galatians 5:19–21	207
Galatians 6:7–8	206
Genesis 3:22–24	171
Hebrews 10:26–27	133
Hebrews 10:30–31	153
Hebrews 3:12–13	133
Hebrews 3:7–13	343
Hebrews 6:4–6	153
Hosea 4:6	37
Isaiah 40:31	238
James 1:12–16	106
James 2:17–20	228
James 3:13–16	129
James 3:13–18	197
Jeremiah 1:17–19	52
Jeremiah 1:5–10	52
Jeremiah 31:31–34	67
John 1:1, 14	61, 172
John 1:12–13	229
John 12:35	285, 348
John 14:6	172
John 16:12–13	57
John 17:22–23	144
John 3:16–17	342
John 3:17–21	168
John 3:5–8; 6:44	229
Joshua 24:15a,c	305
Jude 1:12	89
Jude 1:24–25	138
Luke 12:2–3	169
Luke 22:31–32	93
Luke 22:31–34	145
Luke 4:17–21	340
Luke 8:17–18	231
Luke 8:18	41
Malachi 4:5–6	283
Mark 13:32–33	209
Mark 16:15–18	101
Matthew 12:31–32	153
Matthew 13:18–23	172
Matthew 13:24–30	192
Matthew 13:36–43	193
Matthew 16:21–23	57
Matthew 18:15–16	277
Matthew 21:42–44	210
Matthew 4:1	96, 247
Philippians 1:9–11	136
Philippians 3:10	120
Philippians 3:13–15	130
Proverbs 1:7	198
Proverbs 2:1–5	197
Proverbs 2:6–7	196
Proverbs 27:5–6	199
Proverbs 28:10	141
Proverbs 28:4–5	194
Proverbs 4:14–19	194
Proverbs 5:22	302
Proverbs 8:13	198
Proverbs 8:35–36	207
Psalms 119:92–93	172
Psalms 145:20	189
Psalms 21:8–11	189
Psalms 41:9–13	194
Psalms 5:4–6	189
Revelation 19:7–13	61
Revelation 2:20–23	147
Revelation 20:11–15	235
Revelation 20:14–15	295
Revelation 21:7–8	204
Revelation 21:8	194
Revelation 22:13	345
Revelation 22:13–15	206
Revelation 22:16	25
Revelation 22:17	62
Revelation 3:1–6	233
Romans 1:18–19	237
Romans 10:11	130
Romans 10:9–13	227
Romans 12:1–2	228
Romans 15:4	133, 175
Romans 16:25–27	134
Romans 6:16, 23	237
Romans 8:27–28	98
Titus 3:8–11	230
Zechariah 3:7	294

End Notes

(1) God's Holy Word: The King James Bible, referenced in this book, was published by Thomas Nelson, Inc., copyright 1976. I use the *Strong's Exhaustive Concordance* for more in-depth Bible study, also published by Thomas Nelson Publishers.

The King James Version (KJV), aka the Authorized Version (AV), is in the public domain in most of the world, but in the United Kingdom, the right to print, publish, and distribute the AV is a royal prerogative and the crown licenses publishers to reproduce it under "letters patent."

The AV was translated out of the *original tongues*, with previous translations diligently compared and revised, and has been accepted as the inspired Word of God by Christians down through the ages, unto this day.

The Greek texts used in the AV, known as the Textus Receptus, or Received Texts, consistently agree when compared with one another, except for differences mainly due to copying errors. It is worth noting that the precise meaning of a word in the Hebrew, Greek, or Aramaic languages is not always fully conveyed because there is not an equivalent word in the target language.

One characteristic of the King James Version is the *use of italics*, which the editors added to clarify the meaning and better relate the original language to English. I want to emphasize that the italicized words were not in the original manuscripts, and they sometimes alter the meaning and intentions of the author. Nonetheless, the KJV is a very reliable translation that can be trusted to present sound doctrine. [For this version of my book, I have put the italicized words into brackets.]

For those who are watching, God's Word has been under attack from the beginning, and Satan has been systematically undermining the true gospel of Jesus Christ. He is guilty of mixing truth with lies in order to mislead the unsuspecting soul.

The inclusion of the manuscripts of Westcott and Hort, and other corrupt writings, into modern versions of the Bible has caused great division in the body of Christ, and I see this one issue as *the* major cause of error and deception in the churches.

The corrupted copies, also known as the Alexandrian manuscripts, many times do not even agree with each other. The Vaticanus and Sinaiticus manuscripts are part of this deviant group of manuscripts and are heavily relied upon by most translators.

I am not against modern versions as such, *just the poison in them!* Some versions are very subtle in their mixture (which brings about a slow death), but others are so blatant in their corruption! I am outraged that they are *even* called a Bible!

The debates about the King James Bible and modern versions have been ongoing, and we must not "agree to disagree" any longer; otherwise, Satan will continue to lead people astray. How much "poison" are you willing to take or share with others?

(2) Purim: Esther 9:20–22, 28 "And Mordecai wrote these things, and sent letters unto all the Jews that [were] in all the provinces of the king Ahasuerus, [both] nigh

and far, to stablish [this] among them, that they should keep the fourteenth day of the month Adar, and the fifteenth day of the same, yearly, as the days wherein the Jews rested from their enemies, and the month which was turned unto them from sorrow to joy, and from mourning into a good day: that they should make them days of feasting and joy, and of sending portions one to another, and gifts to the poor....

And [that] these days [should be] remembered and kept throughout every generation, every family, every province, and every city; and [that] these days of Purim should not fail from among the Jews, nor the memorial of them perish from their seed."

(3) Providence House Publishers: The first publisher of *Walking With the Enemy*. I had sent them my manuscript on 31 October 1994, and I was so excited that I was able to complete this work on my enemy's most sacred holiday—Halloween!

What's even more amazing, my book arrived at my doorstep on 28 February 1995, exactly two years to the day that God delivered me from my enemy! I was not yet aware that I had received my book, because the package was left at a door I don't normally use. It was not until after I called Providence House that I realized I had the book in my possession. I was so thrilled when I found it, and I am sure the lady from the publisher remembers because I left her holding on the line while I went to see if it was there. And it was! Praise God!

Over the years, there have been many different people involved in getting this book ready for publication, and I do not know all the names of those who have had a hand in it. But God does, and I pray that He will abundantly bless them for their efforts!

I would especially like to ask the Lord God to bless my dear husband and children for their help with the work of the ministry, whether it was directly or indirectly. All of us have made sacrifices to some degree for this work to be done, and I am so thankful for my loved ones who stood by me, even when they didn't feel like it.

(4) The Message: In previous editions of this book I capitalized "The Message," but at that time, I knew nothing of Eugene H. Peterson and his paraphrase of the Bible. (His book was partially published by NavPress in 1993 and finished in 2002.) And I want to emphasize: I have no affiliation whatsoever with Peterson or his *message*.

These verses come to mind when I consider his so-called Bible. 2 Peter 1:20 "Knowing this first, that no prophecy of the Scripture is of any private interpretation."

Revelation 22:19 "And if any man shall take away from the Words of the book of this prophecy, God shall take away his part out of the Book of Life, and out of the Holy City, and [from] the things which are written in this book."

(5) Ninth of Av: 2 Kings 25:8–9 records that the seventh day of Av is when the Roman general entered into Jerusalem to begin burning "the house of the LORD, and the king's house, and all the houses of Jerusalem." According to the historian Josephus, the second temple was destroyed in AD 70 by the Romans on the tenth of Av. However, many religious Jews observe the Ninth of Av as a day of mourning in remembrance of the destruction of the Jewish temples in Jerusalem.

End Notes

(6) Reference to AD 70: Matthew 24:1–2 "And Jesus went out, and departed from the temple: and His disciples came to [Him] for to shew Him the buildings of the temple. And Jesus said unto them, See ye not all these things? verily I say unto you, There shall not be left here one stone upon another, that shall not be thrown down."

(7) Jesus "will swallow up death in victory!" Isaiah 25:8 "He will swallow up death in victory; and the Lord God will wipe away tears from off all faces; and the rebuke of His people shall He take away from off all the earth: for the Lord hath spoken [it]."

(8) Yeshua HaMashiach: Yeshua is the Hebrew translation for Jesus, and it means, "YHWH is salvation." YHWH are the four consonants that make up the Holy Name of the God of Israel, who is the Most High God, the Great I AM! HaMashiach is the Hebrew word for Christ, meaning *anointed one*.

There are those who would cast a dark shadow over the name of Jesus; however, it's not how you pronounce His beautiful name that is most important, but whether you personally know the Messiah of Israel, the Savior of the world.

(9) Branch Davidian compound: It was located on seventy-seven acres, with the main structure having a fortress-like construction. Prior to David Koresh's takeover of the group, separate housing units lined the road, but he had them dismantled. The building he had constructed did not have indoor plumbing, air conditioning, or heating, but Koresh's room was equipped with all of these amenities and other conveniences.

The Branch Davidians was a movement started by members of the Seventh-day Adventist church. David Koresh and his followers were in the building at the time of the failed raid, which took place on the morning of 28 February 1993, when ATF agents (a force of seventy-six) were attempting to execute lawful search-and-arrest warrants at the Branch Davidian compound near Waco, Texas.

The ATF agents were allegedly ambushed by the members of this religious cult, led by David Koresh. Reportedly, the Davidians opened fire with assault weapons before the agents reached the door. The gunfire continued until the Branch Davidian leaders agreed to a cease-fire. This unsuccessful raid resulted in the deaths of at least two Branch Davidians and four ATF special agents: Conway LeBleu, Todd W. McKeehan, Robert J. Williams, and Steven D. Willis.

After a fifty-one-day standoff with the FBI, ATF, and other law enforcement, the Branch Davidian compound was engulfed in flames and burned to the ground on 19 April 1993. Reportedly, eighty-two people perished in the fire during the siege on that fateful day, including women and children. They said many had gunshot wounds, possibly inflicted by fellow cult members or their own hand.

I am deeply saddened by the many lives lost due to the horrible tragedy that took place in that compound, but I am also greatly concerned about the innocent souls that are being led down the road to death and destruction by the likes of David Koresh. May God's people have eyes to see what *really* happened on that day!

(10) Mount Carmel: This was the name given to the Branch Davidian compound. According to the Scriptures, Mount Carmel was the place where the prophet Elijah

prayed for God to rain down fire upon his sacrifice, rather than on the sacrifices of the prophets of Baal, to prove that they were false prophets.

Elijah's prayer was answered, and the fire of God fell and consumed only his sacrifice and all that surrounded it, which caused God's people to acknowledge that the Lord God Almighty is the only True and Living God (1 Kings 18:17–40).

(11) David Koresh, aka Vernon Howell (17 August 1959–19 April 1993): Reportedly, Vernon Howell filed a petition in the California State Superior Court in Pomona, California, on 15 May 1990, to change his name for publicity and business purposes to David Koresh. The judge granted his petition on 28 August 1990.

Koresh violently took over Mount Carmel in 1987 after a power struggle with the son of the previous leader. David Koresh's followers were extremely devoted to him, and he obviously had a stronghold over them since the men were willing to just hand their wives over to him. His committed followers even killed for him and, ultimately, died for him! All in the name of God!

There are numerous reports, articles, videos, congressional hearings, and books on David Koresh, but one thing we must *never forget*: This man claimed to be "Christ," the Lamb of God, the Messiah. He also claimed to have special knowledge on the seven seals in the book of Revelation, which he was supposedly writing about prior to his death. There is much more I could say about this man, but it is so important for others to know that Koresh was *not* of God, as he professed to be. In fact, he was of the same antichrist spirit as the man sent to try to destroy me and my family!

(12) David Breese (14 October 1926–3 May 2002): He was a well-known prophecy and cult expert. He sent me his thirty-two-page booklet entitled *The Marks of a Cult*, but I must say, it would *not* have prepared me for the cult that I was in.

Based on the conversations I had with Dr. Breese after the interview, he seemed to be a very humble man. And even though I do not necessarily agree with his view of the rapture, I am hoping to meet him in Heaven one glorious day!

(13) A Bible study group: In the radio interview, I revealed the actual name of Bill's ministry, but I have chosen to remove his title from my testimony.

(14) Caller (deceased): Ironically, the next caller was a Pentecostal woman who used to go around town visiting various churches, regardless of the denomination. She was a very strange woman, and I was quite uncomfortable in her presence. She would repeatedly chant the name of Jesus while the preacher was praying from the pulpit, which was extremely annoying to say the least, and evil at best!

(15) Woman (deceased): She was a member of the Eastern Star, and her husband was a Freemason, which explains their hostility toward me after I started sending out my 5 June 1993 letter. Due to the lukewarm decision made in regard to Freemasonry by the Southern Baptist Convention at their gathering in June 1993, my family and I eventually left this church that was in agreement with their ruling. The SBC leadership said that each church should decide if its members could be a part of

End Notes

this secretive organization, regardless of the fact that the SBC Home Mission Board deemed the "god" of Freemasonry to be *Abaddon!*

Revelation 9:11 "And they had a king over them, [which is] the angel of the bottomless pit, whose name in the Hebrew tongue [is] Abaddon, but in the Greek tongue hath [his] name Apollyon."

(16) Main group: Bill (his real name): I have noted some details about Bill so as not to confuse him with others with the same name. His young, unmarried mother gave him up for adoption when he was born, and he was raised by a prominent family.

He said he had been enlisted in the US Army as a chaplain and was a psychology teacher as a civilian. As far as I know, he has five children (three by one wife and two by the other). He has been divorced at least twice. He found his birthmother, but soon after she came to live with him, she had a bad accident and died soon afterward. (This is according to what Ira wrote me.) I was told that he now lives in New York, but I have not verified that information. I hope no other Bill fits this profile.

Ira (not her real name): Please note: Ira, Alisha, and Elisha mentioned in this book are one and the same person.

Candy (not her real name): After I joined the group, she left for a short time, but returned to the group after she attended a birthday party for Bill in December 1990.

Wendell (not his real name): He was one of the newest members of the group. After I left the group, I never heard from him again. I hope he found the Lord!

Thomas (not his real name): He was with the group the whole time that I was, and he eventually left several months after the group broke up. May God be with him!

Kim (not her real name): A young girl who joined at the invitation of a friend.

(17) Listing: After the Bible study group was exposed due to my 5 June 1993 letter that I mailed out, its ministry listing was removed from the church section of the local newspaper (under much protest from Ira, I was told). A year later, its listing showed back up in the newspaper, just as it was before. I spoke with the editor, and he assured me that it was probably due to an error. It was promptly removed again. I am sure that this editor was warned about this cult, but just like me when I first came to Bill's Bible study group, he may not have understood the great danger involved. May this testimony be a wakeup call for all God's people!

(18) Open to the public: After Bill and Ira were exposed, they continued to meet at Ira's home, where the public was invited, but they were forced to disband. I heard that Ira was attending a local United Methodist church, but they eventually resumed going to their former charismatic church. Ira informed me in a letter that she and Bill were going to counseling sessions at that church, which only cemented my distrust for them.

(19) Won't continue walking with Jesus: This assertion by Christian cult leaders is a common ploy to instill fear of leaving the group, by leading people to believe that if they do not stay they are denying Jesus and will be doomed for Hell.

(20) References: Hebrews 13:5; Matthew 28:17–20; Revelation 22:12; Revelation 1:8.

(21) The Sunday morning paper: The article that I had referenced was the second of a series of articles that the *Waco Tribune-Herald* had begun on 27 February 1993, entitled *Sinful Messiah*, specifically targeting David Koresh and his cult.

The headline for that 28 February 1993 article read: "Ex-members say cult 'messiah' abuses children." In that same article, Howell/Koresh is quoted as saying, "If the Bible is true, then I'm Christ."

(22) Claims that he was Christ: The advocates of the late David Koresh say he did not claim to be "Jesus, or even God himself," but they said, and I quote, "He certainly did claim to be this Lamb who opens the sealed scroll, as well as the figure who rides the White Horse when the First Seal is opened, and appears at the end of the book, still mounted on the same White Horse, when the 'marriage of the Lamb' takes place (Revelation 6:1–2; 19:7–19)."

These statements by some of Koresh's remaining advocates are so contradictory because the "Lamb" in the book of Revelation *is the Lord Jesus Christ, the Messiah!*

(23) Psalms 68:1–2 "Let God arise, let His enemies be scattered: let them also that hate Him flee before Him. As smoke is driven away, [so] drive [them] away: as wax melteth before the fire, [so] let the wicked perish at the presence of God."

(24) Prince of the power of the air: In Ephesians 2:2, the Devil is known as the "prince of the power of the air, the spirit that now worketh in the children of disobedience."

(25) Fireplace: In front of the hearth by the fireplace where Bill used to sit and teach, he adopted a ritual from his revered John Osteen, where he mimicked his routine statement at the start of every service. It started out like this: "This is my Bible, I am what it says I am. I can do what it says I can do…" The elder Osteen died in 1999, and his youngest son, Joel, took over where his father left off.

(26) Word for word: On 7 May 1993, God brought back to my memory the very words that were spoken by the Holy Spirit on that remarkable night of 28 February 1993. I truly believe that what happened that night is in fulfillment of the Holy Scriptures, and I am so humbled that God would reveal Himself to me in such a mighty way.

(27) Prophecy of 28 February 1993: Here are a few passages from the Scriptures that help confirm this prophecy: Daniel 2:28a; Joel 2:28; Mark 2:28; Luke 2:28–32; Acts 2:28; Romans 2:28–29; 1 John 2:28; Revelation 2:28–29.

(28) Prophecy of 28 February 1993: Bill was addressed by his last name.

(29) United States Marine Corps: While I was enlisted in the United States Marine Corps, many significant changes took place in my life. When I was on a temporary assignment to Yuma, Arizona, Iranian students seized the American Embassy in Tehran on 4 November 1979, taking sixty-six Americans hostage.

End Notes

The Marines stationed in Japan went on red alert, including my boyfriend. I was worried because his unit could have been called to go to Iran at a moment's notice. Thankfully, he never got the call, and on 20 January 1981, the American hostages were finally released by Iran, right after President Ronald Reagan took office.

Just as 11 September 2001 was a momentous event that greatly affected this nation *and the world,* so too was the Iranian Crisis a day of reckoning for so many people, including myself. I was definitely headed in the wrong direction, and I praise God that He sent one of His servants to direct my way back to Him. In November 1979, I gave my heart to the Lord, and I have been walking with Him ever since. And only by the grace of God will I continue unto the end!

(30) Born again: There is much debate over what it truly means to be "born again" and "filled with the Spirit." To become a child of God and to be born again is solely in the hands of God, and it's the same with being filled with His Spirit. Please prayerfully consider these passages.

John 1:10–13 "He was in the world, and the world was made by Him, and the world knew Him not. He came unto His own, and His own received Him not.

But as many as received Him, to them gave He power to become the sons of God, [even] to them that believe on His name: Which were born, not of blood, nor of the will of the flesh, nor of the will of man, but of God."

John 3:5–8 "Jesus answered, Verily, verily, I say unto thee, Except a man be born of water and [of] the Spirit, he cannot enter the Kingdom of God.

That which is born of the flesh is flesh; and that which is born of the Spirit is spirit. Marvel not that I said unto thee, Ye must be born again.

The wind bloweth where it listeth, and thou hearest the sound thereof, but canst not tell whence it cometh, and whither it goeth: so is every one that is born of the Spirit."

(31) 1 John 4:4 "Ye are of God, little children, and have overcome them: because greater is He that is in you, than he that is in the world."

(32) 5 June 1993: God prompted me to have this letter notarized at the chancery clerk's office on 11 June 1993. I have since discovered that 11 June 1967 was the last day of the Six-Day War between Israel and the Arab nations. And I must proclaim, the God of Abraham, Isaac, and Jacob *is my God too!*

Just a little Israeli war trivia from an article I read in *Israel My Glory* magazine (Volume 55, Number 5, 1997). After centuries of not having a homeland of their own, Israel was "reborn" on 14 May 1948. Egypt, Syria, and Jordan had devised a plan to destroy this small nation, and with no other choice but to defend themselves, the Israeli Air Force attacked Egypt on the morning of 5 June 1967.

Amazingly, they destroyed almost the entire Egyptian Air Force (more than three hundred planes) in less than three hours! And on that same day of 5 June 1967, Israel's armored divisions, under the leadership of Ariel Sharon, destroyed more than eight hundred Egyptian tanks and took thousands of prisoners in just three days!

The second phase of this Six-Day War resulted in the capture of East Jerusalem, to include the Old City, which prior to that had been controlled by the Arab Legion. When under Jordanian control, they decimated the Jewish Quarter of the Old City, blowing up its synagogues and destroying every vestige of Jewish life there. Jewish gravestones on the Mount of Olives had even been used to pave roads!

By 8 June 1967, Israel had access to the Western Wall—the remnant of the wall that once surrounded the ancient Jewish temple. Israel also won back the ancient towns of Shechem, Shiloh, Bethel, Bethlehem, and Hebron—very holy sites, according to biblical history.

Finally, on 10 June 1967, Syria accepted a cease-fire and Israel was now in control of the Golan Heights—a most strategic position. Israel has given back much of what the brave men and women fought and died for—all in the name of peace. But if they ever lose access to the Golan, they are doomed!

The Oslo Accords (13 September 1993 through 28 September 2000) were supposed to bring the people of Israel peace and safety, but they have no peace or safety—only unrest, death, and destruction! Moreover, God's people will never have true peace until they put their trust in the Lord Jesus Christ, the Prince of Peace, who is the Messiah, the Holy One of Israel.

I pray for the day when I see God's chosen people recognize the Messiah of Israel and earnestly call upon the Lord with a sincere and repentant heart. And only until God's people truly repent and depart from all that is evil will they be the holy nation that God intended, and then they can truly be a light unto the nations!

(33) Great White Throne: There is much speculation as to who will be judged at this final judgment, as referenced in Revelation; and I am reluctant to be definitive as to exactly what will happen on that Day, but it is obvious that there are two sets of people being judged—those who belong to God and those who do not. God said you must be "born again" to enter into Heaven, and how you respond to God and His Holy Word will determine your destiny. It's not your bloodline that matters, but whether your name is written in the Book of Life.

Revelation 20:11–15 "And I saw a Great White Throne, and Him that sat on it, from whose face the earth and the Heaven fled away; and there was found no place for them. And I saw the dead, small and great, stand before God; and the books were opened: and another book was opened, which is [the Book] of Life: and the dead were judged out of those things which were written in the books, according to their works.

And the sea gave up the dead which were in it; and death and Hell delivered up the dead which were in them: and they were judged every man according to their works. And death and Hell were cast into the Lake of Fire. This is the second death. And whosoever was not found written in the Book of Life was cast into the Lake of Fire."

(34) Amos 3:3 "Can two walk together, except they be agreed?"

End Notes

(35) FM Station: After leaving Bill's cult group, I have come to understand that the contemporary "Christian" music industry is directly responsible for leading many unsuspecting souls down the road to compromise and worldly living.

Music can manipulate our emotions for good or for evil, and just because it has a Christian label does not mean the company or the artists are true Christians. My prayer is that God's people will truly bow before Him, so that He can reveal what is true and what is false, what is pleasing to Him and what is not. And only *then* will God's people be able to worship Him in Spirit and in truth, as He so deserves!

(36) Friends: The official title for this song is "Friends Are Friends Forever" (1983) by Michael W. Smith, who wrote the music, and his wife, Debbie, wrote the lyrics.

I first heard this song when I lost some friends that I really thought I would know forever. But I was so wrong!

(37) What if you are wrong?: I posed this question to the rabbi during a three-session introductory course on Judaism that Bill, Ira, Candy, and I attended in the first part of February 1993. The question pertained to his rejection of Jesus being the Messiah. I don't remember his response, but I believe he sensed my sincerity.

I have found that many Jewish folks are quite hostile toward Christians, as foretold in the Holy Scriptures (Romans 11:25-33), but one day, God will take away the blinders, and for those who truly love Him, He will give them eyes to see the truth. Please prayerfully consider this prophetic passage that is yet to be:

Zechariah 12:9-10 "And it shall come to pass in that day, [that] I will seek to destroy all the nations that come against Jerusalem.

And I will pour upon the house of David, and upon the inhabitants of Jerusalem, the spirit of grace and of supplications: and they shall look upon Me Whom they have pierced, and they shall mourn for Him, as one mourneth for [his] only [son], and shall be in bitterness for Him, as one that is in bitterness for [his] firstborn."

(38) Blasphemy of the Holy Spirit: This grave sin is mentioned at least three times in the New Testament by three separate witnesses: Matthew 12:31-32; Mark 3:28-29; and Luke 12:10. They all emphatically state that it is the only unforgivable sin.

(39) The Laodicean church is among the seven churches addressed in Revelation 2-3. In Revelation 3:14-22, God was greatly displeased with the people of this church because they had become apathetic, lazy, boastful, arrogant, and self-righteous—the very condition of many people in the present-day church.

God dearly loves His people and will warn us if we are going the wrong way, but we must listen for His voice and strive to obey Him. When God warned the churches in Revelation, He addressed an angel rather than a man because "God [is] a Spirit: and they that worship Him must worship [Him] in spirit and in truth" (John 4:24).

1 Corinthians 2:14-16 "But the natural man receiveth not the things of the Spirit of God: for they are foolishness unto him: neither can he know [them], because they are spiritually discerned. But he that is spiritual judgeth all things, yet he himself is judged of no man. For who hath known the mind of the Lord, that he may instruct Him? But we have the mind of Christ."

All of this gets back to the great need to be born again of God's Spirit. God is knocking at the door. Will you let Him in? "He that hath an ear, let him hear what the Spirit saith unto the churches!" (See Revelation 2:11, 17, 29; 3:6, 13, 22.)

(40) Letter: In December 1996, I sent a letter to a Messianic Jewish rabbi (Jewish teacher who believes in Jesus) regarding the Pensacola Revival. I asked him, "What is your opinion of the Pensacola Revival, which appears to be connected with the Toronto Outpouring?" His response was lukewarm, but due to that first letter, I started sending out the same question to various Christians (Jew and Gentile), particularly those in leadership.

Amazingly, almost everyone responded to me, and the results were quite interesting. About a third were for it, another third were against it, and the rest could go either way. But very few saw these so-called *revivals* for what they really are, *which is* the "working of Satan with all lying wonders" (2 Thessalonians 2:9).

(41) *Walking in the True Light: A Testimony* was published on 5 September 1997, exactly one year after I heard about the revival that took place in Pensacola, Florida, on Father's Day 1995. I learned of this "move of God" after listening to an interview on a Christian radio station of the minister who was promoting a women in ministry conference at his church that was heavily involved with the Pensacola Revival. God led me to attend the conference, and when I saw what was happening at the services, it was reminiscent of what took place at Bill's ministry, but on a much wider scale!

(42) Southern Baptist churches: If I had to choose a denomination that I am closest to, it would be the Baptists, but I am disheartened with them too. So many in the Baptist churches have completely fallen for the evils of this age, which is a major indicator that we are definitely in the "apostasy," as spoken of in the Holy Scriptures.

Moreover, considering that the "strange fire" that began burning in Toronto, Canada, in January 1994, aka the "Toronto Blessing/Outpouring," was actually fueled by a Southern-Baptist-trained man further proves to me that the "great falling away" as spoken of in the Scriptures has been going on for at least twenty years now. (See 2 Thessalonians 2.)

(43) Devin (not his real name): I met this man at a tent revival that I attended while I was with the Bible study group, and he even came to one of our meetings.

(44) 29 June 1993: My husband was on his way to a service call when God prompted him to pull over to the side of the road and write this wonderful letter to me.

(45) Ruby (not her real name.): Ira used to occasionally speak about this lady, who was a member of the Bible study group before I joined.

(46) Dairy Queen: Bill, Ira, Candy, and I had stopped at Dairy Queen prior to going to the synagogue for a Judaism course. While the girls and I were in the bathroom, something strange was happening. It was as if there was a presence surrounding us. Ira told me it was a demonic attack, and she and Candy started praying for me.

End Notes

Even after we got to the synagogue, I still felt this unusual presence, which was causing me to be very anxious and even fearful. Thank God, the feeling did not last, and it left me after I got home when I was no longer with Bill or Ira. In retrospect, I believe the Lord was starting to open up my "spiritual eyes" to be able to discern when I was in the presence of evil.

(47) According to the website www.kingjamesbibleonline.org, Hell is referenced in 54 instances in the King James Bible, and Heaven is mentioned in 551 instances. It would appear that Heaven is of higher importance to God, and *it is* His desired destiny for all men. But sadly, according to the Scriptures, "few there be that find it" (Matthew 7:14).

(48) Judgment seat of Christ: 1 Peter 4:17–18 "For the time [is come] that judgment must begin at the house of God: and if [it] first [begin] at us, what shall the end [be] of them that obey not the gospel of God? And if the righteous scarcely be saved, where shall the ungodly and the sinner appear?"

(49) Baptist Book Store: This store no longer exists, and was replaced by LifeWay, the retail arm of the Southern Baptist Convention, which closed all brick and mortar stores in 2019.

(50) John 1:29 "The next day John seeth Jesus coming unto him, and saith, Behold the Lamb of God, which taketh away the sin of the world."

(51) Preached on the house, uh, mountaintops: Ira said mountaintops, but I wanted to say housetops. Consider what God says about it:
Matthew 10:27 "What I tell you in darkness, [that] speak ye in light: and what ye hear in the ear, [that] preach ye upon the housetops."
Ezekiel 6:13 "Then shall ye know that I [am] the Lord, when their slain [men] shall be among their idols round about their altars, upon every high hill, in all the tops of the mountains, and under every green tree, and under every thick oak, the place where they did offer sweet savour to all their idols."

(52) MasterLife: A discipleship program authored by Avery T. Willis, Jr. and produced by the Church Training Department of The Sunday School Board of the Southern Baptist Convention, 1982, in Nashville, TN.

(53) Hosea 4:6 "My people are destroyed for lack of knowledge: because thou hast rejected knowledge, I will also reject thee, that thou shalt be no priest to Me: seeing thou hast forgotten the law of thy God, I will also forget thy children."

(54) Mark 13:22 "For false Christs and false prophets shall rise, and shall shew signs and wonders, to seduce, if [it were] possible, even the elect."

(55) Demanding that they leave my home: Ira went through my entire house praying and anointing my home by putting oil over every doorway, even closet doors! She said it was to keep the demons away.

(56) 14 May: This was an important date in history for God's chosen people too. The Israeli Declaration of Independence was signed on 14 May 1948 / 5 Iyyar 5708, with the expiration of the British Mandate over Palestine (the land of Israel). David Ben-Gurion, the first prime minister of Israel, declared the establishment of a Jewish state in Eretz Yisrael, known as the State of Israel. This prophetic event is celebrated every year in Israel as a national holiday on 5 Iyyar, according to the Hebrew calendar.

(57) My own husband: Ira was right there when we had this discussion about who Bill was to me, and she is not the innocent victim Bill tries to make her out to be.

(58) That Day: Regarding the great and dreadful day of the Lord, read Malachi 4:5–6.

(59) Only a few are right: This is a very common indoctrination technique used in cults to not only instill fear of leaving the group, but also to produce pride in its members, along with a blind loyalty to the leaders of the cult group.

(60) Husband leaving: He left for active duty on 4 January 1991, and was separated from our family for almost a year and a half. It is important to note that the *only* way the Devil could carry out his evil deeds to the degree that he did with me required the absence of my husband.

(61) *This Present Darkness* (published by Crossway Books, 1986) was written by Frank Peretti, a popular author who has written many fictitious books about God, Satan, and the spiritual world. Ira also encouraged me to read some books by a former witch who claimed to be a Christian. I now understand why.

(62) Sue (not her real name): She was with the Bible study group almost the whole time that I was, but quit coming soon before the group broke up.

(63) Seminar: Charles Simpson was the preacher that night, and he was calling people to the front to be prayed for and filled with the Spirit. According to his website that I visited on 2 March 2015, he still has a very active ministry.

(64) "Filled with the Spirit:" If you find yourself in a service where the ministers are "laying hands" on people as they pray (in a known language or in other tongues), especially if the people are falling to the ground, you need to get out ASAP!

This practice of praying for people and knocking them to the ground is *not* of God, no matter what people say about it. In the charismatic and Pentecostal circles, they call it "slain in the Spirit." They say the reason people fall back is due to the presence and power of the Spirit. It's also called "falling under the anointing," but I must warn you that demonic spirits are the ones touching people, and the ministers who do this are under the influence of the Devil, whether they are aware of it or not. Please beware! Satan is *real*, and he wants to destroy your life any way he can!

(65) Wife and children: At this time, Bill was separated from his wife, and she was planning to divorce him, which she eventually did.

End Notes

(66) Messianic Jewish fellow: Zola Levitt (3 December 1938–19 April 2006): Mr. Levitt professed to be a Jewish convert to Christianity. He founded Zola Levitt Ministries, and TBN (the Trinity Broadcasting Network) was among those that aired his shows filmed in Israel. The fact that TBN is home to many Pentecostal and charismatic ministers proves that they are major facilitators of the apostasy.

(67) Baby shower: I was pregnant with our first son when my husband was ordered to active duty for military training. He was gone for a year and a half, and this was the only time that my husband was not present for the birth of one of our children.

My enemy wanted to claim my firstborn son as his own, but he can't have him because he belongs to God! Bill even tried to be in the room during the birth, but my "great physician" would not allow it! Thank God! I know my son is very special to God, as are all my children, and I see where the Lord was using him even before he was born! Praise God!

(68) From the Lord, 9 June 1991: Try reading this letter as if it was actually Satan speaking to me, and it takes on a completely different meaning.

(69) Once saved, always saved theory: This is a very popular teaching among Baptists, and I believe it has helped to contribute to sin and apathy in the churches. Yes, I believe you can know for certain that you belong to God and that your name is in the Book of Life, but to say you could *never* fall away from God is just not true. You have to discount many passages in the Word of God to believe this fallacy.

(70) In the original letter, I quote the Jewish New Testament, which is now called the Complete Jewish Bible (CJB), a modern version that Bill highly recommended.

(71) 27 February 1992: At the time I heard these words, it was as if I was surrounded by a very dark presence. I now realize that these were the words of the Devil himself! It was also truth mixed with lies, just like God warned about on 28 February 1993.

(72) God's anointed: This is a ploy by cult leaders to cause fear and intimidation so as to discourage dissent among the members. It is based on the following passage. Psalms 105:15 "[Saying,] Touch not Mine anointed, and do My prophets no harm."

Ira would always compare Bill with King Saul, a man that started out serving God, but turned away from God and was eventually rejected by God, even though he was the "Lord's anointed." Ironically, it sounds a lot like Bill, but he was never a king.

1 Samuel 16:14 "But the Spirit of the LORD departed from Saul, and an evil spirit from the LORD troubled him."

(73) Comfort to you: I actually believed that God was speaking to me in that message, dated 27 February 1992. I have since realized it was the Devil that led me to believe I was supposed to be a "comfort" to Bill. As my testimony reveals, it is so important to be able to discern the voice of God versus the many voices of the wicked!

(74) The piano: The Sunday after I left the group, Bill and some of the men from the Bible study group came to get Ira's piano. They were driving a small pickup, and they pulled around to the back of my house where they were going to load the piano. After they got it onto the truck, they were significantly weighed down. They could barely creep through my yard! As they were desperately trying to leave, I started praying in the Spirit. Then I began circling their vehicle while quoting, "If any man preach any other gospel besides the gospel of Jesus Christ, let him be accursed!"

As I followed them all the way to the end of my driveway, I was still quoting the passage from Galatians 1:6–9. When they were finally able to leave my property, it was as if I just threw them out of my presence. As my voice reverberated up into the heavens, they slowly drove off down the road. It was truly another amazing day!

(75) Sermon on national television: As I was working on this edition of my book, I was sad to discover that the minister (of Changed Lives ministry) who preached that important sermon had died at the age of eighty-eight. As currently posted at his website: "On October 24, 2013, Ben Haden went to be with his Heavenly Father."

I know he will be very missed by his family and friends who personally knew him, but *he is* in a much better place. And I look forward to meeting him face to face one great and glorious day, in the place that God has prepared for those who love Him!

(76) Warning letter: I included Reverend Ben Haden's sermon with this letter.

(77) Hebrews 10:26–27 "For if we sin willfully after that we have received the knowledge of the truth, there remaineth no more sacrifice for sins, but a certain fearful looking for of judgment and fiery indignation, which shall devour the adversaries."

(78) Demonic spirit: A person who is truly born again of God's Spirit cannot be possessed by evil spirits or demons, but a Christian can be adversely affected by the agents of Satan, as I experienced firsthand while I was walking with the enemy.

(79) 14 April 1993 warning letter: I did not realize it when I wrote this letter, but the fourteenth of April has great historical significance on many different levels. It was also on that day in 1912 that the warnings were sent to the RMS *Titanic!*

Had those in charge of this once-great ship realized the danger they were in and the dire consequences of ignoring the warnings, they could have spared the lives of so many innocent people from such a horrible and untimely death.

Pride is why they could not hear the warnings then, and it is the same in our day! God has been warning His people, but they just will not listen to Him or to those whom He has sent. And it grieves the heart of God that those He created for His good pleasure do not count His voice worthy of consideration. Just as the many men, women, and children perished in the icy waters that early April morning, so too will many be lost in the pits of Hell because they failed to heed the many warnings.

A few RMS *Titanic* facts: The *Titanic* left Southampton on 10 April 1912 at noon and narrowly escaped a collision with the *New York*—an American ocean liner. On 14 April 1912, the *Titanic* received numerous ice warnings, but all were ignored. (At 10:30 p.m., the temperature of the sea was thirty-one degrees.) At 11:00 p.m.,

END NOTES

the *Californian* warned about the ice but was told to shut up and was cut off by the wireless operator before it gave the location. This final warning never reached the bridge, and at 11:40 p.m., the RMS *Titanic* collided with an iceberg at latitude 41° 46′ N, longitude 50° 14′ W. It sank at 2:20 a.m. on 15 April 1912.

The *Carpathia* rescued 705 survivors between 4:10 a.m. and 8:30 a.m. The exact number of lives lost in the *Titanic* tragedy varies depending on where you get your information, but between 1,635 and 1,490 souls died on that unforgettable night. This horrifying tragedy could have been circumvented had those in charge of this so-called *unsinkable ship* heeded the many warnings, *especially the final warning!*

(80) Rosh Hashanah: On the first day of the seventh Jewish month of Tishrei (late September or early October), the shofar/trumpet is blown during Rosh Hashanah, which signifies that a momentous event is about to take place. And according to Leviticus 23:23–25, this season is an important time to prepare for the Judgment.

This special Sabbath is to be holy unto the Lord, and no work was to be performed on that day. Ten days later, according to the Scriptures, the Day of Atonement (a.k.a. Yom Kippur) is commemorated, which is the highest holy day on the Hebrew calendar. Repentance and forgiveness are the focus of this very special day, and when the temple in Jerusalem was still standing, it was the one day of the year that the Lord God allowed the high priest, and *only him*, to go into the holy place to make atonement for his sins and the sins of the people.

After much prayer, and study of God's Word, I believe that it was on the Day of Atonement that Jesus, the Son of the living God, was miraculously conceived by the power of the Holy Spirit, *within the veil*, where no eyes could see, except the Holy Father.

And it is this same Jesus, "by Whom we have now received the atonement," for all who receive the gift of eternal life through God's dear Son, Whom He raised from the dead, and "Who is gone into Heaven, and is on the right hand of God; angels and authorities and powers being made subject unto Him."

Hebrews 4:14–16 "Seeing then that we have a great high priest, that is passed into the heavens, Jesus the Son of God, let us hold fast [our] profession. (See Romans 5:11; 1 Peter 3:22.)

For we have not a high priest which cannot be touched with the feeling of our infirmities; but was in all points tempted like as [we are, yet] without sin. Let us therefore come boldly unto the throne of grace, that we may obtain mercy, and find grace to help in time of need."

It is so sad to watch people praying at the Western Wall in Jerusalem (via the Kotel), knowing that most of them do not even know the Lord Jesus Christ, the only one who can truly save their souls.

So many Jewish folks have yet to see that Jesus is the true Messiah of Israel, but they will one day! And I am utterly amazed at how God ensured that the very day of Jesus's conception would be highly exalted by the Jewish people without them understanding the ultimate significance of that holy day until the time appointed.

May the Lord have mercy on His people who are not yet able to see that it is Jesus "in Whom we have redemption through His blood, the forgiveness of sins, according to the riches of His grace;" (See Ephesians 1:7.)

For those who say they know the Lord and claim to be "once saved, always saved," yet they can still sin against God and their own bodies, without a major war going on inside, they need to realize that Christ is still on the outside waiting to come in!

1 Corinthians 6:18 "Flee fornication. Every sin that a man doeth is without the body; but he that committeth fornication sinneth against his own body."

John 3:5 Jesus said, "Except a man be born of water and [of] the Spirit, he cannot enter into the Kingdom of God."

And despite what many well-meaning men may teach or believe, to be born of water *and the Spirit* is solely in the hands of God!

(81) Go to church anywhere: After the group broke up, Bill and Ira had eventually resumed going to the charismatic church they used to go to. Some charismatic ministers may say they are nondenominational, but they *are* Pentecostal in practice. The services are characterized by "praise and worship music," and then the ministers "lay hands" on people and pray for them to be "filled with the Spirit."

Vineyard/Word of Faith are charismatic churches, and regardless of how much they talk about God, Jesus, or Israel and how *loved* you may feel, it's not the feeling that's important, but what *spirit* is behind what they say and do, Christ or antichrist?

Promise Keepers is a parachurch organization that was established by charismatic ministers, with an ecumenical emphasis. Considering the ecumenical movement came from the Roman Catholic Church's attempts to reconcile with other religions, particularly with the "separated brethren" in order to get the Protestants back under their control, it is understandable that the founder of PK was a charismatic Roman Catholic.

(82) "I called you because I want you, C.": I *really* don't think Bill meant to say that out loud, but that's just how the Devil works. He will eventually let his true colors shine through if you give him time.

Bill's revealing statement is indicative of who he serves. Consider this passage I referenced at the start of my testimony. Luke 22:31 "And the Lord said, Simon, Simon, behold, Satan hath desired [to have] you, that he may sift [you] as wheat."

I am sure the Devil still *wants me,* so he can destroy me if he can! I just praise God for the rest of that passage.

Luke 22:32 "But I (Jesus) have prayed for thee, that thy faith fail not: and when thou art converted, strengthen thy brethren."

And it is my sincere hope that my testimony *will* strengthen my brethren!

(83) The courtroom: After Kim's mother took Bill and Ira to court to force them to divulge the whereabouts of her teenaged daughter, all the members of the Bible study group were ordered to come to a local court proceeding to testify of their knowledge

End Notes

of the whereabouts of Kim, who obviously had been hidden out. Everyone in the Bible study group showed up, except Eve. (She stayed with the children.) Candy's ex-husband was even there along with his wife.

Ira prepared me beforehand with a note that said, "I refuse to answer on the grounds that I may incriminate myself." She said for me to repeat that statement if questioned, but for some reason, no one from the Bible study group had to testify.

(84) Matthew 7:6 "Give not that which is holy unto the dogs, neither cast ye your pearls before swine, lest they trample them under their feet, and turn again and rend you."

(85) 12 May 1993: Another very important date for me is when God commissioned me to be His servant, which I consider the greatest of honors. I did not realize this until after the fact, but 12 May 1937 was the coronation date of King George VI, the father of Queen Elizabeth II of Great Britain.

(86) Read through the entire Scriptures: After I got out of that cult group, I had an insatiable desire to read through the Word of God without being under an evil influence. By the time I had received Ira's letter, I was almost finished reading the whole Bible.

(87) "They should have known better.": Ira's coldhearted response reminds me of a report about a teenage girl who admitted to a reporter on Valentine's Day (2/14/14) that she was in a satanic cult ever since the age of thirteen, and that she lured men in through seductive means, just as Ira had confessed to me.

This young girl, who is currently facing a murder charge, along with her husband, also admitted to the reporter that she had murdered numerous people over the years after joining the satanic cult. No one seems to believe her, but I wouldn't just discount her story. (Update: This young girl and her husband were sentenced to life in prison for the murder of the man she had seduced into a private rendezvous.)

(88) Rebecca (not her real name): One of the young children in the group.

(89) Adoptive mother: Candy told me that she had adopted Kim, but I never saw any evidence or official documentation to substantiate this claim.

(90) Appearance in the courtroom: All of the current members of the Bible study group were subpoenaed to the court proceeding that took place in May 1993. They seemed to be very uneasy when I walked through the doors of that courtroom, but I was not the least bit intimidated by them, and it is only because of the Lord. I had full confidence that God was with me, and they knew it too! Praise God!

(91) Newborn Christian: I had just been baptized at the local Baptist church where my husband grew up, so it was fair to assume that I was a baby Christian. Had they known the truth, they would have known that ten years prior to that, in November 1979, I had committed my life to Christ while I was in the deserts of Yuma, Arizona.

(92) Proverbs 30:20 "Such [is] the way of an adulterous woman; she eateth, and wipeth her mouth, and saith, I have done no wickedness."

(93) Hebrews 5:14 "But strong meat belongeth to them that are of full age, [even] those who by reason of use have their senses exercised to discern both good and evil."

(94) Philippians 3:18 "(For many walk, of whom I have told you often, and now tell you even weeping, [that they] are the enemies of the cross of Christ: Whose end [is] destruction, whose God [is their] belly, and [whose] glory [is] in their shame, who mind earthly things.)"

(95) Watchman Nee, *The Spiritual Man* (North Chesterfield, VA: Christian Fellowship Publishers, 1968).

(96) Out of order: God granted this request on 28 February 1993, but she rejected it.

(97) 2 Corinthians 5:17 "Therefore if any man [be] in Christ, [he is] a new creature: old things are passed away; behold, all things are become new."

(98) Romans 8:11 "But if the Spirit of Him that raised up Jesus from the dead dwell in you, He that raised up Christ from the dead shall also quicken your mortal bodies by His Spirit that dwelleth in you."

John 14:17 "[Even] the Spirit of truth; Whom the world cannot receive, because it seeth Him not, neither knoweth Him: but ye know Him; for He dwelleth with you, and shall be in you."

(99) Hebrews 10:26–27 "For if we sin wilfully after that we have received the knowledge of the truth, there remaineth no more sacrifice for sins, but a certain fearful looking for of judgment and fiery indignation, which shall devour the adversaries."

(100) "If you receive—:" If you noticed, Ira almost said the way to have your name *blotted out* of the Book of Life. Please consider this very important passage.

Revelation 14:9–11 "And the third angel followed them, saying with a loud voice, If any man worship the beast and his image, and receive [his] mark in his forehead, or in his hand, The same shall drink of the wine of the wrath of God, which is poured out without mixture into the cup of His indignation; and he shall be tormented with fire and brimstone in the presence of the holy angels, and in the presence of the Lamb: And the smoke of their torment ascendeth up for ever and ever: and they have no rest day nor night, who worship the beast and his image, and whosoever receiveth the mark of his name." (Also see: Revelation 13:15–17; 19:20; 20:4.)

(101) 1 Corinthians 1:18: Most modern versions tend to soften this verse, while the King James Version emphatically states that those who believe that Jesus's sacrifice on the cross is foolishness are doomed for destruction, and that the cross of Christ is the power of God working in our lives for those who are saved (*not being saved*).

Romans 5:10 "For if, when we were enemies, we were reconciled to God by the death of His Son, much more, being reconciled, we shall be saved by His life."

End Notes

(102) Eve (not her real name): May God bless her and her loved ones!

(103) Prophecy by Bill, dated 18 November 1992: I recorded this message at my home, and it was one of many taped recordings that Bill encouraged me to record of him.

(104) Transcript of meeting dated 6 March 1993: All names in this dialogue are fictitious except for Bill's. This evidence was used to win a child custody battle, which resulted in removing this little child out of the reach of Bill.

(105) "So this is sort of like a cult?": My response reveals how terribly naive I was about Satan and how he works. Consider this passage regarding the Wicked One.

Isaiah 14:12–17 "How art thou fallen from Heaven, O Lucifer, son of the morning! [how] art thou cut down to the ground, which didst weaken the nations! For thou hast said in thine heart, I will ascend into Heaven, I will exalt my throne above the stars of God: I will sit also upon the mount of the congregation, in the sides of the north: I will ascend above the heights of the clouds; I will be like the most High.

Yet thou shalt be brought down to Hell, to the sides of the pit. They that see thee shall narrowly look upon thee, [and] consider thee, [saying, Is] this the man that made the earth to tremble, that did shake kingdoms; [that] made the world as a wilderness, and destroyed the cities thereof; [that] opened not the house of his prisoners?"

(106) "Whatever a cult is:" At this point, I still did not understand what a cult was, but I do now! Praise God! I truly hope that my testimony will sound a major warning for others to beware of the extreme danger of being involved with these types of groups.

(107) Selected references for the Prophecy of 27 August 1992: Amos 3:7; Amos 9:6; Colossians 2:11; 1 Corinthians 3:13; 1 Corinthians 7:18–20; 1 Corinthians 12:11; 18; 2 Corinthians 3:13–16; Daniel 4:35; Deuteronomy 10:16; Deuteronomy 30:6; Ezekiel 28:18; Ezra 2:59; Hebrews 2:3–4; Hebrews 12:29; Isaiah 4:4; Isaiah 33:14; Isaiah 42:9; Isaiah 47:14; Jeremiah 4:4; Jeremiah 9:26; Jeremiah 16:15; Jeremiah 23:29; Jeremiah 31:22; 1 Kings 18:24; John 4:23–24; John 6:37; John 6:63; John 13:19–20; John 14:3; John 16:13; Luke 9:50; Luke 12:49; Mark 1:34; Matthew 3:11; Matthew 10:1; Matthew 11:29; Matthew 12:30; Matthew 16:24–27; 1 Peter 1:7; 1 Peter 4:1–2; Philippians 3:3; Proverbs 13:13; Psalm 18:17; Psalm 57:4; Psalm 68:11; Revelation 4:5; Revelation 22:16; Romans 1:3; Romans 2:28–29; Romans 10:12–13; 2 Thessalonians 1:8; 1 Timothy 3:15; 2 Timothy 2:3–5; 2 Timothy 2:8–9; Zechariah 11:8; Zechariah 13:8–9; Zephaniah 1:18; Zephaniah 3:8.

(108) When he was confronted: Whenever I saw Bill in public, he would avoid me and pretend as if he didn't know me. I always thought that behavior was very strange.

(109) In-depth study: I did an in-depth study on the "rapture" years ago, and I discovered that the word "might" in this passage (2 Thessalonians 2:10–12) is not

in the original manuscript, nor was it italicized by the KJV editors to show that it was added to the text.

This is how this passage reads word for word from the Greek New Testament that I used for this comparison (Stephens 1550 edition). The syntax is not employed.

My Greek View: 2 Thessalonians 2:10–12 "And with all deceivableness of the unrighteousness in them that perish, because the love of the truth not received, that they be saved therewith. And for this cause therefore, shall send to them of God, strong delusion to those that believe they that lie, so that damned be all who do not believe the truth, but officially sanction, approve, or authorize the injustice."

It has been said that once you have the knowledge, *then* you will be held accountable for what you have heard, but according to God's Word, if you call yourself a man or woman of God, you are already accountable for every Word that has proceeded from the mouth of God. God's Word has been written, His beloved Son lived it out, and those who are born again have been given His Holy Spirit.

Thus, there is no excuse for not doing the will of God, yet many people will perish for lack of knowledge, not only because they rejected the truth and believed the lies of a man, but because they officially sanctioned the deceptions of the Wicked One.

(110) Messiah: Read 2 Corinthians 3:4–9, 12–16; 4:1–5 and Romans 10:21–11:36, along with Isaiah 42:1–9, to better understand what this means.

(111) *The Hornblower:* This was the newsletter that reported this GSUSA event in Minneapolis, Minnesota, in October 1993. The National Council convenes every three years and is the link between Girl Scout councils and the national organization.

(112) Representatives: There was a time when I was active in keeping up with politics and writing our congressional leaders concerning important issues, but it seems to be a futile effort. But that, too, has been foretold in the Holy Scriptures.

(113) Demonic spirits: Ira used to tell me about nightmares she had where she could actually see *and feel* demons touching her. I am reminded of an incident during a prayer meeting that took place right before I got out of the group. Ira was sitting in my den when all of a sudden she started screaming as if in horrific pain. It went on for several minutes, and she finally got up and quickly walked out of the room, still screaming. We never discussed what happened, but obviously, demons have the authority to torment her *because she belongs to them!*

(114) The Lord has not allowed me to do that: Actually, I cannot ignore God and what He asks of me. And by His grace, I will continue to love and serve Him unto the end.

(115) Reprobates: According to the *Strong's Exhaustive Concordance of the Bible*, a reprobate is someone who has been rejected by God as worthless.

(116) Transcript of 17 May 1993: This was recorded in my home and all parties were in agreement with the taping.

End Notes

(117) Arthur (not his real name): I truly appreciate the expediency with which this attorney was able to have this little girl removed from this very dangerous situation.

(118) Fathers: Malachi 4:5–6 "Behold, I will send you Elijah the prophet before the coming of the great and dreadful day of the LORD: And he shall turn the heart of the fathers to the children, and the heart of the children to their fathers, lest I come and smite the earth with a curse."

(119) "All I was, was death.": God's Word confirms why Bill said this about himself. Proverbs 8:36 "But he that sinneth against Me wrongeth his own soul: all they that hate Me love death."

(120) Pensacola thing: A counterfeit revival that has caused many people to be deceived. My private publishing of *Walking in the True Light* goes into greater detail about this so-called "move of God," but suffice it to say, Satan has been very busy!

(121) Battle between God and Satan: Bill did not *even* want to give Satan credit for anything that took place. If you noticed, he was so contradictory with everything he said. Looking back, I am certain that Satan—the ruler of the darkness—was the major influence over the leaders of that group, whether they understood it or not!

(122) The working of Satan: 2 Thessalonians 2:8–9 "And then shall that Wicked be revealed, whom the Lord shall consume with the spirit of His mouth, and shall destroy with the brightness of His coming: [even Him], whose coming is after the working of Satan with all power and signs and lying wonders."

(123) He does not belong to God: La'el Ministries was Bill's ministry title, which is a Hebrew term that means "belonging to God." However, the question that begs to be asked, which god? I hope you can see that the only true God is not *his god!*

(124) The definitive truth: To help the reader of this book to better understand the great danger of being involved with people who actually belong to the Devil and are serving him, I would like to share an excerpt from a message that I heard on the Internet.

The preacher made the following statement to his congregation on Father's Day, Sunday, 15 June 2014. The context of his sermon was his private interpretation of 1 Corinthians 13, and his view of prophecy, tongues, and why people *need* the baptism in the Holy Spirit.

He said, and I quote: "We all are looking through a glass darkly. All of us—You can still see, but when someone starts drawing lines and saying *it is the definitive truth*, then be careful. Because there are very few definitive truths in the Bible. There's a lot of mystical stuff. God says, I'll use whatever I need to use, and do whatever I need to do. He's going to use the things that are just *the oddest, the craziest*. He's going to use people you think shouldn't be used."

I find it interesting that this pastor would do a sermon on the *need* to experience the baptism in the Holy Spirit on Father's Day. I am sure he was quite aware of the

Brownsville Revival (aka Pensacola Outpouring), which took place on Father's Day, 18 June 1995, at Brownsville Assembly of God Church in Pensacola, Florida.

Reportedly, more than four million people attended services at Brownsville from its inception in 1995 to when it ended about five years later. The services included praise and worship music and some preaching. The highlights were the altar calls, where people were encouraged to come to the front to get right with God.

The minister would lay hands on them, while another person stood behind the person being "preyed" upon to catch them when they fell backward. (Pun intended.) Untold thousands hit the ground during the course of that revival, where they either thrashed about or were prostrate on the floor as if in a coma for hours at a time.

The "revivals" in Pensacola, Toronto, Azusa Street in LA, and other so-called "moves of God" are all directly linked to the same antichrist spirit that was present in Bill's ministry, and is also present in other charismatic / Pentecostal churches.

The "Toronto Blessing," aka the "laughing revival," began on 20 January 1994, and was characterized by extremely bizarre manifestations, such as uncontrolled laugher, jerking all over, falling down and passing out, shaking violently, roaring like a lion, barking like a dog, and other very *odd and crazy behavior*, all of which was reminiscent and hauntingly similar to what took place at the "Azusa Street revivals."

The Azusa Street meetings began on 14 April 1906, and they were widely considered the birth of the Pentecostal movement. Consider this firsthand account by a local reporter from Los Angeles who witnessed what took place at the Azusa Street gatherings in September 1906:

"... They cry and make howling noises all day and into the night. They run, jump, shake all over, shout to the top of their voice, spin around in circles, fall out on the sawdust blanketed floor jerking, kicking and rolling all over. Some of them pass out and do not move for hours as though they were dead.

These people appear to be mad, mentally deranged or under a spell. They claim to be filled with the Spirit.... Their preacher who stays on his knees much of the time with his head hidden between the wooden milk crates. He doesn't talk very much, but at times he can be heard shouting, 'Repent!' And he's supposed to be running the thing... They repeatedly sing the same song, 'The Comforter Has Come.'"

Advocates of these revivals claim that they have received a "touch from God," but regardless of what they say about it, or what they call it, I am certain that all of it is of the Devil! And God's people need to have nothing to do with it!

I am greatly concerned that so many people, particularly our youth, are being led away by smooth-talking ministers, who are luring them to their charismatic churches and events. Please be warned, the practice of being "slain in the Spirit" is Satanic in nature, and the spirit behind this so-called "baptism in the Holy Spirit" is *not* the Spirit of God, but is the spirit of antichrist!

Satan is alive and well, and the angel of light continues to be invited into so many of the churches by unwary ministers, and a people that is sound asleep. These wolves in sheep's clothing are walking about seeking whom they may devour, and this is the season that *all* God's people need to be so wary!

End Notes

Even though the body and soul of Vernon Howell / David Koresh was violently removed from this earth on 19 April 1993, the antichrist spirit that was inside of him still lives on in the hearts of some deceived and wicked men! *And that is the definitive truth!*

2 Corinthians 11:14 "And no marvel; for Satan himself is transformed into an angel of light."

(125) Hebrews 12:2 "Looking unto Jesus the author and finisher of [our] faith; who for the joy that was set before Him endured the cross, despising the shame, and is set down at the right hand of the Throne of God."

(126) Evil will not always be with us: Prayerfully consider this very prophetic Word that appears to be coming to pass right before our eyes in these final days.

Psalms 92:7–9 "When the wicked spring as the grass, and when all the workers of iniquity do flourish; [it is] that they shall be destroyed for ever: But Thou, LORD, [art Most] High for evermore. For, lo, Thine enemies, O LORD, for, lo, Thine enemies shall perish; all the workers of iniquity shall be scattered."

ARISE O GOD

Arise O God, let your enemies scatter. Arise O God, let your enemies scatter. For You are exalted King of all the earth! Riding high above the Heavens! Your Name shall be praised in the mighty gates of Zion! Your Kingdom shall reign forever! And ever!

About the Author

C. Read committed her life to Jesus Christ in the fall of 1979 while enlisted in the United States Marine Corps. Her duty station was 1st Marine Brigade Hawaii. While on an assignment to Yuma, Arizona, Iranian students seized the American Embassy in Tehran on 4 November 1979 and took sixty-six American hostages.

A special friend of Read's was on a six-month deployment to Japan and was prepared to go to Iran at a moment's notice. She felt so helpless to do anything about it, and it was such a desperate and uncertain time in her life, and in the lives of so many others.

As unbelievable as it sounds, looking back, Read was actually thankful for the Iran hostage crisis because it was that agonizingly horrific event that caused her to call out to God.

About that same time, a Marine, whom she had never met, came up to her as she was leaving her barracks in Yuma and handed her a Bible. He said, "Here, I think you need to read this," and just walked away. Read never saw him again, but she will never forget him!

That encounter in the deserts of Arizona was a major *turning point* in her life. Read did take his advice and started reading and studying the Bible, but that was just the beginning of her walk with God. It took Read nearly fourteen years to truly understand the truth about God and His heavenly Kingdom, and there is still so much to learn!

It was due to her love and concern for that very special friend that caused Read to see her great need for the LORD Jesus Christ, the only true Savior! They were married almost a year later, and God blessed them with seven beautiful children.

Their love for each other remained all through the "Storms of This Life" and has grown stronger even after the sudden departure of her beloved Husband! And by God's grace their love will be forever!

The Storms of This Life

*My youngest son had just turned three
a month before the storm hit.
My little Justus was trying to be so brave
when his sister took a picture of him
while he was standing beside me
in the doorway of our home on that day.*

*His eyes and face were red from crying,
and he was holding his lips real tight
to keep from getting upset in front of the camera.*

*He, along with his six-year-old brother,
was absolutely terrified when the trees started falling
all around us during the worst part of the storm.*

*My little boys became visibly upset
when an over one-hundred-foot pine tree
fell across our driveway and blocked us in.*

*They were begging me to call someone for help, and I did,
but the lady at City Hall said there was nothing they could do
and that we just needed to ride out the storm.*

*When another pine tree went through the roof
and water started pouring into the kitchen and a bedroom,
all seven of my children became quite distressed.*

Walking with the Enemy

It was then that I realized we could actually die in this storm,
but I also had full confidence that only if it was God's will.

I can honestly say that absolute fear was not with me
on that horribly devastating day,
but a great love and concern for my dear children.

My response to the terror of the storm
was to humbly call upon the Lord,
and His peace was noticeably with us.
I thank God He heard my most earnest plea!

My husband was not able to be with us due to the war,
but soon before he was to arrive home,
my oldest daughter asked my little Justus,
"Are you going to tell Daddy
that you were a big boy during the storm?"

He hung his little head and looked to the ground,
and a few moments later,
with an ashamed look on his face,
he looked up and said,
"No, I was little."

That profound statement, from the mouth of my baby,
reminded me just how small we really are
in the sight of God!

The Storms of This Life

We all need the Lord God in our lives,
and He is the only One who can truly help us
in the midst of the Storms of this Life!

God will use trials and tribulations
to show us how we desperately need Him,
and I hope you won't reject Him when He calls!

For those who have turned to God
and away from sin,
His love will forever live in those
who worship only Him!

The Devil wants to lead you into sin
and fill your heart with hate,
so he can separate you from God
and those who love Him too.

Satan is the one who wants you dead,
so he can destroy your soul in Hell!
I Am pleading, don't give into his lies and deceit!

Jesus Christ is truly the only way to Heaven,
and He gave His life so we could live
with Him, world without end!

Amen!

C. Read

(29 August 2005)

www.ingramcontent.com/pod-product-compliance
Lightning Source LLC
Chambersburg PA
CBHW050612300426
44112CB00012B/1470